Thirty-five years ago d[...] jettisoned the Christian fa[...] [...] childhood for the Afro-centric movement. I viewed Christianity as "the White man's religion." God, in his kindness, eventually rejected my rejection of him. However, if I had a resource like Rev. Cyril Chavis's *The Bible Explained,* I would have been able to engage my false understanding of the Christian faith. Cyril has magnificently brought to bear the beauty of Reformed Theology with the testimony of the African American Christian experience to disciple college students of African descent. I believe many will come to faith in Christ and be strengthened in their faith by reading this book.

DR. IRWYN INCE, AUTHOR OF *THE BEAUTIFUL COMMUNITY: UNITY, DIVERSITY AND THE CHURCH AT ITS BEST*

In my 12 years of full time college ministry on an HBCU, over and over again, I have seen students confused about Jesus because of false information. It's often the same questions, every year, that leave students puzzled when it comes to whether or not they will follow Jesus. Campus ministries need to be a place where students can explore what they believe and why. For ministries seeking to be such, this book is an excellent resource. Do you have questions about the Christian faith? *The Bible Explained* has answers.

LATASHA ALLSTON, CAMPUS STAFF FOR REFORMED UNIVERSITY FELLOWSHIP

If you are a Black college student with questions about the Christian faith, this book is a clear, biblically-grounded, and culturally-relevant guide to deepen your understanding of the core beliefs of the faith.

College creates cause for confusion for many young Christians. Having a college Christian guide is just what we need to encourage us students in our faith walks and promote perseverance. That's why this book is so essential. It teaches, it encourages, it strengthens.

In The Bible Explained, Rev. Cyril Chavis has offered a wonderfully contextual account of the Christian faith for Black college students and young professionals. Many young people in our communities are leaving the Christian faith, not because there is a lack of credibility to the faith, but because there is a lack of accessibility — they have questions that have gone unanswered for far too long. If you were to ask these young folks if they understand the teachings of Scripture, many would reply with the Ethiopian Eunuch, "How can I, unless someone guides me?" We can be glad that Rev. Chavis has offered such needed guidance for the next generation.

THE BIBLE EXPLAINED

A COLLEGE STUDENT'S GUIDE TO UNDERSTANDING THEIR FAITH

CYRIL CHAVIS JR.

FOREWORD BY
ELBERT MCGOWAN JR.

HIDASE
Publishing

TO MY STUDENTS

whose gracious welcome and kindness to a young pastor

and desire to understand the Bible

never cease to amaze me

CONTENTS

PART TWO
RELATIONSHIP

PART THREE
RESCUE'S STORY

ACKNOWLEDGEMENTS

This book would not be what it is without the help and influence of my family, friends, and co-laborers.

To my God, Yahweh, thank you for the privilege of doing this project with you and for you. I still can't believe that I have the honor of serving you. Thank you for always being with me.

To my wife, Jenell, thank you for your love, support, and partnership. Thank you for test reading the book. Thank you for understanding on those late nights when urgent writing bled into the time we usually hang (like now as I'm typing this). Thank you for being mentally present with the family on those days when ideas and syntax clouded my mind. I love you. Don't ever leave my side.

To my kids, Aria, Elise, and Kyrie, thank you for understanding when I say, "Writing my book," after you ask, "Daddy, what are you doing?" in those early hours of the morning. I hope that this book will lead you to the living God when you are able to pick it up and read it on your own.

To my mother, Arwonder, and my father, Cyril Sr., thank you for raising me into a writer, entrepreneur, and a follower of Jesus. Thank you for instilling in me a work ethic and a love for our kinsmen according to the flesh. To my siblings, Wesley, Christina, and Jessica, thank you for your insight and encouragement.

To my students, thank you for welcoming my ministry and trusting me to pastor you. Also, thank you for being test readers when I know you have no lack of reading. This book flows out of my relationship with you. To Nevaeh, thank you for being the first to tell me I should write this book.

To my Reformed University Fellowship squad, Latasha Allston, Jason Francoeur, and Chris Reed, thank you for your encouragement, affirmation, and excitement toward this project. Thank you for understanding on those days when I had less energy for our team because of the demands of writing. It is an honor to serve college students alongside you.

To the whole RUF family, thank you for being a family that has helped me fall more deeply in love with campus ministry and with Jesus.

To Elbert McGowan, thank you for taking a young, brash seminarian under your wings and pastoring him. It is hard to overestimate how much I have learned about serving students from you, and our time together on the campus serves as an enduring model for me today.

To the Grimké Society, thank you for welcoming me and graciously engaging my persistent flow of ideas and thoughts. The idea for Hidase Publishing was birthed among you.

To Shelton Murphy, thank you for pastoring me, baptizing me, and being one of the first to commend my theological writings. Thank you to Donell Woodson and Charlene Brown for graciously putting up with a knuckle headed, young college student who was desperate to grow. To Matt Murphy and Bliss Spillar, thank you for pursuing me and investing in a young Christian who thought he knew way more than he actually did. To Russ Whitfield, thank you for being a coach, an invaluable source of inspiration, and an unfailing vision partner.

To my Hidase Publishing friends, Rome Douglas, Ashley Williams, and Jason Francoeur, thank you for believing in this project.

To my editors, Charles McKnight and Aaron Hicks, thank you for not only deeply enriching this project but also for enthusiastically encouraging me and believing in what God will do through this resource.

FOREWORD

The year was 2007. The place? Jackson State University (JSU). This was long before the Deion Sanders era. However, during that year Jackson State made sports headlines. We won the men's basketball SWAC Championship and advanced to the first round of March Madness.

Though the tournament was huge for JSU, something far more important was happening on the campus in 2007. The rest of the world had no idea. But we did. God had opened a door to start a campus ministry at Jackson State called Reformed University Fellowship (RUF). Through this ministry, we desired to transform the lives of students with the good news of Jesus. God called my wife, Karen, and I to plant it.

Why was starting this ministry on JSU's campus so important? We knew that a student with both an HBCU education and a life transformed by Jesus was a beautifully dangerous thing.

Serving college students on an HBCU wasn't an accident. My wife and I understand how special HBCUs are to the Black community. My grandmother worked at Tougaloo College. I spent every summer on Tougaloo's campus, between 1989-1995, attending various programs that exposed elementary, middle, and high school students to life on the Black campus. They were a safe place to play and learn. My wife holds degrees from two of them – Stillman College and Florida A&M. We actually met on the campus of the HBCU I attended – Alabama A & M University (AAMU). HBCUs have been one of the anchoring and uplifting communities for Black folk. We love them, and I am a better man because of them.

The year was now 2009. The ministry had taken off and was thriving. We saw students believe in Jesus for the first time and saw gospel transformation in the lives of many students. We also had favor with the university administration. For example, a vice president at JSU asked if I had the bandwidth to serve as the director of campus ministries. The volunteer position with the university further ingrained us into the fabric of the school.

Fast forward to the fall of 2014. We now had two biological kids of our own and hundreds of spiritual children on the campus. We had been praying for more laborers. The harvest was plentiful. Our staff was few. Myself and Latasha Allston, also a JSU grad, were the only ones on payroll. One evening, this young Black man showed up at our weekly campus-wide worship service. We prided ourselves on knowing our students – their faces and names – but on this particular night in 2014, there was a new face in the crowd. This new person looked very much like a JSU student, but he was different. He wasn't dressed like a college student and appeared mature. He was locked in, you might even say, intense.

After I finished preaching, he approached me. He waited until students cleared and introduced himself. "I'm Cyril Chavis. I'm a student at Reformed Theological Seminary. A campus pastor at UVA told me to come to Jackson for seminary and then to find you when I got here. Here I am." Little did I know that he was an answer to prayer and how God would use that night to inaugurate a beautiful friendship.

Cyril immediately devoted himself to ministry on our Black campus. Cyril wanted to meet with me. He was relentless. He wanted to learn, serve, and do evangelism with me. He wanted to come around when we spent time with our student leaders; to sit in on Bible studies; preach; and hang out on my back porch with other men and talk about life, repentance, Jesus, justice, marriage, and sports. Cyril loved seminary, but it became crystal clear that he wanted to cut his teeth in ministry, at least for a few years, on the Black campus. After hiring him to minister with us, we officially worked together. Some time later, I felt called to pastor the local church I had been a part of – Redeemer Jackson. Cyril became the campus pastor at Jackson State. Then, the LORD called him to start an RUF chapter at Howard University.

Well, those few years of cutting his teeth have turned into almost a decade of campus work as a Black man, among Black people, on two different Black campuses. Malcolm Gladwell writes, "The key to achieving true expertise in any skill is a matter of doing that skill, the correct way, for 10,000 hours." By my math, Cyril has invested well over 17,280 hours of thinking, reading, praying, writing, learning, preaching, teaching, reflecting, and being with college students on historically Black campuses. And this book proves this.

This book is a must read for college students who want to know the in's and out's of our faith. It is for the college student who wants to strengthen their spiritual foundation. This is a book for skeptics looking for the sweet soundness of the gospel. *The Bible Explained* will help steady your life when hard things happen or when you are forced to wrestle with hard things that have happened to Black folk in our world and country. This book also locates the problem in our own souls. If you listen and read carefully, this book will walk you right into the arms of Jesus. And he will never let you go.

Elbert McGowan Jr.
    Senior Pastor, Redeemer Church in Jackson

WHY SHOULD I READ THIS BOOK?

The goal of this book is for you to *understand*. So often, we accept things because our parents believe them or because they are accepted by people we respect. There is nothing inherently wrong with this; however, we must take it a step further. You must understand for yourself. Why? Because understanding the Bible for yourself is key to embracing a life filled with God's glory and joy. Without understanding, you will not experience the fullness of God.

————

WHO IS THIS BOOK FOR?

The Bible Explained is for the college student who is asking the question, "Is Christianity for me?" Perhaps you are a Christian, but you feel like you have always believed in something that you don't quite understand. You follow Jesus, but you sense that there is so much more to learn and experience in your relationship with him. This book is for you. Maybe you are hungry for God, but you wouldn't call yourself a Christian. You want to explore Christianity to see what Jesus is all about, to see if he can satisfy your spiritual hunger. This book is for you.

FOR GEN Z'S NEED

The need for understanding has shown itself repeatedly in my ministry. I am a pastor whose joy is to reach Generation Z Africans — diaspora and continent — with the gospel on HBCU campuses. I served the Reformed University Fellowship (RUF) chapter at Jackson State University (JSU) from 2014 to 2019 in several different capacities, and I have served the RUF chapter at Howard University for the last four years.

I believe understanding the Christian faith is one of the greatest needs of every Christian college student; you need to know, "Why?"

On a late afternoon one day, I was sitting across from a student, whom we will call Troy, in the JSU student union. I was meeting with him for the first time, and he had only been to one RUF Bible study. His friend, who we will call Jessica, invited him to one of our Large Group Bible Studies. There, she introduced me to him. We connected and scheduled the one on one meeting we were now enjoying. I was eager to find out why Jessica was intentional in connecting me with her friend. Perhaps there was some crisis, some perpetual problem? Whatever the situation, here we were, sitting across from each other, and I was about to find out.

We began chatting, getting to know each other. Eventually, we got to the topic of religious upbringing:

"I walked away from Christianity because I asked my mom, 'Why should we read the Bible?' And she immediately shut me down saying that we aren't supposed to question the Bible. I mean, I was asking simply to understand! . . . So I am going to ask you this question, 'Why should I read the Bible?'"

I gave an answer to his question (find the answer in the next chapter!) and affirmed his curiosity. On that day, Troy became a regular part of our ministry on campus. It felt so simple! Troy's experience is more common than we think. Students want to understand the Christian faith, and many have grown up in churches and families where curious questions and intellectual exploration were condemned.

Allow me to share another story.

I was sitting in the Theater in the JSU Student Center in front of anywhere from 30 to 60 college students. It was a Tuesday night in the middle of the semester. I was sitting on a stool next to a high, circular, restaurant-styled table to my left. On the other side of the table was C.J., my student interviewee for the night. Student interviews were times where we could put the spotlight on a student.

After asking a couple other questions, I asked the final question: "So, tell us about your spiritual walk?" I knew this particular student was not a Christian. In fact, he was open and vocal about not being a Christian. "Well I am not a Christian, but I grew up in a Christian home going to church . . . I don't believe that Jesus is the Son of God, and I don't know if the whole Bible is true . . ." He shared about his religious upbringing, his complex relationship with his parents when it came to religion, and his search for the truth.

After each interview, we would open up the floor for questions from the audience. A student sincerely and graciously asked, "If you are not a Christian, then why do you come to RUF?" You could feel the room tune in and eagerly wait for the answer to the question.

C.J. responded, "I come because I feel like I am actually learning. Growing up, when I would go to church on Sunday, I felt like church would mostly be about motivation to get you through the week. But when I go to a mid-week Bible study, I feel like I am actually growing in my understanding and am learning. So I don't go to church, but I come to things like RUF."

I instantly realized that C.J. expressed something very significant. Intellectual Black Gen Z men and women, the kind who go to a HBCU, want to understand the Christian faith on a deep level! You are not merely satisfied with *doing* or *feeling* Christianity; you want to *think* Christianity. Among many different things, you want an intellectual and theological framework from which to engage your ever-changing world, a framework from which to inform and evaluate your own beliefs and practices. For that reason, in this book, we are going to be doing more science than art. Now, I am not advocating for an intellectual faith at the expense of all the other aspects; no, I want students to live a full-orbed faith. Indeed, the ability to think the Christian faith strengthens one's ability to feel and do the faith.

I think perhaps Gen Z's longing for understanding might be something slightly unique to our Gen Z folks in comparison to previous generations. This generation, many are saying, is the first post-Christian generation.[1] More than ever, people are unfamiliar with the Bible's basic teachings.

FOR YOUR SPIRITUAL JOURNEY AS A COLLEGE STUDENT

Your situation as a college student presents a powerful spiritual opportunity and challenge. What's the opportunity? While in college, often, you are leaving the house for the first time in your life. Or, perhaps you are commuting from your childhood home, but this is the first time you are setting out to build a life independent from your parents. You are on your own. This newfound sense of independence leads you to question, "Who am I outside of my parent's house?" College is an opportunity to figure out who you are and what you believe.

What's the challenge? While exploring these pressing questions, you experience extreme temptations, distractions, trials, and competing beliefs in the college setting. These challenges can make college feel like a very confusing time when it comes to religion and spirituality. In the midst of the opportunity and the challenge, you face an undeniable desire to know God.

Here is the problem that you have: You know that Christianity is the easiest place to start with figuring out God, but you might be wondering, "What is Christianity all about?" Chances are that you have heard conflicting things about Christianity, so you want to know for yourself. You know that the Bible is the primary way to understand the God of the Christian faith, yet you have no idea where to start. You need a guide, and this is it.

The Bible Explained will explain some of the Bible's most basic and essential beliefs. This book will cover what I want every student to know in their four years of college. After gaining understanding, you will see that the Christian faith is more glorious and more enjoyable than you ever knew.

As you read, you will notice that this book focuses on Christian beliefs, not practices. I began to write a book on both, but I realized that I needed to split it into two books. I am currently writing a second book that focuses on the Christian lifestyle. Stay tuned for that one. Though this book focuses on beliefs, I expect that you will still find it useful for your everyday life.

FOR BLACK COLLEGE STUDENTS

I am writing this with African Gen Z college students in mind— African American, Afro-LatinX, West African, Afro-Caribbean, and more. Though I hope to address all Africans, I will address "the American Africa"[2] since this is the context with which I am most familiar. This means that as we apply the unchanging truth of the scriptures, we unapologetically do so as those who are Africans speaking to Africans. This is a Christian book written and published by Africans and written to specifically address African core concerns.

Throughout history, there have been many different ways of referring to those of African descent in America – Negro, Colored, Black, African, Ethiop, Black African, African American, and so forth. I will use Black and African, or a combination of both, largely interchangeably to refer to people of African descent. When I want to be explicit that I am referring to Africans in a particular region of the globe, I will use the term "African Americans," "continental Africans," "Afro-Caribbean," and the like.

Some might think that because this book is written directly to a certain audience it necessarily excludes other audiences. However, this is not the case. Allow me to explain.

This book is theology. Theology is the study of God and how he relates to everything he has created. If theology addresses everybody, it addresses nobody. Why? The information would be so general that it wouldn't piercingly nor specifically address the issues facing any one demographic. Instead of giving you generic applications, the theology in *The Bible Explained* will pointedly address a specific group of people. This is what God intended theology to do and what is actually happening in the Bible. Theology enriches everyone when that particular theology addresses a particular group of people about their particular situations.

For example, the Bible often addresses particular people in particular situations, like the first century Corinthians (e.g. 1st and 2nd Corinthians) or Jewish Christians (e.g. Hebrews). However, 21st century Christians (we) more vividly see how Christian truths apply to ourselves because we see them applied to the Corinthians and other particular peoples in Scripture. This is an essential part of the theological task; every ethnic group or demographic does this, whether they recognize it or not. In writing this book, I am hoping to craft a theology that speaks to African Americans.

I also particularly have the HBCU college student in mind in this book. I am a pastor who has only pastored HBCU college students up to this point. It is an honor to minister on an HBCU campus given HBCUs' rich Christian legacy of African uplift. *The Bible Explained* flows out of my love for my students, and I hope to use it in my service to them.

———

THE ORIGIN STORY

Let me share the story of how this book came to be.

FRESHMAN GAME NIGHT

It began around 8:00 pm on a Monday evening during the fall of 2020, in the depth of the COVID pandemic. I was sitting in my home office getting ready for our first Freshmen Game Night through Zoom. I looked at several first-year students' video streams with a smile as we started our *Black Card Revoked* game night and karaoke.

"Alright, y'all! The person who gets the most points walks away with a . . ." I paused as I considered a potential prize, " . . . a free Christian book!" After some fun and laughter, a student named Déja won our game night.

I checked our GroupMe chat the next day. Déja messaged me saying, "Good morning Cyril! Can you give me some suggestions for the Christian books I have to choose from as the winner of the game night, please?"

My nerdy, book-loving self read this text with delight. I replied, "Morning! Sure, let me give it some thought." What would the perfect book be like for my college students? I realized the perfect book would survey the basics of the Bible. It would have to be accessible for the everyday person and address the needs of a Gen Z African American HBCU college student. Also, I didn't want the book to shy away from explaining biblical topics that might cause disagreement among Christians. It would need to take a stance on some of the Bible's more difficult, but important passages. Though the book would need to be deep enough to engage a thoughtful Christian, the content would also need to be clear and simple enough for a person who had never been exposed to Christian teachings. So, I reflected, "There must be something out there." However, I could not find something that fit the above description.

Though I knew my ideal book was missing, I had not yet come to the conclusion that I should write it. There is more to the story.

ORIENTING A NEW BELIEVER

For several weeks, I met with a student named Nevaeh, who had recently committed to following Jesus. During this time, we would go through Westminster Shorter Catechism (WSC) questions to prepare for her baptism. A catechism allows people to learn Bible truths in a question-answer format, similar to a note card. The WSC is a commonly used summary of the Bible's basic truths for new Christians.

"Alright! Ready to hop into the catechism questions?"

"Yup!" she said.

I responded, "Ok, now at which question did we end?"

I asked the questions, and Nevaeh recited the answers. After reciting the answer, she would summarize what we had just read. Nevaeh is bright, so she could understand a good bit of the questions. Though very sharp, occasionally she would confess with a chuckle, "Yeeaaaaahh I don't know," inviting me to shed light on the catechism answer. After explaining several times, she would reply, "Ohhh, ok. I never knew that," or, "Gotcha, I've never heard that before," or, "I learned something different from the churches I've visited, but this makes so much sense."

I was happy that she was learning and thought, "Man, I wish every student could get an organized and basic overview of the Christian faith in this way."

One day, in response to a light bulb moment, I told her, "Shoot, I might write a book that explains all of this stuff to students."

Kindly and matter-of-factly, she said, "Yeah, you should. The way you explain it is helpful."

At that moment, the idea came to write this book. In addition to the characteristics of the book I mentioned above, I realized I wanted to use the Westminster Shorter Catechism (WSC) as a rough outline. The WSC was written to explain the Christian faith to children or new Christians. Its truths and topics are those that every Christian should know, so I will loosely follow the topics that it covers. As I cover the topics, I will explain its truths in a way that addresses Black Gen Z.

————

JOURNEYING WITH OLD FRIENDS

As we learn the Bible and understand it, I want Black African Christians of previous generations to shape you. Their penetrating insight about the Bible and how it relates to the experiences of their fellow Africans can help us in our task. These old friends can give us wisdom and understanding for our new times. We have access to their wisdom and lives through the things they and others left behind. In each chapter, I will highlight an African Christian – diaspora and continent – and how they help us in our current task.

Allow me to introduce you to our first, old friend – Charles Octavius Boothe.[3] He was born enslaved on June 13, 1845. Rev. Boothe began to learn how to read during his early childhood and gradually learned the Bible throughout the rest of his childhood. Around the age of 21, he decided to follow Jesus and was then baptized. He eventually pastored Dexter Avenue Baptist Church. It is now famously known as The Dexter King Memorial Baptist Church, named in remembrance of another well known pastor who led there, Martin Luther King Jr. as this was the church where Martin Luther King, Jr. pastored. Boothe was a fierce advocate for racial uplift, and education was one of the main ways he sought to uplift newly freed Africans. His book, *Plain Theology for Plain People*, was an outflow of his desire to educate.

Rev. Boothe wrote *Plain Theology for Plain People* to meet a need. He and other church leaders needed a book that explained the Bible's teachings in an orderly and systematic manner, but all the books they found were written by and for academic scholars.

Thus, these books' style were very difficult to read. These books gave little assistance to the ministers and deacons he was training when he was an instructor for the Ministers' and Deacons' Institutes. Many newly freed African Americans had little time and capacity to grit their way through these dense books. He needed a book that was simple and written for everyday people. He knew he needed to craft something special for his students given the lack of another resource. In *Plain Theology for Plain People*, he says, " The doctrines of our holy religion need to be studied in order, according to some definite system; but simplicity should prevail — simplicity of arrangement and simplicity of language . . . this little book's only mission is to help plain people in the study of the first principles of divine truth."[4]

In writing *The Bible Explained*, I am carrying forward the ministry of the African American pastors of old, like Charles Octavius Boothe, who sought to create resources that organized the essentials of the Christian faith for the people they loved and served. Though African Americans in the 2020s are in a different place educationally when compared to the late 1800s, you have little time for more academic books as a college student; you want something simple. And as a Black college student, you want something written with you in mind. *The Bible Explained* seeks to meet both of those needs, as Boothe did so long ago.

―――――

WHAT WE WILL ACCOMPLISH

The Bible Explained is divided into 12 chapters. I follow the outline of the Westminster Shorter Catechism questions 1-38.

Part one explains how God reveals things to us. Chapter one explores how God is giving guidance through the Bible. Chapter two explains how we ought to interpret the Bible correctly so that we can understand God's life-giving word.

Part two explains God and humanity's relationship. Chapter

three surveys who God is and how he is all that you need. Chapter four explains what God is up to in the world and in your life. He is trustworthy, even in the midst of hard circumstances. Chapter five dives into God's glorious purpose for humanity and, therefore, for you. Chapter six argues that sin is what is wrong with the world, and this chapter explores how the world has fallen so far from God's design for it.

Part three explains how God rescues us through Jesus. Chapter seven explains how Jesus is the center and climax of history and how he ought to be the center and climax of your life's story. Chapter eight highlights who Jesus is. It shows how Jesus, being both God and human, is uniquely equipped to save you. Chapter nine highlights what Jesus has and is doing. It explores how Jesus serves us as a prophet, priest, and king.

Part four explains how the effect of God's rescue gets into our lives. Chapter ten explains what it means to be saved and how we become saved. Chapter eleven shows all the blessings that come with being a Christian in this life. Chapter twelve shows us all the blessings that come with being a Christian at death and in the next life.

Though reading the book in order is most helpful, feel free to jump around and read parts that specifically interest you or help you prepare a Bible study or other similar things.

THE HOPE

As a result of African Gen Z students understanding the Christian faith, I pray to see students joyfully embracing Jesus as their life-giving ruler. I hope to see Black college students excited about the church and serving alongside the church to help further the mission of the church.

I yearn to see HBCU campuses saturated with Jesus as students confidently share the good news about him. I long to see Black Gen Z engage all that they do — their jobs, their families, their communities, their friendships, their politics, their finances, and more — in a way that is distinctly and compellingly centered on Christ. In short, I want to see lives transformed and Jesus glorified as a result of this book.

Alright! We know where we are going and what we hope to see along the way. Let's get started.

PART ONE
REVELATION

CHAPTER 1

CAN I GET SOME HELP WITH .. . EVERYTHING?

Have you felt the anger, fear, and confusion that comes with not knowing whether or not you have the proper guidance to succeed at something? It is the feeling of being helpless, walking in the dark, desperately searching for someone to guide you.

"Brooooo, I really need to pass this class 'cause I need this class to graduate! Do you know where I can find a tutor?"

"Girl, I really like him, but I don't know what to do! I want to get his attention, but I don't want to seem weird or thirsty. What should I do?"

"When I tell you the WHOLE CLASS failed the exam . . . and tell me why the professor won't let us retake the exam?! Trippin'. This class is for my major too, so I need to figure out what went wrong."

"It would be so dope if I was a part of that organization, but I hear they are really selective in their intake process. Do you know anyone who's been through it before?"

"It feels like my friends are kind of ghosting me right now. What's the best way to approach them about it?"

As a college student, you are often faced with situations like these above repeatedly. All of these situations have one thing in common – someone needs guidance. This is why having a mentor is such a beautiful thing. A mentor is someone who gives guidance. The perfect mentor has at least three things: 1) they are able to relate to your experience 2) they are wise and therefore able to give powerful direction and 3) they love you and are deeply invested in your flourishing. A mentor can be game changing for your life.

YOUR MENTOR IS YAHWEH

What if I told you that you have a divine mentor? This being is the perfect mentor. He is able to relate to your experience because he became a human and experienced your hardships (except sin). This mentor is wise and gives powerful direction because he is all-knowing, almighty, loves you, and is deeply invested in your flourishing because he himself is love. The Bible calls him many names and titles, but his personal name in the Hebrew alphabet is יהוה which is the name "Yahweh."[1] He is your mentor.

This sounds amazing, but where do I receive wisdom from Yahweh? This wonderful mentor has said everything he wants to say to you in the Bible.

WHERE WE ARE GOING

In a sentence, this chapter will drive home the fact that the Bible is Yahweh's amazing guidance, so let the Bible shape every part of you.

So often, we go to college knowing very little about the Bible. Often, we were exposed to a Bible-less Christianity or a Christianity where the careful explanation and study of the Bible was not prioritized. You have been around the Bible but do not understand why it is necessary or even if it is trustworthy, relevant, or good. As a result, we look for other inspiration and playbooks to direct us. When we hear our peers challenge the Bible's usefulness, truthfulness, or relevance, we really don't know what to say or think.

I want to convince you that the Bible is God's word and therefore more glorious and enjoyable than you ever knew. We will see that the Bible is 1) God revealing himself to you 2) the key to embracing your highest purpose and 3) true and trustworthy. As a result, I pray that you saturate your life with its truths like a full sponge overflows with water.

Without the Bible, you will be without guidance from Yahweh and ultimately lost when it comes to understanding God, yourself, and the world around you. With the Bible, you will have the guidance needed to glorify God and enjoy him in every area of life.

———

HELP FROM AN OLD FRIEND

As we explore the Bible, let me introduce you to an old friend who is a picture of what I would like us to become. Her name is Maria Stewart.

Why Maria Stewart? She was a fierce Christian, an undying servant, a proto-Black nationalist, and a prophetic voice. She was proud of her African heritage, yet was not afraid to challenge other Africans. She saw her career totally in submission to Jesus and was not afraid to give up her life for his mission.

STEWART'S LIFE AS A SPEAKER, EDUCATOR, AND LEADER

Maria Stewart[2] was born free in 1803 in Hartford, Connecticut. At age five she was orphaned and received a Christian education while spending most of her childhood growing up in a clergyman's home. She eventually married James W. Stewart in 1826 in Boston. They became activists and members of Boston's Black middle class under the tutelage of David Walker, who was also a Christian, activist, abolitionist, and author of *David Walker's Appeal*. Her husband died in 1829, and her mentor Walker died very soon after in 1830. She placed her trust in Jesus in 1830 and made a public profession of her faith in 1831. After this, she began to speak and write widely about all different kinds of topics – women's rights, the abolition of slavery, African uplift, judgment upon White America for racism, the ignorance and passivity of Africans, motherhood, morality, discipleship, education – all the while always saturating everything with her faith in God and belief that Jesus was the way to salvation and elevation for Africans. She had a public writing and speaking career from 1831-1833. In 1832, she gave the first recorded public lecture by an American woman (White or Black), which happened before a mixed audience of Whites and Blacks, males and females. After a life of service and education work, she eventually became matron (a chief nurse) at Freedman's Hospital at Howard University. She died in 1879.

STEWART WAS SATURATED WITH THE BIBLE

Why Stewart for this chapter? Dr. Valerie Cooper, associate professor of religion and society and Black church studies at Duke Divinity School, tells us that "Stewart, in fact, speaks a kind of 'Bible-ese': she has so shaped her ideas in scriptural-sounding words and phrases that it is sometimes difficult to tell where the Bible ends and Stewart begins. Again and again, the words that Stewart chooses to speak are the words of the Bible. It has become her mother tongue."[3]

Look at this example from Stewart where she speaks Bible-ese while advocating for oppressed Africans:

Many think, because your skins are tinged with a sable hue, that you are an inferior race of beings; but God does not consider you as such. He hath formed and fashioned you in his own glorious image, and hath bestowed upon you reason and strong powers of intellect. He hath made you to have dominion over the beasts of the field, the fowls of the air, and the fish of the sea. He hath crowned you with glory and honor; hath made you but a little lower than the angels . . . Many will suffer for pleading the cause of oppressed Africa, and I shall glory in being one of her martyrs; for I am firmly persuaded, that the God in whom I trust is able to protect me from the rage and malice of mine enemy, and from them that will rise up against me.[4]

Here, Stewart speaks "Bible-ese" from Genesis 1:26-28; Genesis 2:7; Job 10:8; Psalm 7:6; Psalm 8:5-9; Psalm 18:48; Psalm 59:1; Psalm 144:2; and 2 Timothy 1:12 to empower her fellow Africans in America and express her confidence in God's provision for her mission to serve them. Like Stewart, I want you to be so thoroughly shaped by God's guidance in the Bible that it saturates everything you say, think, and do.

THE BIBLE IS THE ULTIMATE GUIDE

Probates are a hallmark of the HBCU college experience. Probates are ceremonies where fraternities and sororities reveal who their new members are. A group of men or women move across the campus in a tight, single-file line. While they are doing this, older fraternity and sorority members accompany them. And beyond them, there is an even greater crowd often surrounding the older members following the line of new members. But why is this crowd following the line? The new members in the line are masked. The crowd is eagerly waiting for the new members to be revealed, and the new members will reveal themselves in a musical, choreographed, poetic fashion. Probates are about revelation, revealing who the next generation of the organization will be.

Just as probates are about revelation, all of life is about revelation. Whereas probates are revealing the new members of an organization, all of life is revealing God. Life is like one giant divine probate. Why does God reveal himself? We need God to reveal himself if humans are going to know anything about him. Through revealing himself, he is mentoring you into flourishing. Let's look at how the infinite God reveals himself to finite humans.

THE BIBLE IS REVELATION

God gives guidance about himself through the things he has created (Romans 1:19-20), through our inner selves (Romans 2:14-15), and in many extraordinary ways, like miracles and prophecy. One of these extraordinary ways is an inspired written collection (Exodus 24:4), aka. the Bible. The Bible is a written collection of God's revelation that is authoritative for God's people in all places and at all times. God had Scripture written down for remembrance and preservation from generation to generation. There are many ways that God guides us, but the Bible is the highest and final authority in all things.

Only God himself has the authority to add or subtract from his word as humans do not have that authority. God said to his people, "Do not add to or subtract from these commands I am giving you. Just obey the commands of the LORD your God that I am giving you" (Deuteronomy 4:2). Throughout the Bible, there is an understanding that revelation from other gods, religions, or people are not to be held alongside those from Yahweh. Only Yahweh's appointed apostles and prophets (aka God's official messengers and representatives) can give His written revelation (Isaiah 8:19–20).

THE BIBLE GUIDES YOU INTO YOUR PURPOSE

What is the goal of the Bible's guidance? What is God mentoring you for? God, through the Bible, is guiding you into fulfilling your highest purpose. Your highest purpose is twofold. Your purpose is "to glorify God and to enjoy him forever."[5] The Bible is all about glory and joy.

YOUR PURPOSE IS TO ENJOY GOD

Let's start with joy. To enjoy God means more than simply to have joy; it also means to find God satisfying, to delight in him, and to take pleasure from him. Think of the things that you would say you enjoy — the sun hitting your skin on a beautiful mid-spring day as you hear the sound of laughter and music while walking on the campus yard; the low and profound "mmmm" that involuntary escapes your vocal chords as you take a bite of your favorite meal after not eating all day; the warm embrace of a parent who graciously comforts you as you weep from a really long semester.

These are to enjoy, but oh, how much more enjoyable is the one for whom you are created? The one who formed you and shaped you for himself, the one in whom every crevice of your being was designed to delight? David, an Old Testament prophet and king, captures this enjoyment in song and prayer:

> "You make known to me the path of life;
> in your presence there is *fullness of joy*;
> at your right hand are *pleasures forevermore*." (Psalm 16:11
> ESV, emphasis added)

The psalmist speaks of enjoyment, and God is the object of this enjoyment. Elsewhere David speaks of the happiness that comes with knowing God: "*Happy* are the people whose God *is* the LORD!" (Psalm 144:15 NKJV).

God is our pleasurable King, and he designed us to enjoy him. And as the author of Psalm 23 can testify, this enjoyment follows us even into deep suffering: "Yea, though I walk through the valley of the shadow of death, I will fear no evil: for thou art with me; thy rod and thy staff they comfort me" (Psalm 23:4 KJV). Even in a dark and scary place, the sheep can enjoy the shepherd's kingly protection and presence. The prophet Isaiah agrees when he proclaims: "Behold, God is my salvation; I will trust, and will not be afraid; for the LORD GOD is my strength and my song, and he has become my salvation. *With joy* you will draw water from the wells of salvation" (Isaiah 12:2–3 ESV, emphasis added).

Since our purpose is joy, the Bible is all about joy. Jesus tells his disciples, "When you obey my commandments, you remain in my love, just as I obey my Father's commandments and remain in his love. I have told you these things so that you will be *filled with my joy*. Yes, your *joy will overflow!*" (John 15:10–11, emphasis added). John, an apostle and powerful leader in the early church, himself writes, "We are writing these things so that you may fully share our joy" (1 John 1:4). The Bible is written for your joy!

YOUR PURPOSE IS TO GLORIFY GOD

The Bible uses the term "glory" to denote God's worthiness of honor, his splendor, and his majesty. To glorify him is to think, feel, act, and desire in such a way that acknowledges and displays God's glory.

What do we mean when we talk about God's glory? Let us take a journey to 14th-century western Africa. Mansa Musa was a famous mansa (ruler) of the Empire of Mali. Mansa Musa became famous around the world due to his great wealth and lavish living acquired from his empire's strategic role in the trans-Saharan gold trade. In 1324-5 AD, Mansa Musa took a pilgrimage to Mecca traveling with a huge caravan carrying unimaginable amounts of gold. How much gold, you say? As he traveled from West Africa to Mecca, he arrived in Cairo, Egypt. He gave away so much gold that he jolted the economy of Egypt, and it took the economy years to recover.[6]

Can you imagine this? You are a Berber trader standing at a trading post near an oasis in the middle of the hot Saharan desert. And as you look on the horizon, you cannot believe your eyes! You see a golden aura, like a rising sun, emanating from a long train of people who are regal and dazzling as you have ever seen. Gold everywhere was the source of the aura — golden vessels, golden jewelry, golden laced garments. You know who this is, and it can only be one person, the king of the Mali Empire. You gaze at the seemingly endless wealth; the fame that reaches the ends of the earth; the massive control over the world's supply of gold; and the power to crush economies with lavish generosity. In the same way as when we gaze upon the entourages of our favorite celebrity visiting campus, or the commencement ceremonies of graduation, all we can think is, "What I would give to be a part of this display of glory!"

Though Mansa Musa was glorious, even in all of his splendor, Mansa Musa could not touch the glory of the King of kings and Lord of lords! God is the GOAT! God is our glorious King. Like Mansa Musa was incomprehensibly rich, God is even more so. He is rich in mercy (Ephesians 2:4); rich in glory (Romans 9:23); and rich in kindness and patience (Romans 2:4). And he doesn't keep these riches to himself, but he sets "his riches on all who call on him" (Romans 10:12 ESV). Like Mansa Musa lavished his riches on Egypt in such a generous way that it collapsed their economy, God lavishes his riches upon us in such a way that completely collapses the previous empty ways we operated in our lives (Ephesians 1:7). And God has given everything, even his only Son, so you can be a part of his royal entourage. Even further, Jesus sacrificed the outward display of his glory and became a human so that we ourselves might become more glorious: "For you know the grace of our Lord Jesus Christ, that though he was rich, yet for your sake he became poor, so that you by his poverty might become rich" (2

Corinthians 8:9 ESV). Christians live rejoicing in the honor of being a part of his glory.

All through the Bible, it is clear that the highest purpose of humanity is to glorify God. Everything that we do in life has God's glory as its ultimate goal, as Paul, an apostle and significant Bible author, says, "So whether you eat or drink, or whatever you do, do it all for the *glory of God*" (1 Corinthians 10:31, emphasis added).

Since our purpose is glory, the Bible is all about helping us glorify God. Psalm 119 shows us that the Bible is all about the joy that God's word brings and the help it offers in glorifying him:

> The instructions of the LORD are perfect,
> reviving the soul.
> The decrees of the LORD are trustworthy,
> making wise the simple.
> The commandments of the LORD are right,
> *bringing joy to the heart.*
> The commands of the LORD are clear,
> giving insight for living.
> Reverence for the LORD is pure,
> lasting forever.
> The laws of the LORD are true;
> each one is fair.
> They are *more desirable than gold,*
> even the finest gold.
> They are *sweeter than honey,*
> even honey dripping from the comb.
> They are a warning to your servant,
> *a great reward* for those who obey them. (Psalm 19:7–11,
> emphasis added)

The Bible is about glory and joy.

YOUR PURPOSE IS FOREVER

I love a good party. I love good food, fun company, carefree dancing, and a worthy reason to celebrate. You know what my least favorite thing about a party is? It has to end. Even while I am enjoying a good party, I am grieving a little bit that it won't last forever.

What if I told you that God's glory and enjoyment last forever? You won't have to grieve that at some point they will be depleted. It is almost too good to be true that the glory and the enjoyment are to last *forever.* His kingdom is eternal and glorious! The final destination of your life will be to enjoy a glorified body (1 Corinthians 15:43) in a joyously glorified new heavens and new earth (Revelation 21:1) with an all-satisfying, glorious God:

> I heard a loud shout from the throne, saying, "Look, God's home is now among his people! He will live with them, and they will be his people. God himself will be with them. He will wipe every tear from their eyes, and there will be no more death or sorrow or crying or pain. All these things are gone forever." (Revelation 21:3-4)

Eternity is where we will reflect the glory of God in overwhelming joy. And the expectation of this future glory and enjoyment gives us hope in the here-and-now as we look around and see all of the ways that people have rejected God's kingship. Along with Peter, an apostle and Bible author, and the recipients of his second letter, we "are looking forward to the new heavens and new earth he has promised, a world filled with God's righteousness. And so, dear friends, while you are waiting for these things to happen, make every effort to be found living peaceful lives that are pure and blameless in his sight" (2 Peter 3:13–14).

GOD SPEAKS THROUGH THE BIBLE

You have likely heard people call the Bible "God's word," and this is because God speaks through his word. God's speaking is an expression of his goodness. He loves you so much that he doesn't want you to guess about how to glorify and enjoy him, or to guess how to flourish. Therefore, God gives his guidance open and plainly in the Bible. Moses says this about God's word:

> It is not kept in heaven, so distant that you must ask, "Who will go up to heaven and bring it down so we can hear it and obey?" It is not kept beyond the sea, so far away that you must ask, "Who will cross the sea to bring it to us so we can hear it and obey?" No, the message is very close at hand; it is on your lips and in your heart so that you can obey it. (Deuteronomy 30:12–14)

Moses, a prophet and the author of the first five books of the Bible, was speaking to his people about God's guidance, telling them that God gives it plainly and abundantly!

College is a time where you have to make a plethora of choices and figure out life semester by semester. When we are trying to figure out God's will, his word is the primary place we go. Often, we look for a feeling, a sign, or a voice; however, God wants you to do the hard work of studying what he has already said in his word and applying it to your life. You must 1) read God's word 2) ask God to transform you so that you can know how to apply his word to your life and 3) ask other Christians for wisdom. Sometimes God's word approves of two different options and both seem equally good. Praise God! Let go of the anxiety of trying to look into the future to see if things will go well for each option. Make a decision; rejoice that God is pleased; and trust God with your future.

THE BIBLE IS DIVIDED INTO TWO COVENANTS

These plain and abundant words are divided into two sections, the Old Testament and the New Testament. To understand these two sections, we must first understand the concept of a covenant. The Bible is a collection of covenant documents.

What is a covenant? To put it simply, and at the risk of over-simplification, in the Bible a covenant is a formal relationship between two parties. A common example of a covenant is marriage. It is a relationship. Two people have a warm and loving bond that they share. They love, serve, and spend quality time with each other. It is also a *formal* relationship. There are vows that each person makes, and these vows create duties for the relationship. Faithfulness, loyalty, service through thick and thin, and more, are some of the formal duties. These formal vows protect the marriage from hardship and temptation. The formal vows also cause the relationship to flourish.

Covenants are on every page of the Bible, either explicitly mentioned or hanging out in the background, so to speak. Usually there is a relationship that already exists between the two parties — the two parties being either,

- God and human(s) (Genesis 9:9)
- God and inanimate objects (Jeremiah 33:20)
- Human(s) and human(s) (Jeremiah 2:18).

Just like marriage, the two parties make the relationship formal by establishing conditions that each party must fulfill. The parties also establish promised blessings if the conditions (i.e. duties) are fulfilled and promised curses if they are not. Covenants in the Bible often involve an oath (a vow with an "or else"/curse attached to it) ceremony where the covenant is established, and the oath binds one or both parties to the agreement. The covenant ceremony marks a change in the relationship. The ceremony tweaks, affirms, and strengthens the relationship. After forming a covenant, the terms of the covenant are recorded for each party so that neither party forgets the terms of the covenant (this is where we get the two stone tablets of the Ten Commandments). The Bible is a collection of the covenant records for the covenants God has made with humanity.

God has created two major covenants, after which the two major divisions of the Bible are named— the old and new covenants. "Old Testament" is referring to the old covenant and "New Testament" is referring to the new covenant.[7] What's in each testament? The Old Testament is all of God's covenant word before the coming of Jesus, and the New Testament is all of God's covenant word after the birth of Jesus.

GOD SPEAKS THROUGH THE OLD AND NEW TESTAMENTS

First, both the Old Testament and New Testament are God's word. Peter places the OT authors and the NT apostles in the same category: "I want you to remember what the *holy prophets* said long ago and what our Lord and Savior commanded through *your apostles*" (2 Peter 3:2, emphasis added). Peter is acknowledging the fact that God spoke through primarily the prophets in the Old Testament and the apostles in the New Testament. What I want to highlight is this: God spoke in both the New Testament and the Old Testament. God wants to instruct you through the Old Testament just like the New Testament. The New Testament is God's word along with the Old Testament.

Second, the Bible is true because it's God's word. Paul tells Timothy, his prophetic spiritual son, "All Scripture is breathed out by God and profitable for teaching, for reproof, for correction, and for training in righteousness, that the man of God may be complete, equipped for every good work" (2 Timothy 3:16–17 ESV). The phrase "breathed out by God" comes from the word in the Greek language that means "God-breathed." God himself is the origin of the scriptures. The scriptures come from God's mouth, which is why they are called "the word of God." To reject the Bible is to reject God's speaking, and to reject God's speaking is to reject God himself.

Third, *all* of the Bible is true. The passage also says that *"all"* Scripture comes from God. It is not as if there are some parts from God and other parts that are not. The Bible, in its fullness, is from God, and therefore the Bible is true because God neither lies nor is the author of error.

Fourth, God used people to deliver his word. There are 66 books of the Bible and many different authors. Upon first hearing this, we might conclude that the Bible is somehow merely human writing posing as God's words. However, God purposefully used human authors as his tool to communicate to us and guide us. The Apostle Peter teaches us this when he says, "Above all, you must realize that no prophecy in Scripture ever came from the prophet's own understanding, or from human initiative. No, those prophets were moved by the Holy Spirit, and they spoke from God" (2 Peter 1:20–21). God used human authors — with their unique styles, personalities, perspectives, and angles — to produce God's words. The human authors were not a liability but an asset.

Fifth, the Bible is useful and powerful. Paul tells Timothy that the Bible is useful for teaching, training, and correcting. As Timothy was speaking God's words, people were growing. As we are exposed to the Bible through singing, preaching, teaching, praying, chatting with friends, podcasts, panels at Christian conferences, and the like. God is maturing us. Paul also tells Timothy that with the Bible, he was "complete, equipped for every good work" as a "man of God." A "man of God" in the Bible is a prophet. The job of the prophet was to be God's representative. The Bible was all that Timothy needed in order to be equipped to represent God. This is why Timothy is told a few verses after our passage, "Preach the word of God. Be prepared, whether the time is favorable or not. Patiently correct, rebuke, and encourage your people with good teaching" (2 Timothy 4:2). The

Bible is central to Christian ministry and to the Christian life, and this is why we preach it, listen to it, study it, memorize it, meditate upon it, sing it, pray it, and more.

YOU NEED GOD'S SPIRIT

Sixth, you can only understand the Bible with the help of God's Spirit. Paul spends 1 Corinthians 2:6-16 explaining this, saying, "No one can know a person's thoughts except that person's own spirit, and no one can know God's thoughts except God's own Spirit. And we have received God's Spirit (not the world's spirit), so we can know the wonderful things God has freely given us" (1 Corinthians 2:11–12). One cannot understand the wisdom of God's guidance (the Spirit speaking in the Bible) without receiving his Spirit, because "people who aren't spiritual can't receive these truths from God's Spirit. It all sounds foolish to them and they can't understand it, for only those who are spiritual can understand what the Spirit means" (1 Corinthians 2:14). Just like real recognize real, only spirit can understand spirit. So only spiritual people, those who have God's Spirit, can receive God's word. Someone can understand God's word on an intellectual level without the Spirit, but they won't be able to recognize it as God's word and receive it as God's word.

You will only receive the Bible as God's word if the Holy Spirit softens your heart to receive it. Once softened, you will know that it is God's word in the same way that the tongue knows honey is sweet and the same way the eyes know light is luminous — it simply knows. And only from this place will we be able to use our reasoning and observation to confirm what we already knew by the Spirit. Only from this place will we recognize the powerful attributes of the Bible, the historical evidence supporting its reliability and accuracy as a collection of documents, and the clear consensus of the church throughout the ages.

At this point I must acknowledge the fact that I am using the Bible's truths to teach you about the Bible. I am not appealing to scientific theory, secular historians (historians who reject religious or spiritual explanations), or naturalistic philosophers (philosophers who deny the existence of spiritual things) to prove truths about the Bible. Why? The Bible is not under the authority of our human reasoning or observation, nor does the Bible rely on them to be the word of God. However, the Bible invites us to use science, history, and our reasoning to serve its own purposes. For example, the Gospel Accounts are eyewitness evidence (i.e. history) supporting the claim that Jesus is king and worthy of your devotion. Another example: the scriptures tell us several times that Paul reasoned (i.e. philosophy) with people to convince them that Jesus was the Son of God (Acts 17:17, 22-31). Also, the Bible's authors invite us to carefully observe nature (i.e. science) in order to know truths about God (Matthew 6:25-33; Romans 1:20). The Bible is not against science, history, and philosophy, but we must never use them as measuring rods to make the Bible prove itself. The Bible sits in judgment over science, history, and philosophy, not the other way around.

RECAP

We have seen that God gives us his guidance through the Bible. Just like Maria Stewart, the Bible is meant to saturate and shape all of who we are. God is revealing you things in his word, and all of his revelation has something to do with showing you how to glorify and enjoy him. The Bible is structured by covenants. The Bible is totally true, reliable, and useful. We can only understand and receive the Bible when the Holy Spirit opens our eyes to see it and receive it.

Now that we have a basic overview of the Bible, let's talk about how to interpret the Bible.

CHAPTER 2

GOD IS TEXT MESSAGING ME?

Did you know that you interpret things every day? Anytime you read texts or a symbol, you have to figure out what it means.

Let's talk about text messaging. We have to interpret text messages. Isn't this hard sometimes?! We have to figure out someone's tone, intentions, and true meaning. We decipher and put together the context, the back story, and understand the grammar. Let's not even bring up autocorrect! We also have to figure out the order of the text messages and who was responding to what. It's also vital to figure out the purpose of the text.

Did you know that God has sent you text messages? He has sent you 66 of them to be exact. These messages are called "the Bible." In these texts, he is communicating with you the most love-filled and powerful things he wants you to know. Just like texts and any other message, you must figure out the tone and the author's meaning and intentions. You need to know the historical context, the back story, and the grammar of the language. Unlike text messages sent to your phone, the Bible was written to you *through* an original audience, like the Christians in Corinth during the first century (1 Corinthians 10:11). You also have to figure out how the original audience likely received and responded to the particular Bible book. If that wasn't enough, you have to figure out the purpose — what does God want you to think, feel, and do in response?

WHERE WE ARE GOING

In a sentence, the message of this chapter is: The Bible brings a life-giving message to African Americans, so trust it.

African Americans have a complex relationship with the Bible. On the one hand, the Bible deeply shapes our culture and is the foundation of our community. We have interpreted it to be a book of life, hope, and resistance against oppression. On the other hand, the Bible has been a part of an oppressive version of Christianity. White racist Christians have wrongly used the Bible to prop up racist institutions, racist ideologies, and a racist religion. You may not know how the same book can be interpreted so differently at times. So how can you trust it?

If you do not realize that the Bible gives a life-giving message to African Americans, then you will spend your walk with God wondering if he can be trusted. You will view his word with suspicion and will half-heartedly embrace his guidance in your life. To the contrary, God and his word are worthy of full trust. Like someone falling backwards into a trust-fall, I pray that you fall backwards into God's word, betting everything on it. Only then can you embrace God's glory and joy.

In the following sections we will cover 1) what the Bible is about 2) some basic rules of interpretation 3) how interpreting the Bible works 4) false ways the Bible has been interpreted and 5) what it looks like to fight for healthy interpretations of the Bible.

———

THE BIBLE IS LIFE-GIVING BECAUSE IT'S ABOUT GOD

Let's talk about some key things we need to consider in order to interpret the Bible correctly.

First, you must figure out what the Bible is about. People try to make the Bible about a lot of things — science, world history, astrology, racial history, and more. Though the Bible *addresses* these things, the Bible is not *about* these things. The Bible is about Yahweh, the God of the Bible.

THE BIBLE IS ABOUT LIFE-GIVING BELIEFS

The Bible tells us what to *believe* about God. For example, the first words of the Bible invite us to believe that "God created the heavens and the earth" (Genesis 1:1). This verse is a truth-claim that God intends to shape your beliefs! You must choose to either accept or reject the claims. As a book that contains beliefs about God, the Bible will shape your view of reality — who God is, what God's world is like, who you are as God's image, and what God is doing in the world.

THE BIBLE IS ABOUT LIFE-GIVING PRACTICES

The Bible also tells us what to *do* for God. God tells Joshua, who led the Israelites into the Promised Land, "Study this Book of Instruction continually. Meditate on it day and night so you will be sure to obey everything written in it. Only then will you prosper and succeed in all you do" (Joshua 1:8). The Bible is all about your lifestyle — the emotions you feel for God, the choices you make for God, the habits you build for God, and the like. You must choose to either accept or reject the claims in the Bible that God makes on your life.

———

WE MUST INTERPRET THE BIBLE CORRECTLY

In response to this, some of you might be thinking, "How do people come up with so many different beliefs and practices from the Bible, particularly the concept of White church vs. Black church?" This question hits on the process of how we interpret the Bible. Let's touch on this briefly.

First, you must realize the steps to interpreting a passage correctly. Where do we go to find this process? Well, the Bible itself. The later books in the Bible actually interpret the earlier books in the Bible. The New Testament Bible authors are constantly doing this process with the Old Testament. The whole book of Hebrews, a New Testament book of the Bible, is a perfect example of this interpretive process. It often quotes an Old Testament passage and then gives an explanation. The Bible is interpreting itself, and we are to imitate its process.

YOU MUST READ THE BIBLE CAREFULLY

What happens in this process of interpretation? There are at least four steps:

- One, you must observe what is on the page. We often do this step naturally without even thinking about it, but it is nonetheless essential to do it carefully.
- Two, you must determine what the Bible passage's author is actually saying to their original audience.
- Three, you must determine what the author wants the audience to do in response.
- Four, you must figure out what we, in 2023, are to believe and do in response. Why? Bible passages have an original audience (e.g. the book of Romans written to first century Christians in Rome), but Bible passages are also written for future generations, like us, 21st century Christians (Romans 15:4; 1 Corinthians 10:11).

The key to understanding how to interpret the Bible is understanding the difference between the Bible and theology. The Bible is God's word. Theology is our words about God. We are doing theology as we interpret the Bible. The Bible + human interpretation = theology. When doing theology, we must highlight the fact that it involves *human* interpretation. Humans disagree with each other as they interpret the Bible. This is why there is one Bible but many different strains of theology. The goal is to have our theology be as faithful to the Bible as possible.

BLACK INTERPRETATIONS CAN BE DIFFERENT FROM WHITE INTERPRETATIONS

In talking about how the Bible is God's word, I realize that as a Black African you might have a complex relationship with the Bible given how widespread it has been interpreted, for both good and evil purposes. Let's talk about this for a second.

As Black Africans have come to the text of the Bible, we engage in theology. We bring to the text our needs, questions, and concerns that flow from our lived experiences. As we come to the text, the text speaks back, giving us answers to our questions and also giving us different or additional questions to ask. This is why African Americans and Euro-Americans can take away different theological conclusions from the same passage, even when they equally believe the scriptures are true!

For example, with a passage about how Christians should relate to the government, an African American might be asking the unspoken question, "How does this relate to a government that has been active in racist oppression? How do we oppose such governments?" A White American might ask, "How does this relate to a government that promotes freedom and equal opportunity, like our government? How can we be more faithfully patriotic in building up the good works of the government?" Based upon the questions and assumptions about governments that they bring to the passage, they will walk away with different theologies. Both people can walk away with a different idea of what the Bible requires them to do for God in their political life. A similar thing happened to me as I was preaching a sermon during my preaching class in seminary. A Chinese Christian who was listening essentially shared with me that my sermon was too optimistic about Christians participating in public life and politics. Why? He was used to a government that persecuted Christians. His lived experiences would have had him preach a different sermon on the passage. Sometimes two different interpretations can be valid depending on the situation and audience, but at other times, one interpretation is in harmony with the Bible and the other is actually contrary to the Bible.

Given this process of interpretation, different groups of people can walk away with different theologies on slavery, on our responsibility to address racism, the church's role in addressing people's physical condition and social situation, the scope of the gospel's work, the reality of God's judgment, the ethics of community development and restoration, how the end times affect our engagement of the here and now, and more.

Here are a few examples of White Christian interpretations that differ from Black Christian interpretations.

- Some White Christians have interpreted Cain's mark of punishment in Genesis 4:9-15 to be Black people's skin color.
- Some have interpreted the curse of Ham in Genesis 9:20-27 to support the enslavement of Black Africans all over the globe.
- Many White Christian traditions would view talk about race, social class, and ethnicity as a distraction from the gospel.

Most African Americans, in their social spaces and religious traditions, would quickly push against these biblical interpretations. Why? Their personal experiences as African Americans force them to re-engage the scriptures in the face of theologies that support their oppression — the same Bible, competing theologies.

African Americans, generally speaking, have their own religious traditions and ways of interpreting certain passages. Generally, Black Christians have seen the Bible as the source of hope for our community. This hope pushes against the hopelessness of many White Christian interpretations, and it pushes against the Christ-less despair that flows out of other places in Black culture. It is a reading of the Bible that is not only true to the Christian faith but also addresses the real lives of African Americans. As we bring our Black African questions, experiences, and core concerns to the Bible, we put them in conversation with the Bible. God, through the Bible, gives Africans words of hope and transformation.

———

I LOVE AFRICANA AND JESUS. WHERE ARE THE OTHERS?!

One day I was recording an *Africana Manna* episode with one of our students, Alafia. *Africana Manna* is a podcast I started with a couple of students. It explores the wisdom of Christian African ancestors so that we can apply that same wisdom to the current issues of our day. We were doing a special episode where we discussed *The Black Church*, a documentary on the history of the Black church narrated by Dr. Henry Louis Gates. After we recorded the episode, Alafia and I talked. We both agreed that the Black church must remain faithful to the scriptures *and* care about Black African uplift and racial justice. There shouldn't be an "either/or" or a "but." Alafia said, "You know, I really don't know many Christians who are serious about the Bible and really care about africana. Some of the only people I know of are you and me!"

On campus, given the stigma Christianity can have among

your peers, it can really seem like you must choose one or the other. Can I care about africana *and* believe the scriptures at the same time? Throughout the course of this book, I will address African core concerns from the rich resources of the Christian faith. Some of you might be thinking that this aspiration is inconsistent within itself. You might be thinking that Christianity is only for the evil agenda of White people's racism and that Christianity couldn't possibly offer anything of significant value to Africans. I disagree, and let me tell you why.

CHRISTIANITY CAN GET POLLUTED BY CULTURE

First, there have been many who criticize Christianity's relationship with those of African descent. I join them in their efforts to criticize. However, I will *not* criticize the Christianity *of the Bible*. I will criticize some of the various ways Christianity has been manifested and practiced in different variations.

Wherever Christianity goes, it takes on a particular form based upon the beliefs, practices, and stories belonging to the people Christianity encounters. For example, Christianity in China will look different than Christianity in Haiti. Ideally, these Christian traditions will not contradict each other. They will be both authentically Christian and shaped by the culture in which they find themselves. Dr. Carl Ellis, the author of *Free at Last?* and provost's professor of theology and culture at Reformed Theological Seminary, captures this process:

> When the gospel is applied to a particular culture, the result is Christianity. There can be as many varieties of Christianity as there are cultures, but these cultural Christianities will not contradict one another. They will have a complementary relationship as they focus on God's gracious deliverance accomplished in Christ. Hence it is not necessarily wrong to have a White Christianity or a Black Christianity.[1]

The above is why you intuitively know that on a Sunday, a Chinese church experience is going to be different than a worship experience at a Black church, which will be different from a Puerto Rican church. The problem comes when these "Christianities" become so polluted with anti-God beliefs, practices, and stories that it ceases to be Christianity. Dr. Ellis calls this "Christianity-ism." When a Christian tradition becomes polluted by certain anti-God aspects of culture, it starts to become a false version of Christianity. What we often react against in the United States is White Christianity-ism, not Christianity itself.

CHRISTIANS HAVE RECOGNIZED FALSE CHRISTIANITY

David Walker, a prominent Black Christian in the late 1700s and early 1800s, pronounces the judgment of God over an American Christianity-ism, a Christianity infected with racism, in his famous booklet *David Walker's Appeal*:

> Can anything be a greater mockery of religion than the way in which it is conducted by the Americans? . . . Will the Lord suffer this people to go on much longer, taking his holy name in vain? Will he not stop them, PREACHERS and all? O Americans! Americans! ! I call God — I call angels — I call men, to witness, that your DESTRUCTION is *at hand*, and will be speedily consummated unless you REPENT.[2]

It is abundantly clear throughout western church history that there have been many wicked, racist people who have taken the Bible and twisted it for their own purposes and selfish gain. The Bible has been used to support slavery, Jim Crow legislation, and to justify ignoring the oppression of Black people. In fact, to do this, racist White Christians have often had to hide certain portions of the Bible from the enslaved. Walker, along with any one who has an intact sense of justice and an awareness of world history, knows that God is opposed to a religion that crushes the helpless under its feet.

Though we often paint in broad strokes the story of how White Christians used the Bible to oppress, there is a complexity to the story. In fairness, there have been White Christians who have seen the Bible's teachings as the reason why they were compelled to love their Black neighbors as themselves. While some use the scriptures to oppress, others use it to liberate.

The issue of Christians dealing with false Christianity exists on the African continent along with the diaspora as Africans oppress other Africans. Wole Soyinka, a Yoruba writer and recipient of the Nobel Prize in Literature, believes that Christianity and Islam are religions that are preventing the African continent from its own uplift. He says, "As if the continent did not have enough on her plate, enter the shadowy but lethal force determined to re-enslave a continent with its chains of fundamentalist theology!"[3] He criticizes how corrupt governmental powers, groups, and agendas have used extreme versions of Islam and Christianity to justify and further their violence and oppression. However, the version of Christianity that supports corrupt governments on the continent is not the Christianity of the Bible.

When one looks at the history of Christianity, Black people's objection to it is understandable. Understandably, some Black people reject Christianity when observing the shocking abuses and distortions of it at the hands of their oppressors and when observing the ways that all people, including Black people, have failed to live up to Christianity's ideals.

Apostle[4] Peter joins David Walker in judging perverted forms of Christianity. When speaking of the Apostle Paul's writings, the Apostle Peter warns us of people who will try to twist the scriptures to create a version of Christianity that is anti-God: "Some of his comments are hard to understand, and those who are ignorant and unstable have twisted his letters to mean something quite different, just as they do with other parts of Scripture. And this will result in their destruction" (2 Peter 3:16). Peter tells us that there are people who have twisted the scriptures in the effort to make them mean something different from what they are saying. Peter says their instinct to twist the scriptures flows from their spiritual ignorance and instability. Peter assures us that God will destroy those who do so.

We must not let those who perverted Christianity win the day. By using the word of God to justify oppression, they betrayed the word of God itself. The word is a saving word, not an oppressing word. The word is life-giving, not death-bringing. The word is all-supreme, not White supremacist. Those who use the Bible to justify systems of oppression betray the Bible's own character.

———

WE MUST TRUST THE BIBLE

Now, I want to acknowledge the difficulty that many Black folks find themselves in when it comes to Bible interpretation. There are difficult passages that are hard to figure out about slavery, oppression, and suffering. In the face of those difficulties, we can allow false interpretations to persuade us. This poses a dilemma — "Do I accept this interpretation, or do I throw the Bible away?"

We must be careful not to deny the Bible's power and authority in our efforts to make sense of the Black experience. When encountering difficult texts and uncomfortable passages, the answer for some is to deny the authority that these passages hold. Often, these passages are dismissed as merely human words written by those who were backward, not-yet-enlightened, and blinded by their times. However, we must not mute or ignore parts of the scriptures as we try to process our experiences. We must trust God and wrestle with difficult passages, remembering the character of our God. We must adopt an interpretation of Scripture that takes our experience seriously but does not distrust the authority of Scripture.

We must trust the Bible because it is the foundation of our

hope. We sometimes wrongly believe that we must discard the Bible to find liberation as Black people. However, we will find that God's wisdom and ways are much higher than our own. It is not God who must catch up to us in his thinking, rather we must catch up to God. A vision of Black uplift that betrays the authority of the scriptures will eventually lead to Black demise. Many folks will try to disarm White Christian interpretations of the Bible by throwing away the authority of the Bible itself, but the Bible, correctly interpreted, is actually the foundation of Black hope. We must discard racist theology, not the Bible itself.

CHRISTIANITY ISN'T COPIED FROM EGYPT

One way we mistrust the Bible is by creating a false narrative that is seemingly pro-Black but actually damages the Bible. Folks can deny the origin of the scriptures in an attempt to affirm Black culture.

For example, some Black people would claim that the scriptures originated not from Yahweh himself but from Egyptian religions. They do this to show that Christianity doesn't belong to White people but to Black people. Some argue that Moses was in Egypt, received the Old Testament laws from Egyptian religions, and then re-established them at Mt. Sinai. Later, Jews sought to carry forward a revision of Judaism by coming up with a new god – Jesus. Thus, Christianity has its ultimate origins in Egypt.

The problem with these theories is that they reject the Bible's teaching of revelation, the teaching that Yahweh God himself revealed *himself* as *he* inspired the prophets and apostles to write the scriptures. The Bible tells us that God met with Moses to give him the scriptures; Moses didn't have to copy them from the Egyptians. The Israelite spiritual system has many similarities with religions all over the world. However, this does not mean that the spiritual system is a copy of another. Correlation between religions doesn't mean that one caused the other. Correlation doesn't always mean causation. The scriptures tell us that God has made his own nature and will plain to everyone (Romans 1:18-23, 2:12-16), though sin has caused confusion. The correlation between religions flows from what God has made plain to everyone. It is not surprising that other religions have similarities to Christianity.

THE BIBLE WASN'T INVENTED BY WHITE PEOPLE

Others totally reject the scriptures as an invention of White people to oppress Black people. However, they fail to see that White oppressors did not invent the scriptures. All the known authors of the New Testament were brown and tan-skinned Palestinian Jews, and their non-White ancestors wrote the Old Testament. The only author over whom there is debate over is Luke (they debate whether he was a Gentile or a Jew), and even this doesn't mean that he was White. Many, if not most, of the Bible books were written under political, cultural, or religious oppression or written during exile or homeless wanderings. If we run away from the Bible because we believe it is consistent with the "White man's" racist agenda, we allow racist interpretations to win the day. We repeat the same error. How? They rejected the Bible by misinterpreting it into a White supremacist book, and we reject the Bible by believing it could actually be a White supremacist book. In other words, we answer misinterpretation with misinterpretation. We overcome racist White interpretations of the Bible by correctly interpreting it, not by throwing it away.

THE BIBLE INSPIRES BLACK RESISTANCE

Lastly, as we think about the Bible's focus being on our beliefs and practices, we must realize that the Bible has been the bedrock of the ways that African Americans view the world (i.e. worldview), whether you realize it or not. The Bible shapes many of the ideals you hold dear — pan-Africanism, the struggle for Black freedom and uplift, the dignity of humanity, community development, and more. The Bible influences the way that you intuitively see the world, yourself, and God. The question is not whether or not the Bible has shaped you but how the Bible's theological and philosophical influences function within your worldview.

Actually, Christianity is the best system for addressing the issues that are most dear to Black Africans and the issues that most powerfully shape their lives. Dr. Cedric Robinson, the late political science and africana studies professor, points us to the power of Black Christianity among Black Africans in their path to uplift in his book *Black Movements in America*. Robinson notes how Black Christianity has effectively carried and channeled the Black spirit of resistance against injustice and oppression. Christianity was the vehicle for Black freedom. When the American ideals in the Constitution and Declaration of Independence failed the expectations of Black Americans, the church stepped up to be the single most influential institution to advance the journey towards Black flourishing. At the end of his book, his final words point to the power and necessity of the Black church. Robinson states that the church has always been the institution that has contributed to Black flourishing most powerfully. The Black church brings the possibility of a Black social movement that will bring Black people, and perhaps all of America, to the Promised Land of flourishing. A "continuity of Afro-Christian belief and vision" is the way forward for Black people.[5]

A religion that has nothing to say to the "afflicted" and those in the situation of the "orphan and widow," is not of the Bible. Dr. Howard Thurman — the first dean of the chapel of Howard University, among many other things — shares with us the importance of this:

> I can count on the fingers of one hand the number of times that I have heard a sermon on the meaning of religion, of Christianity, to the man who stands with his back against the wall. It is urgent that my meaning be crystal clear. The masses of men live with their backs constantly against the wall. They are the poor, the

disinherited, the dispossessed. What does our religion say to them? The issue is not what it counsels them to do for others whose need may be greater, but what religion offers to meet their own needs. The search for an answer to this question is perhaps the most important religious quest of modern life.[6]

We must ask, "Is there any help to be found for the disinherited in the religion of Jesus?"[7] The answer is, "Yes!" The Christian faith speaks a good word to those who are crushed and afflicted, like many Black Africans have been.

JOHN JEA TEACHES US HOW TO FIGHT FOR THE BIBLE

Let's learn from our old friend, John Jea, who did not let White, oppressive interpreters win the day in his life in what it means to interpret the Bible.

ENSLAVED UNDER HYPOCRITICAL CHRISTIANS

He was a Christian and internationally renowned preacher who lived in the late 1700s and 1800s. John was born in Africa in 1773, was enslaved, and then brought to North America with his mother, father, and siblings. Then, a cruel master bought them in New York. He gave the enslaved repulsive food; made them work brutal hours (they worked during the summer from 2am to 11pm and during the winter from 4am to 10pm. Even the horses rested five hours a day), and tortured them if they complained about the conditions, sometimes beating them to death. Our friend describes what sometimes happened after these punishments:

> After our master had been treating us in this cruel manner, we were obliged to thank him for the punishment he had been

inflicting on us, quoting that Scripture which saith, 'Bless the rod, and him that hath appointed it.' But though he was a professor of religion, he forgot that passage which saith, 'God is love, and whosoever dwelleth in love dwelleth in God, and God in him.'[8]

Jea was noting the hypocrisy of his master. Particularly, his master twisted the scriptures to uphold his own hate-filled intentions. Jea noticed the Christian hypocrisy of many of the White American "Christians" around him. They claimed to believe in the Bible, but used it to justify their own treatment of the enslaved.

JOHN HATES CHRISTIANS

John began to openly and vocally hate Christians. Jea's master, seeing how much Jea hated Christians, made him go to worship as punishment. One day, the minister's preaching inspired Jea to pray for God's presence. John prayed because he wanted to see if there was truly a God. After all, his heart told him there was no God since his heart was filled with rage against the minister and other hypocritical Christians.

Despite his hatred, God was working on John. Later, John became convicted that he was a sinner against God. He was making spiritual progress though he had not yet placed his trust in God. In response, his cruel masters restricted him from going to the chapel. Jea would continue to seek God's word with desperation and go to chapel even though his masters beat him for doing so.

JESUS SAVES JOHN UNDER PERSECUTION

Jea confessed his sins to God and experienced the Spirit's power and renewal. Jesus saved John against overwhelming odds! Of his salvation, Jea speaks in joyous and powerful terms about the change he experienced in his own soul and about how he related to the world. For example, though Jea continued to be beaten by his masters for seeking God's word, he continued to pursue the Lord. John saw the sufferings he endured as the same kind Jesus endured. Jea wanted more of the Bible, and as a result, he endured persecution from hypocritical Christians. Nevertheless, Jesus met and sustained him in the troubles he faced. Jea saw that Jesus was against the slave master and for the oppressed. Even more, he saw his own sufferings as the same kind Jesus experienced. This same Jesus strengthened Jea by the Spirit.

JOHN IS FREE

After being sold and bought several times, our newly converted brother ran away from his last master to be baptized by a minister. In response, John's master was furious because the minister informed the master that "according to the spiritual law of liberty, [Jea] was considered a worthy member of society"[9] and as a result freed. Jea's master took him to the magistrates, and upon Jea making a credible profession of faith, the magistrates declared him freed.

GOD'S MIRACLE FOR JOHN

In response, Jea's master and his sons then set themselves on a mission to convince John that God required him to remain enslaved. They used the Bible to try to convince our African friend. Jea could not read and could not know the scriptures for himself, and this grieved him. He fervently prayed that he would be able to understand it in order to refute his oppressor's interpretation of it.

After fervently praying for six weeks, the Lord sent an angel to Jea, and the angel supernaturally taught Jea how to read the first chapter of the Gospel According to John! God had equipped Jea to resist his oppressors.

The next day, Jea was rejoicing and praising God. After his day's work, he went to the minister's house to share what had happened. After the minister refused to believe John, he tested him. Jea skillfully read aloud the first chapter of John's Gospel Account. Continuing the test, the minister gave Jea other books. Jea displayed he could not read those. In response, the minister and his wife concluded God gave Jea the ability to miraculously read the Bible and the Bible alone.

In all of this, God saw Jea and favored him. Jea said, "This caused them to spread a rumor all over the city of New York saying, that the Lord had worked great miracles on a poor Black man . . . From that hour, in which the Lord taught me to read, until the present, I have not been able to read in any book, nor any reading whatsoever, but such as contain the word of God."[10]

Like Jea, do not let the abusers of the Bible have the last word over it. Seek God, and trust that he will lead you into truth.

RECAP

We have seen that the Bible gives a life-giving message for African Americans. The Bible is about God. We learn from it what to believe about him and what to do for him. As we interpret the Bible, we interpret it carefully and realize that oftentimes human interpretations can differ from one another. These interpretations can lead to versions of Christianity that are so polluted that they become false versions of Christianity. Though Bible interpretation has been polluted by White racism, African American Christians, along with notable others, have recognized the Bible's true interpretation in the face of racism. As Black interpreters of the Bible, we must be careful not to deny the authority of the Bible in the face of the ways that people have abused the Bible. We must fight for healthy biblical interpretation and place our trust in the Bible.

Now that we have considered God's word, let's turn to God himself.

PART TWO
RELATIONSHIP

CHAPTER 3

FIRST DATES AND HEART BREAKS

Have you ever had a crush on someone? Now let me ask you another question. How well did you know that person before you had a crush on them?! When you are first interested in someone, you often know very little about them. Maybe you scrolled through their *Instagram* page or asked your friends about your crush, but that is not nearly enough to actually know who someone is. So often, we are infatuated with our idea of our crushes, not the reality of them. As you get to know your crush, you learn who they really are, not your perception of them, and you learn how to love the real them.

For many of us, God is like that crush we see and like but whom we know very little about. You are infatuated with your idea of God, not his whole reality. Or perhaps you are infatuated with someone else's idea of God. In this chapter, I want to sit down on our "first date" with God.

As you get to know God, you will have your heart broken in little ways or big ways. That's okay because we all have false conceptions of God that need correcting. You will have to bury some parts of that view of God you had, some parts you might've loved. Some of us will have to say "goodbye" to the God that is distant, or the God that wants us to follow a few sets of rules and merely intervenes in life to make us feel better. Some of us will have to say "goodbye" to that God who agreed with all of our religious preferences and fit perfectly into our already existing lives. Some of us will have to say "goodbye" to that God who we believed was really the same God of every other religion. However, your heart will learn to love someone better than you ever imagined.

You might be thinking, "Of course I have gotten to know God himself. I talk to him everyday, and I go to Bible study regularly. I grew up in church. I have been more than acquainted with God." Nevertheless we know that spending time around someone doesn't mean we know them. Someone can be your best friend, yet you can know little about them. Shoot, you can be *married* to someone and know very little about them.

I thought I knew God well until I read my first book on the character of God. It was A.W. Tozer's *The Knowledge of the Holy,* a small book about the attributes of God (attributes are things that are always true of God at all times). I was probably in my fourth year at the University of Virginia. Up until that point, I thought I knew God well until the book started blowing my mind. As I was reading the chapters on God's goodness, faithfulness, self-existence, transcendence, and other attributes, I was amazed at how much I was learning about God's attributes and how understanding each of them was massively important for the Christian life. If God himself is central to the universe, it is absolutely vital to know who he is, truly.

WHERE WE ARE GOING

In a sentence, this chapter will show you that God is everything you need, so satisfy yourself with him.

On Black campuses, Christianity is a commonly found religion. Whenever people talk about God, we assume that they are talking about the same God as the Christian God. For example, often, people will say, "I see the God from Judaism, Islam, and

Christianity as all the same God." However, there are many things that people say about "God" that are not true about the God of the Bible. On top of this, oftentimes people are using the same words but mean different things. "God is good" can mean two different things to two different people. Among all of the misconceptions, we need to be careful to study who God is.

Often, Black suffering can will be an occasion for people to lose hope in God. Dr. Benjamin Mays – civil rights leader, pastor, Howard University's founding dean of the School of Religion, a former Morehouse president, and mentor of Dr. King – highlights this pattern after World War I, when Black people's high hopes of equality were crushed. "Out of this situation came floods of Negro literature expressing a lack of faith in God never before witnessed in the history of the Negro in this country. The Negro . . . began to develop literature after 1920 fraught with agnosticism and atheism."[1] Ta-Nehisi Coates is an example of this in our current day. When retrospectively reflecting upon himself sitting in Howard's Rankin Chapel, mourning the death of a loved one, he tells us,

> And raised conscious, in rejection of the Christian God, I could see no higher purpose in Prince's death. I believed, and still do, that our bodies are our selves, that my soul is the voltage conducted through neurons and nerves, and that my spirit is my flesh . . . When the assembled mourners bowed their heads in prayer, I was divided from them because I believed the void would not answer back.[2]

Coates believed, at the time of writing *Between the World and Me*, that there is nothing more to existence than physical matter. It is a view that holds no hope in a God outside of ourselves.

I want to convince you that Yahweh, the God of the Bible, is more glorious and enjoyable than any other version of God. In the face of suffering, the answer is not to throw God away but to press deeper into the knowledge of him. There is no hope without him. In the next chapter we will deal more with God's relationships to suffering, but in this chapter we will dive into God himself. Understanding God's character is one of the most important things we can understand because it is behind every other teaching in the Bible. If God himself is central to the universe, then he is central to your own life, whether you know it or not. If this is true, then it is absolutely vital to know who he is. We will see that 1) God is everything you ever needed, with some help from Augustine 2) he is always with his people 3) he is the only one you will ever need 4) and he is inviting you into his inner-life of love.

WE KNOW GOD THROUGH THE BIBLE

How do we get to know who God is? In any relationship, we know about a person largely through what they share with us. The same is true of God. This is why we spent so much time explaining the Bible. We need him to speak to us if we are going to get to know him, and we need to have our ideas about who he is centered primarily on what he says about himself in his own words. So what does God say about himself?

————

AUGUSTINE TEACHES US THAT WE DESPERATELY NEED GOD

Allow me to introduce you to Augustine of Hippo, our old friend for this chapter. He can relate to many Black college students; according to our modern-day United States racial framework, he was a Black man. He experienced DuBois' double consciousness being both African and ambitious in a Roman world. Also, he knows what it is like to be both ambitious and spiritually hungry. Moreover, he is undoubtedly the most influential theologian in the western church and one of the top then most influential people in the global West in general. If you live in the global West, you are Augustinian and don't know it. You need to know Augustine.

AUGUSTINE'S AMBITION

Augustine was born in the year 354 AD and grew up in Thagaste, a city in modern-day Algeria near what we now call the North African[3] coast. He was of mixed heritage: He was born to a Roman father, named Patricius, and a Berber mother named Monica. His Roman father, Patricius, was not a Christian until right before his death, and his African mother, Monica, was a devout Christian. Both Monica and Patricius pushed Augustine hard in school, wanting him to move up the social ladder in the Greco-Roman world. As Augustine was climbing the social ladder, he was far away from Jesus. However, Monica was extremely devout and was always praying to the point of tears that Augustine would find Jesus. Eventually, he then moved to Rome to teach rhetoric and then to Milan, which was kind of like a modern day New York or DC, at the center of influence and power. Augustine had made it! He was successful, yet without God.

AUGUSTINE BELIEVES IN JESUS

In Milan, Augustine would sit under the preaching of Ambrose the Christian bishop of Milan. Augustine was initially uninterested in Christianity because it wasn't sophisticated enough for him, but he found in Ambrose a person who was able to present Christianity in an intellectually satisfying way. After a beautiful journey searching for God, he eventually is converted to Jesus through reading Romans 13:13-14: "Don't participate in the darkness of wild parties and drunkenness, or in sexual promiscuity and immoral living, or in quarreling and jealousy. Instead, clothe yourself with the presence of the Lord Jesus Christ. And don't let yourself think about ways to indulge your evil desires." He goes on to become many things – a member of the church, an elder, a bishop, a defender of the Christian faith, and a giant in philosophy.

AUGUSTINE IS SATISFIED IN GOD

He wrote a book called *Confessions* which tells his journey in the form of a prayer. He begins it by saying:

> Can any praise be worthy of the Lord's majesty? How magnificent his strength! How inscrutable his wisdom! Man is one of your creatures, Lord, and his instinct is to praise you. He bears about him the mark of death, the sign of his own sin, to remind him that you thwart the proud. But still, since he is a part of your creation, he wishes to praise you. The thought of you stirs him so deeply that he cannot be content unless he praises you, because you made us for yourself and our hearts find no peace until they rest in you.[4]

The last sentence is one of Augustine's most famous quotes. You will not find satisfaction in life unless your heart rests in God. We live our lives searching, discontent, knowing that there must be more. We are restless, not able to know peace and satisfaction. It is only when we center our lives on God and his glory that we can find contentment and rest. This chapter is the first step – understanding God.

––––––

GOD IS EVERYTHING YOU NEED

An attribute of God is something that is core to his being, something that he always is at all times and in all that he does. For those who grew up in the Black church, you likely often acknowledged this with God's goodness during church. The leader of the service would exclaim, "God is good?!"

The congregation would respond, "All the time!"

The leader would again trumpet, "And all the time?!"

"God is good!"

Goodness is an attribute of God therefore God is always good and good in all he does. Why is knowing his attributes so important? God is everything you need. Each one of his attributes is deeply satisfying and absolutely vital for living life abundantly. Let's look at some attributes of God.

GOD IS THE SOURCE OF ALL EXISTENCE

God is not an imaginary friend nor is he an abstract principle, a symbol, a thought, or an idea. He is real. Furthermore, like a livestream TV show needs the internet, you need God's existence for your own existence. For starters, God is the creator and foundation of all existence, so if he didn't exist, nothing would exist. In fact, our own existence flows from his existence, for "in him we live and move and exist" (Acts 17:28). Also, if God is not real, then all of the other attributes we will discuss cannot bless us. If God is not real, his goodness, wisdom, power, justice, and more, are nothing. However, we praise God that he is real! The author of Hebrews tells us that "it is impossible to please God without faith. Anyone who wants to come to him must believe that God exists and that he rewards those who sincerely seek him" (Hebrews 11:6). If we do not believe God exists, his goodness cannot reach us.

GOD IS SPIRIT

God is Spirit, and you need his Spirit for your own spirit. The Gospel According to John tells us that "God is Spirit, so those who worship him must worship in spirit and in truth'" (John 4:24). Being spirit means that God is not visible or made of physical matter like you and I, as Jesus says, "a spirit does not have flesh and bones" (Luke 24:39 ESV). Therefore as the Apostle Paul says, "we shouldn't think of God as an idol designed by craftsmen from gold or silver or stone" (Acts 17:29). You may be thinking, "Didn't God appear to people in the Old Testament? Didn't they see him?" Yes, God appeared to people in the Old Testament, but it was always with a layer of physical matter that "clothed" his presence to people. God, in a way, clothed himself with physical matter so that we would not behold him directly. Sometimes this was a firestorm (Deuteronomy 4:11-19), the angel of the LORD (Exodus 3:1-4), or even the appearance of a human (Genesis 18:1-2).

So what do we make of the passages that mention where people talk to God face-to-face (Genesis 32:30, Exodus 33:11)? As the *IVP Bible Background Commentary* tells us, "Speaking face to face is an idiom suggesting an honest and open relationship."[5] "Face-to-face" should not be taken literally. There is a limit to the degree that humanity can know God.

The reality that God is spirit is why Jesus' ministry is so beautiful. Jesus is "the visible image of the invisible God" (Colossians 1:15). Through Jesus' humanity, the invisible God is made visible to us. In Jesus, we can see what God is like perfectly because, "No one has ever seen God. But the unique One, who is himself God, is near to the Father's heart. He has revealed God to us" (John 1:18). Also, Jesus sends us God's spirit in order to revive our own spirit. God's spirit gives birth to a new spirit within us (John 3:4-6) so that we can truly worship God in spirit and truth (John 4:24). Just like a phone call can't work with one dead phone and one charged phone, to have a true connection with God, you need Jesus to "charge up" your dead spirit. And Jesus' charge is one that never runs out.

GOD IS LIMITLESS

God has no limits, and you need his limitlessness for your own limitations. Having no limits means God is infinite. There is nothing greater than him in any way. He has no limitations as far as space (1 Kings 8:27; Psalm 139:7), his greatness (Psalm 145:3), his knowledge (Psalm 147:5), his power, and all of his other attributes. His only limitation is his own nature, meaning God cannot do what is against his nature. For example, since there is no evil within God, God cannot do evil. Having no limits means that our limited minds cannot fully understand him. We exclaim with the Apostle Paul, "Oh, how great are God's riches and wisdom and knowledge! How impossible it is for us to understand his decisions and his ways!" (Romans 11:33).

As people who have limits, we depend on God who has no limits. When my daughters throw their toy and it accidentally gets stuck in a high place, they need me, someone whose height has less of a limitation, in order to recover that toy. The same is so of God when we are in need, except God has no limitations. Our own power fails us, but God's power never fails. Our own goodness escapes us in tough moments, but God's goodness overflows from a bottomless pit. Our own wisdom is like mist, but God has wisdom upon wisdom for all those who need it. Our lack looks to his lavish, limitless attributes.

Jesus brings this unlimited God to us. Jesus brings us into connection with God. Jesus, who has been the eternal Son of God, is the one who embraces the limitations of a human so that we can know our infinite God in the flesh.

GOD IS ETERNAL

God's eternality gives us hope in a world that is passing away. God has no beginning and no end. The psalmist says, "Before the mountains were born, before you gave birth to the earth and the world, from beginning to end, you are God" (Psalm 90:2). The psalmist also says, "But I cried to him, 'O my God, who lives forever," (Psalm 102:24). God existed before anything was created, and he will exist forever.

As people whose "life is like the morning fog—it's here a little while, then it's gone," (James 4:14) the fact that we belong to an eternal God comforts us in the midst of a world full of death. Our eternal God will not let us truly die if we belong to him. I typically buy my wife normal roses, but one time I bought her a forever rose. One category of roses dies, the other stays vibrant forever due to a preservative. God's timelessness means that when we die as normal roses, he will make us forever roses, and his very own life-source is the preservative. Jesus is the way we move from eternal death to eternal life with God in his eternity. Jesus says, "I tell you the truth, anyone who believes has eternal life. Yes, I am the bread of life! Your ancestors ate manna in the wilderness, but they all died. Anyone who eats the bread from heaven, however, will never die" (John 6:47–50). Jesus, as one who was resurrected from the dead, will raise us up from the dead (John 6:40) so that we will live forever. He will carry us into eternity as our amazing ruler.

GOD DOES NOT CHANGE

In a world full of change, God's unchanging nature is a comfort. God is "always the same" (Hebrews 1:12). Therefore, "the LORD's plans stand firm forever; his intentions can never be shaken" (Psalm 33:11). Even if from our human perspective it seems as if God's plans change, from his perspective, he has always known what is going to happen. This is important because the Bible means nothing to us if God changes, has new thoughts, or makes mistakes that he must then correct. Why should we trust what he says if he could change his mind tomorrow? Also, why should we trust him when he reveals his nature if his nature could change? He would then conceivably be good one day and then evil the next. God's unchangeableness, or immutability, is often an over-looked but nonetheless precious attribute of God.

We can be sure that God is good because with his goodness "there is no variation or shadow due to change" (James 1:17 ESV). Jesus himself "is the same yesterday, today, and forever. So do not be attracted by strange, new ideas" (Hebrews 13:8–9). The Jesus of the Bible is the same Jesus today, and in the midst of life where we feel the anxiety that comes with change, you can rest assured that Jesus will not change. We sing with the gospel hymn, "Time is filled with swift transition, Naught of earth unmoved can stand, Build your hopes on things eternal, Hold to God's unchanging hand!"[6]

GOD UNDERSTANDS EVERYTHING

God's wisdom is necessary for our lack of knowledge. God is the only one who is truly a "know-it-all." When we think of wisdom, we usually think primarily of practical knowledge that comes from life experience, but the Bible describes wisdom more expansively. To have wisdom is to understand the world. This means that God has understanding and knowledge of all things, which influences everything he does. He created the world by his wisdom, as the psalmist says, "O LORD, what a variety of things you have made! In wisdom you have made them all" (Psalm 104:24). Wisdom also connects to God's ability to govern and judge the universe since he must understand all things to promote justice. "Nothing in all creation is hidden from God. Everything is naked and exposed before his eyes, and he is the one to whom we are accountable" (Hebrews 4:13). This means we are to look to God to understand if we are right or wrong in every situation.

Though we often foolishly sin, God has saved us through the person and work of Jesus, "who became to us wisdom from God . . . a secret and hidden wisdom of God, which God decreed before the ages for our glory" (1 Corinthians 1:30, 2:7 ESV). God saving the world through Jesus seems foolish to the world but is an expression of the wisdom of God.

GOD IS ALL POWERFUL

Like a home hooked up to a generator or a computer with a charger, God's power supplies our weakness. This is why the name "God Almighty" is such a popular name for God. All throughout the Bible, we see clearly "that power belongs to God" (Psalm 62:11 ESV). God can do anything, and nothing can ever compete with him in accomplishing his will. Indeed, as Jeremiah has said to God, "Nothing is too hard for you!" (Jeremiah 32:17), and with Jesus we declare, "With God everything is possible" (Matthew 19:26). This is a beautiful truth because no enemy nor evil spiritual force can get between God and the good that he is planning for his people. No one can ever defeat him or frustrate the things he sets out to do.

Jesus brought the power of God to the world. Apostle Paul tells us, "Christ is the power of God . . . God's weakness is stronger than the greatest of human strength" (1 Corinthians 1:24–25). The world sees a crucified savior as a weak savior. The typical person thinks, "A criminal savior condemned to capital punishment is too weak to bring any kind of powerful salvation!" However, God intentionally wanted the way of salvation to look weak in order to put to shame the world's idea of power. God will save the world through weakness in order for those who think they are strong to realize they actually must give up their own conception of power and embrace God's power. We must embrace God's "weakness" to embrace God's powerful salvation.

GOD IS SPECIAL

God is holy, and this holiness is the answer to our commonness. "Who will not fear you, Lord, and glorify your name? For you alone are holy" (Revelation 15:4). God initially created us to live in his presence and, therefore, be holy. But instead of being set apart for a special purpose, instead of being complete and devoted to God, we embraced commonness. In other words, we became unholy.

When I think of holiness, I think of an art museum. All of these works of art are set apart and special. But why? Because they belong to artists who are set apart and have a special place in history. If any of these pieces were discovered as fakes, they would become common, unholy. We, as pieces of art, become valuable and set apart (holy) as we are connected with the holy artist, God himself.

Out of all of God's attributes, defining the holiness of God, in my experience, sparks the most disagreement. The "holy" or "sacred" is a category that exists in many different religions. In short, different religions often divide all of existence into the holy and unholy. Holy things are those connected to the gods or higher planes of existence, and the unholy things are not connected to the gods or higher planes of existence. In the Christian faith, God is the only one who is holy. God being holy means that he is special and complete. It also means that he is set apart unto himself, to accomplish his own purposes and to glorify himself.

Jesus, "the Holy One of God" (Mark 1:24), united us with himself and restored our holiness. In Christ, we become set apart, gradually complete, and devoted to God.

GOD IS JUST AND RIGHTEOUS

God's justice is what we need for injustice. Saying God is just is also another way of saying that God is righteous. The LORD "is just and fair. He is a faithful God who does no wrong; how just and upright he is!" (Deuteronomy 32:4). Because God is just, he is the judge of the universe who gives to everyone as their deeds deserve. As Abraham says, "Surely you wouldn't do such a thing, destroying the righteous along with the wicked. Why, you would be treating the righteous and the wicked exactly the same! Surely you wouldn't do that! Should not the Judge of all the earth do what is right?'" (Genesis 18:25). This means that God has the sole right to decide what is right and wrong. God always rewards the righteous and punishes the unrighteous because he "will judge everyone according to what they have done" (Romans 2:6).

Some of us think of God's justice as a scary thing, and it can be. However, the fact that God is just is a good thing. We instinctively know this when we as African Americans rejoice at justice in the face of racial injustice. The psalmist says, "Let the fields and their crops burst out with joy! Let the trees of the forest sing for joy before the LORD, for he is coming! He is coming to judge the earth. He will judge the world with justice, and the nations with his truth" (Psalm 96:12–13). God's justice is what brings wholeness to a world filled with injustice.

God's wrath is related to God's justice; God's wrath is God's justice exercised on those who are doing injustice. Advocates of justice must also be advocates of wrath. The Apostle Paul connects God's wrath and justice when he says to those who ignore God,

> But because you are stubborn and refuse to turn from your sin, you are storing up terrible punishment for yourself. For a day of anger is coming, when God's righteous judgment will be revealed . . . he will pour out his anger and wrath on those who live for themselves, who refuse to obey the truth and instead live lives of wickedness. (Romans 2:5–8)

God exercises his justice on the earth through Jesus. First, he displays his justice to the world in the death of Jesus (more on this later), and he will judge the world through his resurrected Son, Jesus (also more on this later). God expresses his judgment through Christ.

GOD IS GOOD

God's goodness is satisfying in a corrupt and dark world. Although God is morally good, this attribute is more than just a moral category in the Bible. The word for "good" in the Bible, especially in the Old Testament, often means "pleasant" or "delightful." This means that God always does what is pleasing (whether we find it to be so or not); thus the psalmist declares, "He fills my life with good things. My youth is renewed like the eagle's!" (Psalm 103:5). It also means that God and all that flows from him are worthy of acceptance. As the Apostle Paul says, "Since everything God created is good, we should not reject any of it but receive it with thanks" (1 Timothy 4:4-5). Like hot comfort food, a cool breeze on a warm spring day, or a beautiful song, God is good.

Oftentimes, we confuse God being good with God being nice. Though God is "kind, tolerant, and patient" (Romans 2:4), God is not always "nice" in the ways that we typically imagine. We often view God's wrath and are confused at how God can be both good and furious at the same time because his wrath does not seem nice. Although God's wrath is not "nice," it is good because it is pleasing and worthy of acceptance for God to oppose the wicked to receive their punishment.

You might wonder, "Where are the attributes of grace, mercy, and patience?" In the Bible, these things are God's love, which is actually God's goodness exercised towards others. Thus, we can declare with the Apostle John that "God is love" (1 John 4:8) since God's goodness is always exercised towards others. God's grace is God's love exercised towards people who deserve God's wrath. God's mercy is God's love exercised towards suffering and miserable people. God's patience is God's love exercised towards difficult people over an extended period of time. As we look at all the different ways God loves us, we confess with North African Church Father Augustine, "For your goodness is almighty; you take good care of each of us as if you had no others in your care, and you look after all as you look after each."[7]

God's goodness has been primarily exercised towards humanity through Jesus, for "this is how God loved the world: He gave his one and only Son, so that everyone who believes in him will not perish but have eternal life" (John 3:16).

GOD IS FAITHFUL

God's trueness is needed in a world full of lies and disappointment. Saying God is "true" is another way of saying that God is faithful. We declare with the psalmist, "His unfailing love for us is powerful; the LORD's faithfulness endures forever" (Psalm 117:2). The terms "lovingkindness" and "steadfast love" in our Bibles are ways of speaking about God's commitment to his covenant promises, in other words, his faithfulness. He can never lie. Everything that he says is absolutely true, and he will always do what he says he will do. This is a foundational truth for humanity because how will we know if we can trust God's promises or what he says in the Bible if he is a liar? Jesus is the ultimate display of God's faithfulness because "all of God's promises have been fulfilled in Christ with a resounding 'Yes!' And through Christ, our 'Amen' (which means 'Yes') ascends to God for his glory" (2 Corinthians 1:20). We will see more about how Christ has fulfilled God's promises later.

When looking at all of these attributes, it is important to note that all of them are united. Because every attribute describes all of who God is all the time, each attribute can describe the other. For example, God's love is a just love, and his justice is a loving justice.

GOD IS ALL YOU NEED

All of these attributes encourage the Christian in the midst of life's troubles and struggles. Are you wondering if you'll be able to pay your balance for school? God is good and will be generous. Are you looking for wisdom on what your major should be? God is wise and will grant wisdom. Are you heartbroken after a hard break up? God is unchanging and, therefore, won't leave you. Did your friend betray you or a professor wrong you? God will work justice. Are you wondering if you'll be able to get your mental health in a good place? God nothing is too hard for our powerful God. Are you worried about life after graduation? God is already in your future. I could go on. Satisfy yourself with Yahweh.

I remember a moment that changed the way I thought about names for the rest of my life. At an African dance class during a Jack and Jill Teen Conference, the instructor taught us the significance of a name.

The instructor said, "When you introduce yourself, never say, 'My name is . . .' No, no, no. Whenever I introduce myself, I say, 'I am . . .' Your name is not just a name! Your name has significance! It was given to you to tell you who you are!"

He then made us say our names out loud with authority.

"I am Cyril!" My name means, "Lordly." Do you know what your name means?

The instructor captured an important truth about names in many societies worldwide today and certainly among God's people — names are important. They are given to you to communicate who you are! And the Bible tells us that God often changed people's names as he gave them a new purpose, like when God changed Abram's name to Abraham. "Abram" means "exalted father," but "Abraham" means "father of a multitude" (Genesis 17:5). God changed his name when God promised him that he would become the forefather of many nations in spite of his and his wife's infertility.

But here is a question you may have never thought of: what is God's name? Exodus 3:1-16 is where God reveals his own name. As God is empowering Moses to go rescue the Israelites, God gives Moses the divine name.

First, he gives Moses his nickname. God says, "I AM WHO I

AM. Say this to the people of Israel: 'I AM has sent me to you'" (Exodus 3:14). What does this mean? Revelation helps us out here. The author, John, when referring to God, says, "Grace to you and peace, from Him who is and who was and who is to come" (Revelation 1:4 NASB). This is a play on God's nickname; it is God's nickname in reference to the past, present, and future. It means that God is present with his people throughout every stage of history. The author is saying, "God is the one who is always with his people!" To paraphrase, God is telling Moses the same thing: "You cannot understand me until you understand that I have been, and I am, and I will be with my people! All of my power, wisdom, goodness, faithfulness, immutability, and limitlessness will be with my people to deliver them! Even when things look dark, when their backs are against the wall, I will be with them!"

God then gives Moses, and therefore us, his name, "Say this to the people of Israel: *Yahweh*, the God of your ancestors—the God of Abraham, the God of Isaac, and the God of Jacob—has sent me to you" (Exodus 3:15, emphasis added). Yahweh means "he will be." God declares that this name is to be used forever to remind the people that God has always been with them and that God will always be with them.

GOD IS WORTHY OF ALL OF YOU

We have seen some characteristics of God and must now ask the question whose answer we often take for granted, "Are there more Gods than one?" Nowadays, traditional African religions are becoming popular, particularly Yoruba religions and the different variations of Yoruba religion, like Santeria. Yoruba has one supreme God, Olodumare, with other gods in a pantheon, such as Esu, Chango, and Ogun. What does God have to say about this and other spiritual systems with multiple gods?

Yahweh claims that he is the only God, meaning there is only one being in all creation who is like him. Thus the Apostle Paul says,

> There may be so-called gods both in heaven and on earth,
> and some people actually worship many gods and many
> lords. But for us,
> There is one God, the Father,
> by whom all things were created,
> and for whom we live" (1 Corinthians 8:5–6).

No spiritual beings are in the same category as him. Indeed, a part of what Jesus calls the greatest commandment is this: "Listen, O Israel! The LORD is our God, the LORD alone" (Deuteronomy 6:4). He shares his power with no one and competes with no other god for the exclusive right to receive worship. In many ways, the Bible is God's glorious efforts to show people prone to worship other things that he is the only God and the only one worthy of worship.

GOD IS INVITING YOU INTO HIS SOCIAL CLUB

Not only does God want all of you, God's goal in your life is to bring you into his social club. His social club consists of three persons – the Father, the Son, and the Spirit. They exist eternally together as one. The scriptures teach that God is simultaneously one and three. Let's look at how this all works.

The Apostle Peter acknowledges the three persons of the Trinity in his first letter, "God the *Father* knew you and chose you long ago, and his *Spirit* has made you holy. As a result, you have obeyed him and have been cleansed by the blood of *Jesus* Christ" (1 Peter 1:2, emphasis added). There is the Father, the Son, and the Holy Spirit. These three together are called "the Trinity." God the Father is the first person; God the Son is the second person; and

God the Spirit is the third person. We already know the Father is God from the reference above in Peter's letter, which explicitly calls the Father, "God." What about the Son and the Spirit? Are they also God?

THE SPIRIT IS GOD

The Holy Spirit is God. Here the words of Peter again recorded in Acts:

> Then Peter said, "Ananias, why have you let Satan fill your heart? You lied to the *Holy Spirit*, and you kept some of the money for yourself. The property was yours to sell or not sell, as you wished. And after selling it, the money was also yours to give away. How could you do a thing like this? You weren't lying to us but to *God*! (Acts 5:3–4, emphasis added)

In the early church, people were giving generously to the church. Ananias lied by pretending to give all the proceeds from a sale of property, but he kept a piece for himself. In verse 3, Peter tells Ananias that he lied to the Holy Spirit. Verse 4 repeats this same truth, yet now Peter says he has lied to God. Peter uses "The Spirit" and "God" interchangeably. If this is not convincing, throughout the Bible, we see the Spirit speaking to people as God (Acts 13:2), the Spirit having emotions as God (Ephesians 4:30), possessing the attributes of God (Hebrews 9:14), and working upon people in union with the other two persons of the Trinity (John 14:26, 15:26; 2 Corinthians 3:17-18).

THE SON IS GOD

But what about the Son? The Apostle John can help us out here, "In the beginning was the Word, and the Word was with God, and the Word was God. He was in the beginning with God. All things were made through him, and without him was not any thing made that was made" (John 1:1–3 ESV). As soon as John begins by saying, "In the beginning," we should think about the first verse in the Bible, "*In the beginning* God created the heavens and the earth" (Genesis 1:1 ESV, emphasis added). In John 1:1-3, you would expect John to finish "in the beginning" by making a reference to "God," but instead he says, "The Word." The Word is closely associated with God.

Who is this Word? In the Old Testament, God's word was basically God in action. Whenever God did something, his word was involved. God's word created, revealed, and re-created broken things. We know that the Word has something to do with God in action, but what else does John tell us about the Word? First, the Word was *with* God. In order for me to be with something, that means that I am something distinct from that thing. If Cyril is with Jenell (my wife), then this implies we are two distinct persons. But John tells us also that the Word *was* God! Whoa! The Word is a distinct person from God, yet he is identical with God. What else do we learn about the Word? This Word — who is distinct from God but also God — "became human and made his home among us. He was full of unfailing love and faithfulness. And we have seen his glory, the glory of the Father's one and only Son" (John 1:14). The Word is the same person as the Son! This Son's name is Jesus.

Connecting the dots, Jesus is the Son of God and God. He is God the Son. John explicitly tells us this in John 1:18, "No one has ever seen God. But the unique One, who is himself God, is near to the Father's heart. He has revealed God to us." God the Son came to the earth to reveal God the Father to us. God the Son is uniquely qualified to reveal God the Father because God the Son is the only one who has seen God.

ALL THREE PERSONS ARE ONE GOD

Here, we see John is starting to give us the teaching of the Trinity. The Father is a distinct person, yet he is God. The Spirit is a distinct person, yet is God. The Son is a distinct person, yet God. You have three persons, but they all have the same being. God is three and one. And it is not as if God is split in three — Jesus as a third, the Father as a third, and the Spirit as a third. All of who God is dwells in each person! In other words, each person of the Trinity fully possesses every attribute of God. They all have the same essence. This is why we can baptize people in "the name of the Father and the Son and the Holy Spirit" (Matthew 28:19) along with baptizing them in "in the name of Jesus Christ"(Acts 2:38). To be baptized into the discipleship of any of the three persons is to be baptized in the name of God, and to be baptized into the one God is to be baptized into all of the three persons.

This is hard to understand because we are creatures; this goes beyond our human experience. If you have a two-dimensional person, say a stick figure human, it will be easy to describe a circle to him, and a triangle would be easy too (I know this is unscientific, but stick with me science folks). But if you tried to describe a cone, a three-dimensional object, to them then it would be mind-blowing to them! It is outside their realm of experience! The best way that you could describe a cone is, "It is like a triangle, but it is also like a circle!" That will be helpful, but they will never truly and fully grasp what a cone is. That is what it is like with God. He is one essence, and he is also three persons! We will have an idea, but we will never fully grasp it. We can *apprehend* the Trinity, but we will never fully *comprehend* it.

YOU CAN FELLOWSHIP WITH THE THREE

As you are saved, you are invited to experience a taste of the Trinity. It is not as if you become the fourth person of the Trinity. No, but you are invited to fellowship with all three persons at the same time. Jesus explains this to his disciples in John 14:16-23. When Jesus dies, rises, and goes into heaven, the disciples will still need the help that Jesus gave them while he was on earth. Jesus explains that he will send the Holy Spirit as another Helper

(John 16:7). The Spirit will dwell in them. This is how the disciples will continue to fellowship with Jesus even though he is in heaven and they on earth – through Jesus' Spirit. Jesus leaves them with a piece of himself, so to speak. Jesus will live in the disciples through his Spirit. And because Jesus and the Father are one, the disciples get a two-for-one deal. They are fellowshipping with both Jesus and the Father through the Spirit. The same night Jesus explained this to his disciples, he prayed for them, saying, " . . . that they may all be one, just as you, Father, are in me, and I in you, that they also may be in us, so that the world may believe that you have sent me" (John 17:21 ESV). It is Jesus' desire that you be "in" – that you have fellowship with – the three persons of the Trinity. It is through this divine union with God that you enjoy him and start to glorify him by becoming like him.

RECAP

So we have seen that God reveals himself clearly through the Bible. We have seen his many attributes, his claim to exclusivity, and his triune nature. We have seen who God is. Let us now focus on what God likes to do.

CHAPTER 4

BUT WHY DO CERTAIN THINGS HAPPEN?

spent most of my church-going childhood in a Black Baptist church. I have fond memories of going to church and being around a Christian community. The community, the prayers, the preaching, and the praise and worship, all deeply shaped me. I learned a lot, but there was at least one thing that always confused me. Let me explain.

Black folks have a very earthy faith. It is beautiful. We aren't so "spiritual" that we look down upon celebrating God's material and physical blessings. We praise God and thank God for providing food, clothing, deliverance from bad situations, and more. Black Christians realize that God is very much at work in all things, in both "spiritual" and "material" ways. Growing up in the Black church, I accepted this truth and praised God for his material and physical blessings. Yet in the midst of praising God for these things, I still had the question, "How is God doing these things? How does God work in the world?"

In prayers, people would say, "God, thank you for putting clothes on our backs!" I would think, "Didn't I put those on my back? Didn't my parents pay for them?" Folks would say, "God is a doctor in the sick room and a lawyer in the courtroom!" I would think, "Well, there is an actual doctor who heals and an actual lawyer who argues. Aren't they the doctor and lawyer?" People would "say grace" over food and exclaim, "God, thank you for putting food on our tables!" I would think, "Why are we thanking God? Didn't we buy and make the food?" We would praise God, saying, "God, thank you for delivering me!" I would think, "Well, didn't x, y, and z happen to get you out of that bad situation?" Someone would testify how they were one of the only ones to survive a tragedy that took the lives of many. I would wonder, "Well, aren't you just lucky? Because God didn't save everyone else." I didn't understand these questions until college, which is when I started to understand God's sovereignty and God's providence. In this chapter, we are going to answer these types of questions.

I consistently hear my students say, "God is up to something," "Everything is divine timing," "Everything happens for a reason," or, "God always has a plan." I agree! But I pose to you the question, "What does this actually mean?"

Understanding God's decrees, his creative actions, and his providence are key to understanding how God works in the world.

WHERE WE ARE GOING

In a sentence, I want you to know that God is at work in your life, so trust him.

We can sometimes doubt that God is at work. As Black Africans view the world around us, it can feel overwhelming. Our people have had the truth of their dignity stolen, their power and agency stripped from them, and their bodies and lives trampled upon. Even now, we are overcoming the legacy of this tragic story. The world can feel as if it has no rhyme or reason. This same confusion about what God is doing is also present in our own lives. Why, what, and how will God move and be at work in my life in the midst of sin and suffering? The apparent senselessness of everything can have us wondering if God is "out there." If God is "out there," it can be hard to figure out what he is doing and how he is doing it.

You can trust God because God is always up to something more glorious and enjoyable than you ever knew. Whether good or bad, we often ask, "Why do certain things happen and certain things don't?" The answer is — God. God is ultimately behind everything in one way or another. God is so big that his good plan includes evil and suffering; he is so good that this evil and suffering ultimately work towards God's good purposes that he's planned for the world. In order to understand how God works in the world, we will look at 1) the reason behind everything he has planned 2) what he did when he created everything 3) what he is doing right now 4) what he is doing in the midst of African suffering and 5) how you become a part of his plan. As a result of understanding how God works, we must endure suffering with patience and trust in God. The God who controls all things is for us and not against us. Let's dive in.

———

GOD HAS PLANNED EVERYTHING IN YOUR LIFE

Understanding God's decrees is crucial to understanding how God works in the world and in your life. Why? Before anything happens, it is decreed by God. Like an executive order given by the United States president or a change in the academic calendar from your university, a decree is a decision or order given by an authority. Decrees are God's purposeful and wise plan for the world. Psalm 33:11 speaks of God's decrees when it says, "But the LORD's plans stand firm forever; his intentions can never be shaken" (Psalm 33:11). God having decrees means that he has planned out everything that happens in the world in advance; anything that happens occurs because God has decreed it. The scriptures often refer to this as God's "foreknowledge" or God's "predestined plan" (Acts 2:23, 4:28; Romans 8:29; Ephesians 1:5; 1

Peter 1:2). If God has decreed it, it will surely come to pass, and his decrees will never change (Psalm 33:11).

GOD HAS PLANNED EVERYTHING TO AMAZE YOU

For what purpose does God make decrees and execute them? God decrees all things ultimately for his own glory. In other words, God wants you to stand in awe of all the attributes we learned about in chapter three. The Christian life is to be filled with the wonder of God. We are to be captivated by his glorious power, his glorious wisdom, his glorious good, and more. The ultimate goal of humanity is to glorify God, and God's ultimate goal is to glorify himself.

Does this not seem cocky and selfish? Why would God be so concerned with his own glory? Well, in the world, it is generally a good thing to show off something amazing, something beautiful. A night sky without light pollution, a gorgeous full moon, a dazzling gem – we gladly point others to them to enjoy them. What if this beautiful thing was yourself? God is the only one in this situation. If you or I became self-centered, no one would be the better for it, but God is the most beautiful and spectacular thing to exist. God is spectacularly good when he directs us to himself and all of his glorious beauty. If God did anything else, it would be a crime. To know God is to gain a newfound obsession with giving him glory, and we are most fully alive when we are doing so. Throughout the Bible, from Genesis to Revelation, we see that Yahweh's goal is to display his glory to humanity.

―――――

GOD CARRIES OUT HIS PLAN

So if God has planned all things in his decree, how does his plan become a reality? God himself executes his plan through his own action. Each year, many of us make New Year's resolutions and vision boards. Despite our plans, we have a problem with executing what we have decided will happen in our lives. God has no issue executing his resolutions and vision boards, and he does it gloriously.

GOD HAS CARRIED OUT HIS CREATION PLANS

First, God executes his plan for creation. The fact that God decreed creation means that God is master over the whole universe. He planned and created everything. There are no places in creation that are outside of the reach of his power and goodness. Therefore, there are no places in your life that are outside of God's hands.

There are many things we can say about how God created the universe. Like a genius who comes up with a mind-blowing invention, God has created everything in his own wisdom. "By wisdom the LORD founded the earth; by understanding he created the heavens. By his knowledge the deep fountains of the earth burst forth, and the dew settles beneath the night sky" (Proverbs 3:19–20). God's creation flowed from his wisdom.

Let's do a quick overview of how creation happened. The eternal God who has no beginning was the only thing that existed. Though no one forced him to and though he didn't need to, God decided to create for himself a palace, a theater where his kingly glory would shine: "Heaven is my throne, and the earth is my footstool. Could you build me a temple as good as that? Could you build me such a resting place?" (Isaiah 66:1). God then began to create all things. God "made the world and everything in it" (Acts 17:24). How long did it take him? In "six days the LORD made the heavens, the earth, the sea, and everything in them" (Exodus 20:11). How did God create? God created all of these things by the power of his word: "By the word of the LORD the heavens were made, their starry host by the breath of his mouth" (Psalms 33:6). When a person speaks, words and breath come out of their mouths. In the same way, when God speaks, the Word (John 1:4-5) and the Spirit ("spirit" is closely connected to the word "breath") go forth. God's Word and Spirit have creative power. God spoke and his Word (John 1:4-5) and his Spirit, who was "hovering over the surface of the waters" (Genesis 1:2), powerfully moved to create.

Now, let's look at how creation happened step by step, in chronological order. After God created all of the physical matter by his command, Genesis tells us that it was "formless and empty, and darkness covered the deep waters" (Genesis 1:2). Over the course of six days, God turned the formlessness into form and the emptiness into fullness.

In the first three days, God is primarily turning formlessness into form. Like a messy room that needs to be organized, God is organizing his royal palace. On the first day, God created light and separated light and darkness. On the second day, God separated the water from top to bottom, creating the oceans below and the clouds above. The space in between is the sky. On the third day, God pushed the waters back so that land would be exposed.

On days four through six, God is filling the emptiness in the places he has formed. Like an empty dorm room that needs furniture and decorations, God fills his royal palace. On the fourth day, God fills the light and darkness with the sun, moon, and stars to manage and mark the days, nights, and seasons of time. On the fifth day, God created sea creatures to fill the sea, and flying creatures to fill the sky. On the sixth day, God creates land creatures and humans.

At the end of creating everything in six days, God looked at everything and judged it to be "very good!" (Genesis 1:31). Dr. Irwyn Ince tells us that "the goodness of each day was about more than its usefulness for God's purposes. Goodness wasn't simply about utility. What God created was good because it brought pleasure."[1] The earth was a pleasant place, filled with pleasure. On the seventh day, God rested. When the Bible tells us God rested, we should not think that God was tired and needed a break. Rather, the scriptures are telling us that God stopped creating. Also, oftentimes in the Bible, "to rest" means to inhabit or to bring your presence to a place (Numbers 11:26). God inhabits his newly constructed palace, having his presence rest in his new home to rule over all creation.

Remember, God has decreed everything to glorify himself, and this includes creation. Have you ever looked up at the stars or looked at the seas and said, "Wow, God is amazing." God designs his creation to have this effect on us! The LORD created the sky, or "the heavens," to bring him glory: "The heavens proclaim the glory of God" (Psalm 19:1). Romans 1 tells us that everything God created screams, "This is the eternal power and divine nature of God!" (Romans 1:20). Psalm 148 calls all of creation to worship God by using the phrase, "Praise!" or "*Hallelu!*" in the Hebrew language.

God's work of creation didn't just happen "back then," but it is happening right now in people's hearts! When you place your faith in Christ, the same work of creation that he did in the beginning of time, he does in you. "For God, who said, 'Let there be light in the darkness,' has made this light shine in our hearts so we could know the glory of God that is seen in the face of Jesus Christ" (2 Corinthians 4:6). And this new work in your heart was decreed before creation itself, as we will see in chapter ten.

GOD IS CARRYING OUT HIS PLANS IN YOUR LIFE

God executes his plan for everything after creation. His execution of everything after creation is called "providence." The fact that God decrees literally everything means that nothing that happens is outside of God's will and sovereignty. This is good news in suffering, as we will see in a minute, because if God is not God over my suffering, then he must've lost control over my suffering. If God has lost control over my suffering, then there is no hope that it will end or that it, a bad thing, could ever work towards a "happy ending." It means that either Satan is in control over it or I am a victim to the cruel chances and random happenings of life. But if God is over my suffering, then I can keep going through it, with God's help, to the other side.

First, in God's providence, he preserves all things. The scriptures tell us this when it says that the LORD God "sustains everything by the mighty power of his command" (Hebrews 1:3). God's people exclaim, "You made the skies and the heavens and all the stars. You made the earth and the seas and everything in them. *You preserve them all*, and the angels of heaven worship you" (Nehemiah 9:6, emphasis added). Like a battery preserves the function of a machine or a fridge preserves food, everything would fall apart without God. He keeps everything going, including your lungs, your heart beat, and the activity of your muscles day by day, second by second. Do you see how intimately involved God is in the world and in your life?

Second, God governs all things in his providence (Psalm 135:5-12), which means nothing we do or that happens is outside of God's sovereign control. All of nature moves by his instruction, like "fire and hail, snow and mist, stormy wind fulfilling his word!" (Psalm 148:8). God governs both the big things and the small things in life. God organized the formation of nations and ethnicities according to his governance (Acts 17:25-28), and he organized even the smallest thing — like the casting of lots[2] (Proverbs 16:33) and like the number of hairs on your head (Matthew 10:29-31). All of these things are within the providence of the LORD.

Lastly, though God can preserve and govern directly, God ordinarily uses means to carry out his decrees. In other words, God uses things to accomplish his purposes. For example, God judged Judah by sending them into exile, but he used the Babylonian invasion to do it (2 Kings 24:1-5). God is the first cause; the Babylonians are the secondary cause. God caused Judah's judgment by his decree, but the Babylonians caused Judah's judgment by invading them. Both God and the Babylonians caused Judah's judgment, but the Babylonians caused it only because God first caused it.

God's cooperation with all things is ordinarily how God does things in our lives. God puts food on the table, clothes on our back, a roof over our heads, and he heals in the sickroom and is a lawyer in the courtroom. God is doing things through other things. This is how prayer makes sense. Why pray if God already knows what's going to happen? Well, God has chosen to use your prayers in the ways he governs the world. Revelation 5:8, 8:1-5 shows us that God uses the prayers of his people to move his plans in the world forward. He chooses to do things in response to your prayers. God causes things, and your prayers do too. In his sovereignty and mystery, God has decreed that your prayers will make a difference in his plan.

Again, remember, God has decreed everything he does in his providence to glorify himself. Let's look at a few biblical examples.

In his providence, God glorifies himself through defeating his people's enemies. In the book of Exodus, we see that God, for his own glory, brings judgment against his people's enemies: "And once again I will harden Pharaoh's heart, and he will chase after you. I have planned this in order to *display my glory* through Pharaoh and his whole army. After this the Egyptians will know that I am the LORD!" (Exodus 14:4, emphasis added). Moses demanded that Pharaoh, the slavemaster, let the Israelites go from slavery. Pharaoh refused, and this refusal led to an opportunity for God to judge Pharaoh. God tells us that he did all of this to display his glory and to let everyone know who he is.

Also, in his providence, God glorifies himself through saving his people: "In him we have obtained an inheritance, having been predestined . . . so that we who were the first to hope in Christ might be to the *praise of his glory*" (Ephesians 1:12 ESV, emphasis added). God predestines, literally decided beforehand, people to be saved so that we could praise his glory! Relatedly, for his own glory, Isaiah's prophecy tells us that God will bring widespread restoration to his people: "All your people will be righteous. They will possess their land forever, for I will plant them there with my own hands in order *to bring myself glory*" (Isaiah 60:21, emphasis added). God even thinks about future generations when he saves people in the present generation:

> For he raised us from the dead along with Christ and seated us with him in the heavenly realms because we are united with Christ Jesus. So God can point to us in all future ages as examples of the incredible wealth of his grace and kindness toward us, as shown in all he has done for us who are united with Christ Jesus. (Ephesians 2:6–7)

All of God's providence is for his own glory, so that you can behold his beautiful majesty. God is spectacular in his decrees!

YOU ARE A PART OF GOD'S STORY

God, in his providence, is preserving and governing world history as a narrative. God is the producer, writer, and director of the streaming show called, "History." This show has a beginning, a middle, and an end. The show also has four seasons – creation, de-creation, re-creation, and new creation. Season 1 is creation, which happens in Genesis chapters 1-2. God creates everything. Season 2 is de-creation, which happens in Genesis 3 when humanity sins against God. Humanity's rebellion against God undoes (de-creates) how God created everything (coming in chapter six). Season 3 is re-creation. Through Christ, God is restoring everything to how he intended it to be (coming in chapters 7-12). In the Bible, Genesis 4 all the way to the beginning of Revelation is re-creation. Last season is the new creation, where God's recreation will be made complete. In fact, things will be even better than they were initially at creation. We will live with God in a perfect world where we will glorify him and enjoy him perfectly forever (remember this from chapter one?). This is the story of both history and the Bible.

God is at work in every season of the story and in every character. Though the world is not what it should be after de-creation, in his providence, God exercises common grace. What's common grace? Like common sense is the sense that everyone has, common grace is grace that everyone receives from God. It is God's gracious love for everyone. Jesus speaks of common grace when he teaches his disciples that God "gives his sunlight to both the evil and the good, and he sends rain on the just and the unjust alike" (Matthew 5:45). Even in the worst and darkest places, God is at work in his providence.

God re-creates people by his providence. Those who are being recreated are made new by special grace, grace that is only for those who have received Christ, who is "full of grace and truth" (John 1:14 ESV). You are being re-created in a world that has been de-created. Apostle Paul speaks about this special grace often: "God saved you by his grace when you believed. And you can't take credit for this; it is a gift from God" (Ephesians 2:8). God's amazing, special grace saves those who believe in Jesus the savior (more in chapter seven).

Common grace and special grace are connected in God's providence. God's common grace is meant to lead people to embrace special grace. Apostle Paul tells the hypocritical Christians in first century Rome, "Don't you see how wonderfully kind, tolerant, and patient God is with you? Does this mean nothing to you? Can't you see that his kindness is intended to turn you from your sin?" (Romans 2:4). God's goodness to you is supposed to lead you to Christ! God is wooing you to himself.

———

PHILLIS WHEATLEY TEACHES US HOW TO STAND IN WONDER

At this point, we must be careful because we can easily forget that all the things we have talked about are supposed to inspire praise in us! Phillis Wheatley teaches us that God's providence is not something that we coldly analyze; we must stand in wonder and awe at Yahweh God's royal majesty as he governs all things.

Wheatley[3] was born in Africa in 1753. She was abducted into the slave trade and then bought in Boston by John and Susanna Wheatley in 1761. Phillis was named after the ship that brought her to America, *Phillis*, and her masters. The Wheatleys made sure that Phillis was educated. By the age of fourteen, Phillis had published a couple pieces of poetry and, as a result, received attention both at home and overseas. After receiving barriers to her work in America, her poems were published in 1773 in England as *Poems on Various Subjects, Religious & Moral.* Phillis Wheatley was the first African woman in America to publish a book of poems, free or enslaved. She returned to Boston as a famous poet. One of the poems in this collection was "Thoughts on the Works of Providence" where she adores God for how he orchestrates all things. Look at a section of this poem:

Ador'd for ever be the God unseen,
Which round the sun revolves this vast machine,
Though to his eye its mass a point appears:
Ador'd the God that whirls surrounding spheres,
Which first ordained'd that mighty Sol should reign
The peerless monarch of the ethereal train.[4]

She calls her audience to adore God for how he governs the earth and the sun. This God revolves the earth around the sun and appointed the sun, poetically called "Sol," to rule in the skies. Wheatley looks at God's preserving and governing works and is moved to poetic praise! She continues to praise him later in the poem:

> Almighty, in these wond'rous works of thine,
> What Pow'r, what Wisdom, and what Goodness shine!
> And are thy wonders, Lord, by men explor'd,
> And yet creating glory unador'd![5]

She delights in God's might, power, wisdom, and goodness that are put on display in his providence over the sun and earth. Even though people can explore and adore God's wonders, there is yet even more to be seen! His glory knows no limits. Wheatley then, later, praises God for the fact that he wakes people up in the morning:

> What mental hand returns the mental train,
> And gives improv'd thine active pow'rs again?
> From thee, O man, what gratitude should rise!
> And, when from balmy sleep thou op'st thine eyes,
> Let thy first thoughts be praises to the skies.
> How merciful our God who thus imparts
> O'erflowing tides of joy to human hearts,
> When wants and woes might be our righteous lot,
> Our God forgetting, by our God forgot![6]

Wheatley highlights the mercy of God in his providence! She marvels at how God puts to sleep and wakes up. In response, we should praise God and wake up with joy! She then rejoices in how God is merciful in his providence. He could justly punish us for our sins by bringing only pain and unfulfilled desires, but because of Jesus, he shows saving mercy! Perceiving providence leads to praise.

———

GOD IS GOOD EVEN IN DIFFICULT CIRCUMSTANCES

For some, it is hard to praise God's providence. The fact that God has planned everything may bring about a moral dilemma, "How does God decree horrible things without being morally responsible for them?" We can often doubt God's wisdom, holiness, and power when we see the things he is doing in his providence, especially when we go through deep, personal suffering.

GOD IS AT WORK EVEN IN HORRIBLE THINGS

We must understand that there are two different ways that the Bible describes God's will. Theologians sometimes call these God's "moral will" and God's "sovereign will." God's moral will is his ideal for us, what he would ideally have us do in obedience to him. Jesus speaks of God's moral will when he says, "My nourishment comes from doing the will of God, who sent me, and from finishing his work" (John 4:34). However, God's sovereign will is anything that comes to pass. Why? Because if God governs all things, all things must be according to his will in some shape or form. Paul mentions God's sovereign will to the Romans: "Pray that I will be rescued . . . Then, *by the will of God*, I will be able to come to you with a joyful heart, and we will be an encouragement to each other" (Romans 15:31–32, emphasis added). Paul also mentions it again as he leaves the Ephesians: "But on taking leave of them he said, 'I will return to you *if God wills*,' and he set sail from Ephesus" (Acts 18:21, emphasis added).

So how does this all relate to evil? Evil is outside of God's moral will. If humanity always followed God's moral will, everything would be perfect. Although evil is outside of God's moral will, it is inside of God's sovereign will. But how can evil be inside of God's sovereign will without him being evil himself? The answer is that there are generally two different kinds of decrees — God's active decree and God's permissive decree. To permit something means to allow it. God's active decrees are the decrees that God proactively and directly carries out. God's permissive decrees are the things that God has planned and purposed without producing the evil intentions, evil desires, and evil actions involved in those plans. The evil comes from us. For example, Adam and Eve's sin was a permissive decree of God. God is not responsible for sin, is not the author of it, nor is the approver of it; yet, God planned and governed Adam and Eve's sin. Confused yet? You should be confused because the phrase "permissive decree" is an oxymoron! To decree something is an active action, but to permit something is a passive action. How can someone actively decree something but passively permit it at the same time? This contradictory phrase is the human language's attempt to capture something we can apprehend but never fully comprehend. God decrees evil; yet, the sin and the evil do not come from him. It comes from the human doing it.

What are some examples in the Bible that we see that can help us understand this? James – a Bible book author and apostle – answers a similar problem when teaching how God can be good yet allow us to be tempted:

> And remember, when you are being tempted, do not say, "God is tempting me." God is never tempted to do wrong, and he never tempts anyone else. Temptation comes from our own desires, which entice us and drag us away. These desires give birth to sinful actions. And when sin is allowed to grow, it gives birth to death. So don't be misled, my dear brothers and sisters. Whatever is good and perfect is a gift coming down to us from God our Father, who created all the lights in the heavens. He never changes or casts a shifting shadow. (James 1:13–17)

Even though God allows people to go through tests and temptations, God is not the originator of any evil. The human committing the evil is morally responsible for what God has permitted in his plan.

Another example is God's own death! Hear the Apostle Peter's Holy Spirit-inspired explanation of Jesus' death: "this Jesus, delivered up according to the definite plan and foreknowledge of God, you crucified and killed by the hands of lawless men" (Acts 2:23 ESV). Did you catch it? Jesus' death was decreed by God, being in his "definite plan." However, the moral responsibility is on the people who killed him because God did not create nor stir the evil that led those people to crucify Jesus. Knowing this, the apostles attribute the death of Jesus to the people but attribute the resurrection of Jesus to God: "Let me clearly state to all of you and to all the people of Israel that he was healed by the powerful name of Jesus Christ the Nazarene, the man *you crucified* but whom *God raised* from the dead" (Acts 4:10, emphasis added).

Joseph, a key figure in Genesis 37-50, captures this reality when he tells his brothers, who sold him into slavery, that God decreed all their evil: "As for you, you meant evil against me, but God meant it for good, to bring it about that many people should be kept alive, as they are today" (Genesis 50:20 ESV). Although the brothers are responsible for their evil, which led Joseph to become a slave in Egypt, it was all in God's plan so that Joseph could rise to power in Egypt and save his family from starvation. God is so big and sovereign that all things are in his plan, even those that are evil, although he is not the originator of nor morally responsible for the evil. Although horrible things happen within God's providence, God is still "most holy, wise, and powerful" in all he does.

God's sovereignty over suffering is good news for those who are united to Jesus by faith. Behold the reality that re-creation brings: "And we know that for those who love God all things work together for good, for those who are called according to his purpose" (Romans 8:28 ESV). For those who are united with Christ, it is impossible for God to *not* be for them. Why? Because "God has put all things under the authority of Christ and has made him head over all things for the benefit of the church" (Ephesians 1:22). All things, even the horrible ones, will work together for the re-creation of his people. Evil must lose, and good must win for those who have placed their trust in Christ. Their stories are defined by re-creation and are moving towards eternal blessedness. It is with this confidence that Apostle Paul declares, "If God is for us, who can ever be against us? Since he did not spare even his own Son but gave him up for us all, won't he also give us everything else?" (Romans 8:31–32). He continues his worshipful trust in God's providence for those who belong to him by saying, "Can anything ever separate us from Christ's love? Does it mean he no longer loves us if we have trouble or calamity, or are persecuted, or hungry, or destitute, or in danger, or threatened with death? . . . No, despite all these things, overwhelming victory is ours through Christ, who loved us" (Romans 8:35–37).

For those who have not placed their trust in Christ, they have not moved into God's re-creating plan. Their suffering is merely a result of how broken our world is, and their suffering is without any promise of a greater meaning or victory that comes from God's saving grace. Their stories and suffering are still defined by de-creation and are moving towards eternal judgment (again, more on this in chapter six). However, God does not want you to stay there. He invites you to entrust yourself to him so that re-creation can be the theme of your suffering, so that your suffering can be a part of a different story.

GOD BOTH PLANNED AND HATES AFRICAN SUFFERING

What does the fact that suffering is in God's providence mean for the history of Black African suffering all around the globe? We must acknowledge and affirm that Black suffering has been a part of God's sovereign will and permissive decree. However, we must also acknowledge that our suffering has been against God's moral will. Horrific and evil things happened. The things done against Africans are disgusting to him, and it angers and grieves him. The scriptures also teach that God does not leave blameless the ones responsible for suffering. He holds those who actively brought about the suffering accountable. While we acknowledge God permits Black suffering, we emphasize that God is against the oppression of Black people. Both of these are true at the same time. In his providence, he pours out his judgment against those who practice evil. When we speak about how God has ordained all things, we must quickly speak of his compassion, sorrow, and vengeance.

To think of a God who had some sort of active role in Black suffering is difficult, or even a God who tolerates it is extremely difficult. The Bible's authors acknowledge this: Job, Habakkuk, and David wrestle with this reality. They painfully desire to know why God has brought suffering on them and even, in some cases, used evil people to do so. However, the same God who allows suffering is the same God who decrees deliverance. The same God who brought it is the same God who can remove it. This is the comfort of the sufferer. The suffering person prays to God only because they know God is God over their sufferings. We will never know what is happening behind the scenes in the mind of God, but we must trust that he is wise, good, and powerful in spite of what we might feel or see. This was the hope of those like Job (Job 42:1-6), Habakkuk (Habakkuk 3), and David (Psalm 22:1-5).

We also must acknowledge that the teaching of God's providence has been abused. It has often been used to justify the enslavement and abuse of enslaved Africans. Oppressors taught Black people that their oppression was due to God's will and that they should not resist the oppression of their masters. This is an abuse of God's doctrine of providence, for while God can permissively decree something, his furious anger can also be against that thing simultaneously. So, one can acknowledge that something is a part of God's providence and resist it in the name of God at the same time.

Black Africans, the only way we know that our struggle means anything is if we receive Yahweh, the God of providence, as our

God. But how do I know that he is worthy of my trust when injustice has happened under his watch? God has shown us that he is worthy of our trust by taking on unjust suffering himself. He took on a human body in order to suffer and die for us. In the person and work of his Son, God came down to the earth to face abuse, oppression, and all kinds of evil at the hands of those who hated him. Why? So that God's love, not wrath, might be ours and so that Christ's power might move all things for our good. Christ's death and resurrection has secured God's saving grace toward you so that, by faith, you can receive the gift of having your story always move towards good. Dr. Esau McCaulley – associate professor of New Testament at Wheaton College and theologian in residence at Progressive Baptist Church, a historically Black congregation in Chicago – expresses this fact beautifully:

> What is God's first answer to Black suffering (and the wider human suffering and the rage that comes alongside it)? It is to enter that suffering alongside us as a friend and a redeemer. The answer to Black rage is the calming words of the Word made flesh. The incarnation that comes all the way down, even unto death, has been enough for us to say yes, God, we trust you. We have decided to trust God because he knows what it means to be at the mercy of a corrupt state that knows little of human rights.[7]

Dr. McCaulley is saying that God earns our trust by entering into our suffering with us. God entered into our suffering as if to say, "I am here in this with you. I love you. Trust me." God entered into our suffering so that he could show how much he loves you. God entered into our suffering so that he could give you a new story, one that ends in eternal salvation and a new creation. Will you trust him?

———

RECAP

God is at work in your life, so trust him. God has planned and purposed all things. God created all things. God preserves and governs all things. He often preserves and governs using people and other means. Whether through common or special grace, or both, God is at work in your life. God governs even the evil in our lives, but this evil does not destroy God's good purposes for his people. We become a part of these good purposes by believing in Jesus. In the person and work of Jesus, God has come to us in the midst of our suffering, showing us that we can trust him.

Now that we have considered how God works in the world, let's zoom in on creation. Let's look at how he created us.

CHAPTER 5

WHEN THE LIGHTING ON GOD'S SELFIE IS JUST RIGHT

I still remember the days of flip phones and actual cameras that weren't attached to our phones. But in the past few years, with the rise of social media apps readily available on our phones and with the increasing quality of phone cameras, selfies have become a thing. You can take a selfie of yourself or a selfie with a group of people. When they want to capture an image of themselves, someone simply grabs their phone, extends their arms, and captures an image of their face. And often it takes several tries to get a selfie where the lighting is on point, the angle is just right, and your facial expression communicates what you want it to. Then, after scrolling through all of the pictures you just took, you find the perfect one to place on *Instagram*.

Did you know that God took a selfie of himself on the sixth day of creation? God wanted an image of himself to show off his glory in his brand-new creation. So, God the Spirit took the phone, yelled to God the Father and God the Son, "Aye come here! Let's get a selfie." The Father came up with the idea; the Son coordinated the moment; and the Spirit took the divine phone and focused the shot on God the Son. All three of them were in the photo. Click! And we were created. His *Instagram* page is the whole world. He posts you on his page to display who he is. You are God's selfie, his image that he wants to use to share his own glory. Hard to believe? Check out Genesis:

> Then God said, "Let us make human beings in our image, to be like us. They will reign over the fish in the sea, the birds in the sky, the livestock, all the wild animals on the earth, and the small animals that scurry along the ground."
> So God created human beings in his own image.
> In the image of God he created them;
> male and female he created them. (Genesis 1:26–27)

We have already seen in chapter four that God has created everything, and during the six days of creation, he is organizing his creation and filling it with life forms. On the sixth day, God created humanity. Before creating them, God expressed his glorious purpose for humanity. This purpose is to create humanity in his image. The Bible explains what it means to be in his image by saying, "After our likeness," as the English Standard Version (ESV) of the Bible translates it. God has created humanity to be like him! In Genesis 2, we see that he created us by forming and breathing his spirit into us. Job confesses, "For the Spirit of God has made me, and the breath of the Almighty gives me life" (Job 33:4).

WHERE WE ARE GOING

In a sentence, this chapter will teach: *You* are created with a wonderful design, so live for God.

Black Africans have been a part of a history that has tried to take away the knowledge of our dignity and humanity. So often the world has screamed, "Less than human!" or, "Not human!" If that wasn't enough, we often focus on humanity's sin and flaws in the church to the large neglect of humanity's glory and beauty.

God has created you to be the perfect image to post. You need to know that Yahweh God has created you gloriously and has a beautiful design and purpose for your life. You are precious to him. If we fail to know this, we will listen to the world's voice over us, which is too often one of disgust and disrespect. If we fail to know this, we will fail to know what God is calling us into. We often know he is calling us *away* from sin, but what is he calling us to? He is calling us *toward* glory and joy.

————

YOU MUST BE LIKE GOD

What does it look like to be in the image of God? What does it mean to be like God? There are three illustrations that the Bible uses to explain how we are to be like God; I think of it in terms of three "K" sounds – kin, kings and queens, and clergy.

BE LIKE GOD AS HIS CHILDREN

First, we are created to be God's kin as God's image. The Bible uses "image" and "likeness" language to describe the relationship between a parent and a child: "When Adam had lived 130 years, he fathered a son in his own likeness, after his image, and named him Seth" (Genesis 5:3 ESV). Here we see that Seth was made after the image and likeness of Adam. To be after someone's image and likeness is to be that person's child. This makes sense when you think of the fact that people's children look like them! As God's children[1], we are like him and are designed to act like him.

Let God's original design for us dictate our future instead of what everybody around us is saying and doing. Don't follow what's trending in the world around you; be true to what God wants posted! God has created you as his kin — to be like him in all areas of life, yet we often want to be like everybody else who have wholesale rejected God's purpose for their life.

BE LIKE GOD AS HIS KINGS AND QUEENS

Second, God created us to be mini-kings and mini-queens as God's image. We are meant to rule all of creation on behalf of God. King David recognizes this:

> Yet you made them only a little lower than God
> and crowned them with glory and honor.
> You gave them charge of everything you made,
> putting all things under their authority. (Psalm 8:5–6)

God himself has made us royalty, just like him! When God created you, he blue-check-verified you as his kings and queens. This means that you are full of dignity and glory as an image-bearer. And as royalty, we are to manage God's creation. Genesis 1:28 gives us more detail, "'Be fruitful and multiply. Fill the earth and govern it. Reign over the fish in the sea, the birds in the sky, and all the animals that scurry along the ground'" (Genesis 1:28). In the Bible, fruitfulness means to produce good things, especially bearing children. Multiplying and filling the earth means to become numerous; in other words, have babies and raise them to be good image-bearers. Governing and reigning over the earth means that humanity is supposed to order and build this world into a glorious home for all of God's glorious image-bearers.

God has created you as kings and queens — to use all of your gifts and talents to make this world a place that reflects God's truth, goodness, beauty, justice, and wisdom. Yet we sometimes subconsciously believe the voices that tell us we will be nothing. We secretly believe that we will amount to nothing, never make a difference, will be a dead-beat dad or irresponsible mother, and will either be in jail or die in the streets. Yet, God created us for so much more!

BE LIKE GOD AS HIS CLERGY

Lastly, we are created to be God's clergy as God's image. A clergy-person is someone appointed for official, sacred duties, usually in a sacred space. Where was humanity appointed for religious duties? "The LORD God took the man and put him in the garden of Eden to work it and keep it" (Genesis 2:15 ESV). God created the first human, Adam, and put him in a garden.

What was the sacred space for Adam and Eve? The garden was God's temple, the place on earth where he lived. Sounds strange? Take a look at Ezekiel 28:13-19. In verse 13, "Eden, the garden of God," refers to the same place as "the holy mountain of God" in verse 14. What is the significance of a holy mountain? Mountains were often places where the gods met with people. The garden was on a mountain, and as a *holy* mountain, it was the place where heaven and earth met, "the place of God's presence, a cosmic Holy of Holies."[2] The garden of Eden was a garden-temple-mountain.

What was Eden, this garden-temple-mountain, like? There were animals, but there were also heavenly beings with animal-like features, like cherubim (Genesis 3:24; Ezekiel 28:14, 16). Genesis 2:10-14 tells us that a river flowed through this garden and broke into four different rivers to water the earth. Life itself flowed from the garden-temple to the rest of the earth. It is not a coincidence that later in the Bible story, God's tabernacle/temple had garden imagery and carvings of cherubim (1 Kings 6:29-31). The temple imagery and carvings were echoes of the garden of Eden. The garden of Eden was a temple-garden, the most holy place on planet earth where God would dwell. What a beautiful place!

We see that Adam and Eve were supposed to work in the LORD's cosmic temple. In what ways? What were their sacred duties?

As God's image, Adam and Eve were temple images. In the ancient Near East, when someone created an image of the gods, they would take a statue and put it through a birthing/manufacturing process. As a result, a visible manifestation of the god was born. This image was used in the temple, and people would come to worship it. Something similar is happening with Adam and Eve, but different. God created humanity to be his image, but instead of being gods themselves receiving worship in the cosmic temple, they were distinct from God and designed to point all the glory to God.

Adam and Eve were also priests as God's image. Priests labored in the presence of God and brought others into the presence of God. Genesis 2:15 tells us that Adam and Eve were supposed to "work" and "keep" the garden. Working and keeping a temple are priestly duties. Let me explain.

Working the garden was a religious/priestly duty. The Hebrew word translated as "work" in Genesis 2:15 (עבד) is most often translated as "serve" where the Hebrew word occurs in other places of the Bible. The term "serve" has a religious flavor when it describes actions in service of a god. In fact, the same Hebrew word for "serve" is sometimes translated as "worship" or "minister" when it is used in connection with gods or God (Exodus 12:31), and the word for "serve" is often used in connection with other words that mean "worship" (Exodus 20:5; Numbers 3:7). "Working" for a god had a religious flavor.

Keeping the garden was a religious/priestly duty. The Hebrew word translated as "keep" means "to guard or to watch." The priests in the Old Testament were appointed to do the same in God's dwelling place.

Working and keeping are two essential ways to describe the duties of a priest (Numbers 3:5-10). Like Adam and Eve, God designed you to serve God as a priest. You are meant to worship God in his presence; labor for him in his presence; protect his presence; and bring others into his presence. If you are human, you are designed as a spiritual creature!

BE LIKE GOD AS A UNITED HUMANITY

The image of God manifests as we, *together*, are like God. "God created *humankind* in his own image, in the image of God he created *them*, male and female he created *them*" (Genesis 1:27 NET, emphasis added). Some translations say, "So God created *man* in his own image, in the image of God he created *him*" (Genesis 1:27 ESV, emphasis added). Translations like this clearly miss the point that God is referring to humanity collectively when he created them in his image! It is together that humans image God and rule over the creation.

The fact that God made humanity in his image means that it is important to God that humans are united. We all need each other! Humanity cannot fulfill its duty to God unless it is at peace with each other. More specifically, of huge importance is unity between males and females. Not only is this the fundamental division among humanity but also the most important place for unity, for many reasons. For example, male and female unity in marriage is what God uses even to create "a humanity" and to fill the earth with his image. Also, all ethnicities and people groups share in God's image. By God's design no people group inherently reflects the image of God more vibrantly than others. All of humanity receives the same design and purpose from God.

BE LIKE GOD AS A DIVERSE HUMANITY

Though we represent the image of God together, we are different. The image of God is manifested as we embrace diversity. Dr. Irwyn Ince, a Black Presbyterian pastor and author, tells us,

> . . . for humanity to be the image of God, it must embody beautiful community — unity in diversity, diversity in unity. If God displays his beauty in his trinitarian life, we should expect that beauty to be reflected in the humanity that images him. While

each person is royalty, we find the fullest expression of the image of God together in community.[3]

Dr. Ince is telling us that unity-in-diversity reflects the nature of God. In the same way that the three persons of the Trinity are different persons united as one God, so humanity is to imitate God in this unity. It is this unity-in-diversity that Jesus asks the Father to give to his followers as a new humanity: "I am praying not only for these disciples but also for all who will ever believe in me through their message. I pray that they will all be *one, just as you and I are one*—as you are in me, Father, and I am in you" (John 17:20–21, emphasis added).

―――――

CHRISTIANS MUST ENGAGE THE WORLD'S DIVISIONS

As Adam and Eve had children and filled the earth, the different nations and families were supposed to glorify God together. However, in Genesis 11, humanity came together to unite against God at Babel, not under him. They were able to do this because they all spoke one language. So in judgment, God gave them all different languages and then scattered them over the world to stop their efforts against him. God hopes that humanity, in the midst of their separation and sin, will find him to be healed of its disunity in diversity. Apostle Paul sums up this whole story: "From one man he created all the nations throughout the whole earth. He decided beforehand when they should rise and fall, and he determined their boundaries. His purpose was for the nations to seek after God and perhaps feel their way toward him and find him—though he is not far from any one of us" (Acts 17:26–27).

Given the divisions that resulted from Babel, how do we engage them as Christians? God is ruler over all the happenings of world history, including our culture and ethnicity. We have found ourselves as Africans — diaspora or continental — in this particular time and place. What does it mean to be African and to be a Christian? Let me build a biblical framework for how to view yourself as both a Christian and an African. This passage is key for understanding our identity:

> Don't forget that you Gentiles used to be outsiders. You were called "uncircumcised heathens" by the Jews, who were proud of their circumcision, even though it affected only their bodies and not their hearts. In those days you were living apart from Christ. You were excluded from citizenship among the people of Israel, and you did not know the covenant promises God had made to them. You lived in this world without God and without hope. But now you have been united with Christ Jesus. Once you were far away from God, but now you have been brought near to him through the blood of Christ. For Christ himself has brought peace to us. He united Jews and Gentiles into one people when, in his own body on the cross, he broke down the wall of hostility that separated us. (Ephesians 2:11-14)

In this passage, the Apostle Paul explains how Christ accomplishes unity in the midst of division. Let's explore this passage for a moment.

ISRAEL IS GOD'S WAKANDA

As we all know, *Black Panther* is one of the most popular movies ever. Wakanda is a place with vibranium, an element that allows Wakandans to craft highly advanced technology. Vibranium can absorb and release energy, bestow supernatural qualities to things like flowers, and enhance mystical powers. Because of the vibranium and the genius of the Wakandans, Wakanda has become a place of beauty, prosperity, power, and glory.

The issue is that the blessings of Wakanda are hidden from the world; they have a strict policy of not opening their borders to outsiders. As a result, all of the people around the globe, notably the oppressed communities of the African Diaspora – like African Americans – are barred from the blessings that would have helped them in the past and currently.

King T'Challa saw the plight of the communities around the world, and he was disgusted with how Wakanda turned their back on the world when they had the resources to help. Consequently, he decided to open the doors of Wakanda to aid impoverished communities all over the world.

Throughout history, Israel was God's Wakanda, and the vibranium which was the promises, covenants, the glory, the law, the worship, and the patriarchs made this people the greatest nation on the face of the planet. They were blessed. When I say "Israel," I am not talking about the modern political nation-state called Israel. I am talking about the ancient Near Eastern nation described in the Bible. And by the time this letter was written, Israel was no longer officially an independent kingdom. It became under Roman rule in 63 BC.

THIS WORLD IS DEFINED BY DIVISIONS

But like Wakanda, they had a strict code. This strict code that was a part of the Mosaic law was designed to keep Israelites separate from the Gentiles[4] (nations) not only morally but also culturally. All throughout biblical history, the Gentiles, who are those who are not a part of God's people, became a part of God's people only as they left behind their cultures to adopt the ceremonial and civil laws of the Mosaic law,[5] like not eating pork and the death penalty for beastiality. The cleanliness codes, the dietary laws, the sacrificial system, and the detailed rules were great obstacles to the Gentiles. There was division between the Gentiles and the Jews.

There were also other major divisions of the world back then in the Roman Empire, like Greeks and non-Greeks, bondservant and free, and man and woman (Galatians 3:27-28; Colossians

3:11). Many of these same divisions exist now, but some of them look different. Deep down we all feel the pain of division, don't we? Everyone is looking for world peace, but it often escapes us, despite all of the answers we might give to attain it. Every country and every culture has these kinds of divisions. The United States has racial and class divisions, India with their caste system, Nigeria with their tribes.

What the Bible calls "this present evil age" (Galatians 1:3) is defined by divisions. And if it is Jesus' goal to unite the whole world under his lordship (Ephesians 1:7-10), then divisions are a problem.

CHRIST BRINGS UNITY

But now that Christ has come and died, there was a shift in what it meant to be a part of God's Wakanda, God's Israel. You no longer had to be a Jew in order to be a part of God's people. It's like the last scene of the movie when the Wakandan technology comes to the kids on the basketball court; the blessings of Israel were now being brought to the nations! How did this happen?

The Mosaic law was the wall that divided Jew and Gentile, but Christ tore it down! Through Christ's death, all people groups are being reconciled to him, and because they are all being reconciled to him, they are being reconciled with each other. The two that were formerly divided by the Mosaic law, Christ has now made them one. Paul says in Ephesians 2:17 that Christ, through the apostles, is preaching peace to those who were far (i.e. Gentiles) and those who were near (i.e. Jews). They are now one new people!

When Christ came to the earth, he established a new way of being. He brings the new creation into the here and now. The future age has broken into the present age, like light shining through a crack into a dark room or water trickling out of a leak onto dry ground. We still live in the present age (Titus 2:12) and have real ties to present age realities, such as our sexuality, occupations, social class, and the like (Galatians 3:28; Colossians 3:11). However, we are also a part of a new creation and are citizens of God's kingdom (2 Corinthians 5:17; Ephesians 2:19) right here and right now if we are united with Jesus. Christians are a part of a new creation (a future age) and this present age at the same time. We live as a new creation people while engaging and living in this present evil age. One of the central goals of the New Testament is to help Christians live as dual citizens – of the new creation and the present age. This means we live in unity even in the midst of division.

THERE IS NEW CREATION UNITY

I am delighted to be Black, but now that I am in Christ, Black is no longer my most significant identity marker. When I was saved by Christ, I was not only brought into a new status with him, but I was also brought into a new nation. I am now a citizen of Israel, which is God's new creation people. I am an Israelite. Israel – as the Bible defines it - is a multiethnic, cross-cultural, cross-racial, multilingual group of people everywhere and at all times who have confessed Jesus as their Lord and Savior.

This means that I am an Israelite and an African American at the same time. This means I am a part of two peoples. Though I am delighted and proud to be an African American, my primary allegiance is to Israel, God's kingdom people. There are things a part of African American culture that I will have to leave behind because I am an Israelite, and there are things that I must keep because I am an Israelite. Also, I have two histories. I celebrate Black history, and I celebrate biblical history every time I read the Bible. These two histories intersect as I celebrate the African American Christian tradition. I celebrate two sets of holidays. For example, I celebrate Juneteenth, and I celebrate every Sunday, which is Israel's national independence day celebration as we celebrate Christ's resurrection victory.

Though Israel is one people, we are also many different

peoples. In Genesis 12, God told Abraham, "I will bless those who bless you, and him who dishonors you I will curse, and in you all the families of the earth shall be blessed" (Genesis 12:3 ESV). God's goal has always been to bless every single people group on the globe. And we see that God accomplishes this in Revelation 7:9-12 as people from all over the globe stand and worship Jesus at his throne. It is Jesus' vision to unite all people into one people under his lordship. Through Jesus, people who would otherwise not be family become family.

———

FIGHTING FOR HUMANITY WITH C. HERBERT OLIVER

Our old friend for this chapter is Rev. C. Herbert Oliver.[6] He sincerely believed in the Bible's view of humanity, and this led him to dedicate a large portion of his life to the fight against segregation and White supremacist violence. He believed that one could not be a consistent Christian and a segregationist at the same time.

SEGREGATION IS AGAINST THE BIBLE'S TEACHING ON HUMANITY

Oliver was born in 1925 in Birmingham, Alabama. He was a Black Presbyterian pastor and is most widely known as a civil right leader in Birmingham, Alabama where he documented cases of police brutality with the Inter-Citizens Committee in the early 1960s, many which happened under Eugene "Bull" Connor.

Oliver wrote *No Flesh Shall Glory: How the Bible Destroys the Foundations of Racism* in 1959, which sought to destroy racism by striking at its ideological foundations. He gives a biblical framework for humanity and race relations:

Racism of any kind, whether Black, White, or anything in between is destructive of good human relations and should be repudiated by all thinking people. He who would be at a loss without the feelings of race solidarity needs to reconsider the basis of his hope. If his hope is in racial solidarity, it is a vain hope as it does not have the support of God. If his hope is in God, he does not need the prop of racial solidarity to bolster him, for he who has God has all, and he who has not God has nothing. With the rejection of racism in all its forms there should be put in its place a balanced emphasis on the unity of the whole human race.[7]

Oliver is saying that racial solidarity, which is another way of referring to racial superiority and racial segregationist thinking, is against God. The way to heal racism is to make God the hope of your life, not the superiority of your race. When you place God as the hope of your life, then you will replace racism with God's teaching of human unity. Seeing and believing in this unity is the first step of engaging in racial justice work that not only recognizes the differences between races but also works towards healing.

UNITY IS THE GOAL OF RACIAL JUSTICE

Like Oliver, I must fight for racial justice, but my fight looks different than those who are not yet Christians. African American Christians have a very rich and powerful legacy of Christian activism related to racism. Our motivation is Jesus and our end goal is to see everyone united under the beautiful reign of Christ. The way that we do this is to call people to change their ways, to align their ways with the love that Christ exemplified. We also call them to believe in Christ, the only one who has the power to transform us into the kind of people who can actually sustain unity in the midst of really hard division. For example, the ideal is Black Christians and White Christian worshiping and fellowshipping together, but it will take a lot of repentance and a radically new way of viewing ourselves and each other. We must be honest about and acknowledge the present age divisions while we make the necessary changes that must happen to see new creation unity.

———

LIVE FOR GOD IN A RELATIONSHIP WITH HIM

We have seen that God created humanity in his image and that we are designed to image God together. Before we move to the next chapter, we must understand that God has created us for a relationship with himself. The first thing God did with humanity was put them in the place of relationship (the garden) and set the terms of the relationship with his word. We see this in Genesis 2:15-17: "The LORD God placed the man in the Garden of Eden to tend and watch over it. But the LORD God warned him, 'You may freely eat the fruit of every tree in the garden— except the tree of the knowledge of good and evil. If you eat its fruit, you are sure to die.'" We take this for granted, but this is a key part in understanding humanity.

God created humans to relate with him, and God defines this relationship through a covenant. Remember, a covenant is a formal relationship, and the Bible is structured around two major covenants – the old and new. Although these are two very important covenants, there are many other covenants about which the Bible speaks.

GOD'S RECORD LABEL

So I recently watched the *Jeen-Yuhs* documentary, and I think it can help us understand the concept of a covenant. I particularly liked the first episode, which follows Kanye West from his days as solely a producer to a famous artist. A huge part of Kanye's story was getting a record deal with one of the hottest labels at the time – Roc-A-Fella Records.

Kanye started as a producer for them, making beats. However, his hard work and dedication got the attention of the label executives, and he received the opportunity to sign a contract, which is similar to a covenant. There was a "covenant ceremony" to make the covenant official. The lawyers and executives of Roc-A-Fella met with Kanye as he signed the contract.

The Roc-A-Fella "covenant" came with conditions. Kanye had to submit to the label's authority and trust the label with ownership over certain aspects of his art. The "covenant" came with "blessings" if he met all the conditions. The label would use all of its resources, clout, power, and relational connections to help make Kanye a successful artist — awards, money, and having his music distributed all over the world. And the "covenant" came with promised "curses" if the conditions were broken. The artist would be cut off from the label and all of its resources.

Roc-A-Fella established a formal relationship, aka a covenant, with Kanye for the good of music lovers and the glory of Roc-A-Fella. The covenant formalized a relationship so that musical dreams could become a reality.

Sort of like a music contract, but better, God created a covenant with humanity. Record labels can be shady, but God is astoundingly good. Contracts take advantage of desperate artists, but God is radically generous. Record labels are sometimes unnecessary, but God is more important than the air we breathe. Record labels often think about themselves over the artist, but God thinks about us over himself.

GOD CREATED A COVENANT OF LIFE WITH HUMANITY

Of special importance in understanding the role of humanity in God's creation is the first "contract" he created with them. This covenant is commonly called "the covenant of works" or "the covenant of life." Now you may be thinking, "Why have I never heard of this covenant before?" It is because the word "covenant" actually never shows up in Genesis chapter two where God sets up Adam and Eve in the garden! However, although the word "covenant" is absent, it does not mean that a covenant is absent.

In Genesis 3-4, we see two parties, conditions, and promised blessings and curses. The formal establishment of this covenant happens in Genesis 2:16-17, which says, "But the LORD God warned him, 'You may freely eat the fruit of every tree in the garden— except the tree of the knowledge of good and evil. If you eat its fruit, you are sure to die'" (Genesis 2:16–17). Here we see the two parties — God and Adam, and by extension Eve, who is not yet created. We see conditions — Adam and Eve are not to eat the fruit of the tree of the knowledge of good and evil. Although God explicitly commanded them not to eat of the tree, it is implicit that they also fulfill their responsibilities as image-bearers. We see a promised curse if they do not meet the conditions — death. We also see an implicit blessing of meeting the condition — life with God and, eventually, eternal life. The tree of life symbolized this eternal reward. Adam and Eve, as we will see, never attained this eternal life because they never had the chance to eat from the tree of life (spoiler alert: In Christ we will get a chance to eat the fruit they never ate).

Understanding the tree of the knowledge of good and evil and the tree of life is an important part in understanding humanity's relationship with God. These two trees represented two things that God has sole claim over. God alone was the giver of life, and God alone was the one who defined the difference between good and evil. The serpent — who is the spiritual being who opposes God, "the Satan," which means "adversary" (Revelation 12:9; 20:2) — convinced them that God was keeping them from eating the forbidden fruit because God was trying to hold them back from truly being all that they could be. Adam and Eve ate the forbidden fruit. They fell into the temptation and decided that they wanted to be God themselves, being their own discerners of good and evil instead of relying on God for such discernment.

When they ate the fruit, everything unraveled. They became

ashamed of their nakedness: "Obedience was their covering, their righteousness, their robe of heavenly citizenship. While this remained untorn they were honorable, appearing in royal apparel. But now it is torn, and their nakedness shames them."[8] They became scared of God and each other. After Adam and Eve sinned, the serpent, Adam, and Eve received curses from God (Genesis 3). Human relationships, including marriage, are now cursed, along with childbearing (Genesis 3:16); humans are far from God (Genesis 3:10, 23-24); the ground is cursed (Genesis 3:18); and labor becomes very difficult (Genesis 3:19). Everything fell apart.

———

RECAP

We have seen that God has created us with a wonderful design, so we should live for him. We have been created to live for him as kin, king and queens, and clergy. As humans fulfill these roles, we do them together as a diverse humanity. Given our calling as God's image-bearers, we must fight division and embrace the unity that Christ brings. As image-bearers, God has wonderfully designed us for a relationship with himself.

Does this sound amazing to you? Well, what went so wrong with humanity? Let's explore this next.

CHAPTER 6
WHY IS LIFE SO HARD?

We all know that Lebron James is one of the greatest basketball players who ever lived. He has played for the Cavaliers, the Heat, and the Lakers. Whenever he switches teams, he gets beautiful murals painted of him in the cities he goes to. He had a mural painted of him in Miami when he played for the Heat. He also had a mural of him painted in Los Angeles when he came to the Lakers.

But many of these images have been marred. To mar something means to damage its appearance. The one in Miami was marred after he left the Heat. Also, the one in Los Angeles was marred when he came to the Lakers. On the picture it says, "We don't want you"; his losing finals record, "3-6"; "LeFraud"; and "No king."

God has painted you as a beautiful mural of himself, designing you to show off his glory to the whole world, but sin has marred his image in you. Sin is the unwanted spray paint that partially blocks the beautiful image that you once were. Sin has written, "no king, no queen," "no longer loved," "you're a fake," and "loser," onto you. The image of God is still there, but it is marred. You have a glorious purpose, but there is no way that you can fulfill it.

This happened the moment that Adam and Eve sinned. Theologians often call this moment "the fall of humanity." Humanity fell from the glorious state they were in, inside God's temple-garden.

WHERE WE ARE GOING

In a sentence, this chapter will show you that sin is your greatest problem, so confess it to God.

The world is messed up. We know that things aren't the way that God created them to be. There is suffering all around us and in our own lives. We and others fail to live up to what God created us to be. Life is hard! How can God be good and allow the world to be like this? This chapter is going to help you understand how the world got to be the way it is.

I want to convince you that sin is what is wrong with the world. Sin has made everything, including ourselves, corrupt and in deep need of restoration. In medicine, if you are not able to diagnose the disease, you won't know what kind of treatment you need. In the same way, if you do not understand how sin has ruined everything, you won't truly understand your need for a savior. It is only when you understand your profound need for a savior that you can embrace the glory and joy of being saved. We will talk about how 1) sin is what caused everything to fall apart 2) the world is cursed 3) the earth itself is cursed 4) evil spirits have power in this world 5) sin enslaves 6) sin brings pain and 7) sin makes the world more complex than our simplistic narratives. This chapter will set us up to be able to understand the rest of this book.

THE WORLD IS VERY DIFFERENT FROM THE BEGINNING

Due to the fall, the world became "fallen." Before we get into the details of what a fallen world is like, let's make sense of the realities that deeply shape the fall of humanity.

SIN CAUSED THE FALL OF HUMANITY

Humanity fell by sinning against God. Sin, in a word, is failure, and it is two-sided. One, sin is failing to do what God requires. James tells us this in his letter when he says, "Remember, it is sin to know what you ought to do and then not do it" (James 4:17). For example, failing to be generous is a sin because God requires us to be generous. Two, sin is failing to refrain from what God forbids. For example, stealing is a sin because God has forbidden us to do it. To summarize, sin is anything that breaks God's law (1 John 3:4). Though sin is breaking God's law, sin is always personal because it is *God's* law. In sinning, we are sinning against God himself. Sin is not simply breaking an abstract and impersonal set of rules. When Adam and Eve sinned, they submitted to the serpent and his word instead of God and his word. They took up weapons against God and rebelled against him.

Some people might say, "If the big deal with sin is that God is personally offended, why doesn't God just get over himself?" This mentality shows that we don't understand just how serious sin is. Sin destroys ourselves, destroys our world, and destroys others because it is a rejection of God's kingship, which is the source of all life. When you have rejected the source of life, what remains is death and destruction. A righteous, loving, just God must take sin seriously!

YOU ARE EXPERIENCING THE EFFECTS OF A BROKEN COVENANT

Adam and Eve broke the covenant, so now we are under the covenant curses. With Adam and Eve, we fell too. Why did humanity fall if only Adam and Eve sinned? Shouldn't their children have started out with a clean slate?

Sports can help us understand this. I wrestled when I was in middle school and high school. Each person who wrestled did so at a certain weight class. Each class was named by the maximum weight. For example, the first part of my junior year, I wrestled at 119 pounds, so I had to be 119 pounds, or under, in order to wrestle in a wrestling match. Before a wrestling match, everyone had to cut weight in order to weigh within their weight class. Either the day before or the day of a match, every wrestler would "weigh in" on the scale to make sure they were at the right weight. I was usually cutting a good bit of weight in order to get under 119 pounds.

In order to prevent any surprise instances where someone was overweight at weigh-ins, my coach wanted to make sure we were all close to the right weight at practice the day before the match. Before this practice, coach would check our weight in his office. After this, we would go warm up in the mat room where we practiced. After weighing everyone, coach would walk in the mat room and list those who were far above weight by saying, "Chavis, so and so, and so and so are three pounds overweight. We are practicing until they get within one pound of their weight class." The whole team would groan. The whole team faced the consequences of a few people's negligence. The whole team was a *team*. The rewards of one person's success was experienced by the whole team, and the consequences of one person's failure was experienced by the whole team.

In a similar way, Adam was the one on whom rested the success or failure of team humanity. His success meant all of our success, and his failure meant all of our failure. When Adam entered into the covenant of life with God, he did not just make the covenant as an individual, he created it as a representative of all of humanity to be born, including Eve, who was not yet created. When Adam sinned, humanity collectively sinned; when Adam fell, humanity collectively fell. Romans 5:12-21 and 1 Corinthians 15:22 explains the mechanics of this. Just as Jesus brings blessings to all who are in him, Adam brings cursing to all who are in him. Thus, Paul tells the Corinthians, "For as in Adam all die, so also in Christ all will be made alive" (1 Corinthians 15:22 NASB). The covenant curse, which was death, should have only happened to Adam if God considered only Adam as the sole individual party in the covenant of life. No, all of humanity shares in the covenant curses because when Adam broke the covenant condition, all of humanity broke the condition of the covenant. This is why the covenant didn't reset with Adam and Eve's children. The children had no opportunity to try to fix what Adam and Eve destroyed; they were recipients of the curse of the covenant because they were a party in the covenant through Adam.

As a result of the broken covenant, all of humanity experiences the captivity to sin and immersion into suffering that comes with rebelling against God. God cursed humanity and their domain, which was the earth. In cursing humanity, God is just and true to the conditions of the covenant he made with humanity.

OWNING OUR PART WITH PHILLIS WHEATLEY

Phillis Wheatley will help us again in this chapter. She teaches us how to see ourselves as a part of the problem. It is easy to look at sin and look at the problems of the world and then say, "Things are horrible out there!" while we forget that things are also horrible within us. We contribute to the sinfulness, pain, and curse of our fallen world because we ourselves are also fallen.

Wheatley's poem "On Recollection" is a poem addressed to Mneme. In Greek mythology, Mneme is a muse, which is a goddess over an art. Mneme is the muse of memory (i.e. recollection). Wheatley would often explore Christian themes by poetically using figures from Greek mythology. As she addresses Mneme, Wheatley talks about how memory (personified by Mneme) functions in the inner-life of a person. Wheatley poetically talks about a sleeping person, who Mneme visits in their dreams. At night, Mneme comes and paints pictures of what we have done. Wheatley says, "Mneme, enthron'd within the human breast, Has vice condemn'd, and ev'ry virtue blest."[1] Memory, which functions as our conscience in this poem, condemns the wrong things we have done and celebrates the good we have done. When the sleeper hears memory applaud their good deeds, it gives them great joy. When memory shows how the sleeper has misspent their lives, torture and bitterness face them. Wheatley tells us what our response should be when we see our sin:

> In Recollection see them fresh return,
> And sure 'tis mine to be asham'd, and mourn.
> O Virtue, smiling in immortal green,
> Do thou exert thy pow'r, and change the scene;
> Be thine employ to guide my future days,
> And mine to pay the tribute of my praise.[2]

Wheatley tells us that as memory shows us our sin, we should experience a deep shame and sadness. When we look at what is wrong with the world, we should see what is wrong with us. It should spiritually crush us to see that our sin has a role to play in this fallen world. Along with this, there should be a pulsing desire to pursue virtue, justice, and wholeness as a way of turning our lives around. We should fall in love with what is good, true, and righteous when we truly realize how ugly sin is. What happens after seeing our sin and wanting righteousness? We should confess our sins to God and desperately ask him for a savior. As we read the rest of this chapter, I pray you develop a weighty sense of how fallen you are, an awesome longing for something more, and a trust that God is the one to pursue for the way forward.

————

WE ARE SINFUL AND MISERABLE

Genesis 3:14-19 describes the curses that God laid upon all of the actors in the cosmic rebellion — the serpent, then Eve, and then Adam. As a result of the curses, all that is bad about humanity's experience on earth can be summarized with two words — "sin" and "misery." God's covenant curse is upon us, which is the outworking of his wrath (Galatians 3:10). Let us look at some aspects of the curse on the world.

SIN MADE THE WHOLE EARTH A HORRIBLE PLACE

Because of Adam and Eve's sin, the whole world is cursed, not just humans. When Adam and Eve sinned, God cursed both humanity and the realm over which we were supposed to have ruling authority, which is all of physical creation. Adam and Eve ceased to be like God, so the earth ceased to be a reflection of God's initial design for it. To illustrate this, if the sun ceased to give light, life would cease.

In God's plan, our destiny is tied to the destiny of our realm. This is why Apostle Paul speaks about creation waiting for the total renewal of humanity. When humanity is renewed, then creation will be renewed. Paul says, "For the creation waits in eager expectation for the children of God to be revealed. For the creation was subjected to frustration, not by its own choice, but by the will of the one who subjected it, in hope that the creation itself will be liberated from its bondage to decay and brought into the freedom and glory of the children of God" (Romans 8:19–21 NIV). The "children of God to be revealed" and "glory of the children of God" are references to the time where Jesus will judge all people. In this judgment, Jesus will reveal those who are his children and renew them. With the renewal of humanity will come the renewal of humanity's realm, creation. But as of now, because humanity is under a curse, creation is under a curse.

The fall of humanity is kind of like the game *Jenga*. You build a tower of long rectangular blocks, and each game player has to remove a piece until the tower falls. The person who removes the piece that makes the tower come crashing down loses. Usually, many blocks are removed from the tower before it comes crashing down. Such is not so with the universe. Only one block was removed from the universe, and that block is Adam's one act of faithlessness and disobedience. And the universe comes tumbling down. Our world was "very good" (Genesis 1:31), but now we live in a ruined world.

Sin is never purely an individual thing. In Adam and Eve's case, their sin affected everything. This is hard for us to grasp because we often think of our relationship with God in hyper-individualistic terms, but the Bible does not look at human relationships in this way.

SIN IS THE SOURCE OF POVERTY

Humans all over the globe experience the pain of not having enough of what they need to live. When Adam and Eve rebelled against him, God cursed the ground. Before, the ground would yield all types of beautiful, nourishing, delicious food for humanity, and humans would easily care for it. Now, the ground would yield, ugly, malnourishing, painful food for humanity along with edible food, and humans will work the ground with much pain and exhaustion (Genesis 3:17-18). The curse on the ground is partly where poverty on earth flows from. Along with this, humanity no longer knows how to manage the earth's resources.

We are greedy and oppressive toward one another, to the point that some have an abundance and others die from lack. God's material provisions are a grace that he gives, but everyone possessing enough is no longer a given fact in a cursed world. Don't you experience this in the college lifestyle? Often, a part of being a college student is financial struggle, biting our nails wondering how we are going to handle our school balance. This was not how it was supposed to be.

SIN GAVE EVIL SPIRITS POWER OVER THE WORLD

Humanity lives under the influence of evil spiritual powers. The fact that evil spiritual forces took control of the earthly realms is the source of much of humanity's sinfulness and misery. Part of the curse is that God has permitted Satan to take the throne, which formerly belonged to Adam and Eve as kings and queens. This is why Satan is called the ruler of this world (John 12:31, 16:11), the prince of the power of the air (Ephesians 2:2), and the prince of demons (Matthew 9:34). Satan has rulers, authorities, and "cosmic powers over this present darkness" (Ephesians 6:12) that are assigned to kingdoms and nations to fulfill the will of Satan in the world (Daniel 10:13, 20-21). God himself also has angelic beings assigned to different nations (Deuteronomy 32:8) to wage war against Satan's demons, with Michael being the angel over God's people (Daniel 12:1, Jude 9, Revelation 12:7). The spirit of Satan is at work in those who disobey God (Ephesian 2:2). The spirit of the antichrist, a mysterious figure who will oppose the church in the future, is at work in those who reject Christ (1 John 2:22, 4:3). The demonic powers over the world both enslave us to sin and inflict misery.

Is this a surprise to us? When we read the news and look at the world, it is easy to see that there must be some kind of intelligent design, some kind of deeper purpose behind evil. When we look at all the wild things happening on campus, we often use the word "darkness." God's enemy is behind it in the world and in our lives. Let us explore this sin and misery further.

SIN SEEKS TO ENSLAVE US

Some of the most horrific images of slavery come from the trans-Atlantic slave trade. Humans in chains marching; people packed into disgusting conditions on slave ships; men, women, and children brutally forced to work until they die. Sin seeks to do the same thing to us. Sin isn't just something that we do; it is a force that wants to enslave, to take us as captives (Romans 6:16-22). Jesus once said, "I tell you the truth, everyone who sins is a slave of sin" (John 8:34). Let's look at what this captivity to sin means for humanity.

First, sin enslaves us to guilt. As sinners, we are guilty before God (Romans 5:12, 19). Being guilty means that we are liable to punishment from God. The guilt of humanity means that everyone, apart from a savior, stands guilty before God as a member of humanity. As Christians, we often invite people to "have a relationship with God." Although I understand what we are trying to do, we miss that the Bible teaches that everyone already has a relationship with God! It is either based upon the covenant curses or the covenant blessings. To borrow the Bible's language, you are either in Adam or in Christ (1 Corinthians 15:22).

Second, sin enslaves us to imperfection. Sin has taken away any chance of being born perfect. Like J. Cole's second album title, we are born sinners. Although Adam was born with complete innocence and the ability to be completely righteous before God, this is no longer a possibility for humanity. We are all born without the possibility of being perfectly righteous, which is the Apostle Paul's point in Romans 3:9-20.

Third, sin enslaves us to a corrupted nature. The whole of human nature is corrupted by sin. This does not mean that humanity is as sinful as it could be. No, God, by his grace, restrains evil in us. What this does mean is that there is no part of a human that is perfect or "pre-fall." For example, it is impossible for a human to be born with a perfectly righteous mind but with a corrupted will, nor is it possible for someone's mind to be corrupted yet their emotions are perfectly righteous. Every part of us is touched by sin. Indeed, Paul tells us that every single human is held captive to sin, "For we have already charged that all, both Jews and Greeks, are under sin, as it is written: 'None is righteous, no, not one; no one understands; no one seeks for God. All have turned aside; together they have become worthless; no one does good, not even one'" (Romans 3:9–12 ESV).

Theologians call these three things – humanity's guilt, loss of righteousness, and corrupted nature – "original sin" because they are directly related to the original sin that brought on the covenant curses, which was Adam's eating of the fruit. It isn't hard to follow Jesus in college only because of the temptations that come with the college lifestyle. No, it is also hard to follow Jesus because original sin has made it hard. We no longer have a natural-born ability to make our campuses beautiful places. There will always be something lacking.

Fourth, sin enslaves us to do sinful actions. The fourth and last aspect of humanity's sinfulness flows from the first three. Because of original sin, each of us commit our own sinful actions (Romans 3:23). Paul says to a group of Christians, describing their lives before they were saved by Christ, "As for you, you were dead in your transgressions and sins . . . Like the rest, we were by nature deserving of wrath" (Ephesians 2:1–3 NIV). Sinning against God and being subject to God's wrath are two states of being that describe humanity. On top of this, we are unable to do anything other than sin, for "the mind that is set on the flesh is hostile to God, for it does not submit to God's law; indeed, it cannot. Those who are in the flesh cannot please God" (Romans 8:7–8 ESV). The flesh is ourselves "in Adam," the self that is not saved (Galatians 5:19-21). Even our best actions are corrupted by sinful motives or are done not in total conformity to God's will. Boothe (remember him from the book introduction?) sums it up when he says, "Sin of every name, and disease of every form, come upon [Adam's] seed through his crime. But we are not coerced sinners; for each man is a sinner in his own will, a sinner of his own choice."[3]

SIN BROUGHT PAIN

Another part of the curse is misery. Misery is another word for pain. From the mild pain of a blazing hot summer day, to the extreme pain of losing a loved one, pain is a part of our world. Let's look at this pain.

First, we experience the pain of being far away from God. We have lost the direct access to the presence of God that Adam and Eve originally enjoyed. Adam and Eve were scared of God and were kicked out of the garden, where God dwelled, never to return again in this life (Genesis 3:8, 24). This is the state that all unsaved humanity is in as it relates to God's presence. We go through life in the dark, hands outreached, feeling for God (Acts 17:27). We know we were created to be in God's presence, yet we do not know how to get there. Paul describes unsaved humanity that never were a part of God's people (aka Gentiles) in such language: "You were excluded from citizenship among the people of Israel, and you did not know the covenant promises God had made to them. You lived in this world without God and without hope" (Ephesians 2:12). And Jesus describes some who were a part of God's people (aka Jews) in this way: "If God were your Father, you would love me, because I have come to you from God . . . you are the children of your father the devil, and you love to do the evil things he does" (John 8:42–44). Apart from Christ, we are far away from God.

Second, we experience the pain of having God against us. We are under God's wrath and curse. Like we have already mentioned, his wrath is his justice responding to our injustice, and his curse is the bad things that happen to us as punishment for our unfaithfulness to our covenants with him. Jesus describes all those who do not believe in him as under wrath: "And anyone who believes in God's Son has eternal life. Anyone who doesn't obey the Son will never experience eternal life but remains under God's angry judgment" (John 3:36). Some will say that God will not punish evil, but don't "be fooled by those who try to excuse these sins, for the anger of God will fall on all who disobey him" (Ephesians 5:6). As those who are sinners, we are covenant breakers and, therefore, recipients of God's curse. Moses says to those who have just heard a reading of God's covenant with them, "Cursed is he who does not confirm the words of this law by doing them" (Deuteronomy 27:26 NASB). All of unsaved humanity stand as covenant breakers and, therefore, are guilty before God.

Third, we experience the pains of just living life. These come from the fact that the world is far away from God and under his wrath and curse. Suffering defines our lives here on earth. Paul teaches us such when he says,

> Yet what we suffer now is nothing compared to the glory he will reveal to us later . . . For we know that all creation has been groaning as in the pains of childbirth right up to the present time. And we believers also groan, even though we have the Holy Spirit within us as a foretaste of future glory, for we long for our bodies to be released from sin and suffering. (Romans 8:18–23)

We experience hard toil, poverty, sorrow, loss, destruction, mental illness, and more. This is why creation groans in agony. God has intentionally subjected all of creation to this suffering as a punishment for our rebellion (Romans 8:20).

Fourth, we will experience the pain of death. We all eventually will physically cease to live. Although we typically think of death as the cessation of the body's functions, death in the Bible is a much more broad category. Death is at work in us at all times — when we sin, when we get sick, when we experience mental illness, when our bodies decay, and when we are laid in our graves. Jesus references this conception of death when he says, "I tell you the truth, those who listen to my message and believe in God who sent me have eternal life. They will never be condemned for their sins, but they have already *passed from death* into life" (John 5:24, emphasis added).

Lastly, humanity is destined for eternal pain, which is the pains of experiencing God's wrath forever. Related to this punishment, Paul says of Jesus, "He will come with his mighty angels, in flaming fire, bringing judgment on those who don't know God and on those who refuse to obey the Good News of our Lord Jesus. They will be punished with eternal destruction, forever separated from the Lord and from his glorious power" (2 Thessalonians 1:7–9). Jesus himself also says of those in the same group of people, "And they will go away into eternal punishment, but the righteous will go into eternal life" (Matthew 25:46). God is an eternal being and is unapologetically opposed to wrongdoing; therefore he eternally and unapologetically will punish wrongdoing.

THE IMAGE OF GOD IS BROKEN

We can also think of sinfulness and misery in terms of the image of God. As a result of the curse, our calling to be God's kin, kings and queens, and clergy is severely hindered.

Though we are kings and queens, we are kings and queens who have been dethroned. As a result, God has cursed our efforts to fill the earth, subdue it, and have dominion over it. It is hard to fill the earth when you have pain in childbearing (Genesis 3:16), when the earth is cursed and does not yield food as it should (Genesis 3:19), and when Satan is now sitting on our throne (John 12:31).

Though we are kin, we are children who have been disowned. Adam and Eve are no longer able to properly love God as their Father (Genesis 3:10) nor love each other in imitation of God's love (Genesis 3:16). Although the Father still loves us, we now no longer have a place in his home and no longer look like his children. Not only that, but the Bible actually calls us children of the devil (1 John 3:10). We are at home in Satan's company and look like him since, after all, we chose to submit to his word about God.

Lastly, though we are still designed to labor in God's presence as God's clergy, we have been exiled from the sanctuary. In Genesis 3:24, God bars us from entering into his presence. We were supposed to labor in God's presence and bring others into his presence, but God is no longer close. We have lost intimacy with God and the ability to usher others into his presence.

Do you see your glorious design? To be fully human is to be glorious and righteous. When we sin, we often say, "Hey, I'm only human." I get what we are trying to say, but this is not good theology. It is not, "I'm only human." It is, "I'm so far from human." All have sinned and have fallen short of the glory of God.

LIFE IS MORE COMPLEX THAN "GOOD VS. EVIL"

In our current culture, it is tempting to paint history with the simple narrative of oppressor vs. the oppressed, White vs. Black, European vs. African, good vs. evil. However, the sinfulness and misery of humanity has touched every single person. Everyone is a combination of both good and bad because we were created in the image of God yet are corrupted because of sin and the curse.

This means we cannot paint a simple narrative when we look at our own history of oppression as Africans. In search of dignity and worth as Black people, we often are tempted to idealize our African ancestry. We look at the African kingdoms of the past and say, "Look! We were free! We were kings and queens!" Yes, we were these things in Africa, and there is much beauty in our connection to the continent. However, there is a danger in idealizing our past in order to claim dignity for ourselves. The continent of Africa's history is filled with glory, but it is also filled with violence, dehumanization, and evil, as are other histories. To forget our history is to repeat it.

Wole Soyinka, in his book, *Of Africa,* speaks to this. In his chapters "Fictioning the Fourth Dimension" and "Tree of Forgetfulness," he urges Africans — both diaspora and continent — to be honest about how they remember the continent's history. Soyinka claims that in pursuit of reparations, some Africans paint history as a simplistic "they" versus "us," and "the danger is that in pursuit of this agenda, an Africa that never did exist is created, history is distorted, and even memory abused."[4] Soyinka goes on to state that though both sides are not blameless, an argument for reparations can still stand. The "they" party is most definitely guilty, and this fact is well documented. However, we must reckon honestly with the "us."

Soyinka then lists people and places where Africans participated and profited from the slave trade. He mentions the "Tree of Forgetfulness, around which the slaves were made to do a ritual dance for . . . induction of amnesia."[5]

Of the Tree of Forgetfulness, Soyinka says, "The purpose was to make them forget their land, their homes, their kinfolk, and even the very occupations they once knew — in short, forget their former existence, wipe their minds clean of the past and be receptive to the stamps of strange places."[6] The perpetrators against these enslaved Africans were "the African slave hunters and middlemen. *They* thought up that ritual, not the alien invaders."[7] And ironically, Soyinka states that most

> Africans would prefer to forget the Tree of Forgetfulness, just as their descendants in the United States would also choose to forget . . . that the Tree of Forgetfulness has its roots on African soil, and that the processes — ritualistic and commercial — that desecrated so much of Africa's humanity implicated, ironically and embarrassingly, the very race that produced millions of such victims.[8]

Soyinka states that Africans — continent and diaspora — willingly choose to forget that Africans themselves were complicit in the trans-Atlantic slave trade. It is easier to forget, thereby making the "us" versus "them" narrative simple. However, it is much harder to move forward with a realistic yet complex narrative of Africa.

My point is this: As Africans, we must realize that our own human history as a continent cannot be the primary or only place where we point for evidence of our dignity and beauty. Although our history is filled with beauty and glory, it is also filled with evil and oppression, just like other areas of the world. The primary place to point to our dignity and glory as humans in the face of racism is God creating us in his own image as kings and queens. And as we remember this fact, we can boldly declare the ways that we reflect God's glorious design *and* our deep need for a savior — just like the rest of humanity.

———

A FORESHADOW OF GRACE

But, amidst all the bad news, there is good news! Genesis 3:15 says, "I will put enmity between you and the woman, and between your offspring and her offspring; he shall bruise your head and you shall bruise his heel." Here God artistically promises a final victory over the devil through a descendant of the woman. There are four parties in the above verse: 1) "you," which is the serpent 2) "the woman," who is named "Eve" a few verses later 3) the serpent's offspring and 4) the woman's offspring. The serpent's offspring will be enemies with the woman's offspring. One day there will be a person among the woman's offspring who will deal a fatal blow to the serpent but at a cost. This is a fore-shadowing of the gospel. The story of the whole Bible from Genesis 3 to the end of the Bible is either in expectation of this savior, describing the person and work of this savior, or looking back on the finished work of this savior, the promised offspring.

There is also another foreshadowing of the grace to come. Verses 20-21 say, "Then the man—Adam—named his wife Eve, because she would be the mother of all who live. And the LORD God made clothing from animal skins for Adam and his wife" (Genesis 3:20–21). Just after God had listed out the covenant curses in Genesis 3:14-19, Adam named his wife "Eve," which is similar to the Hebrew word for "life." Just after God tells Adam that he will die and return to dust, Adam thinks about their future and decides that life will come from his wife. They look forward to a hope in the midst of despair, a light in the midst of darkness, life in the midst of death. Then, God gave Adam and Eve new clothes. In Genesis 3:7, Adam and Eve tried to make clothes out of fig leaves to cover their guilt and shame. This is a picture of what we all try to do out of our sense of fear, guilt, and shame. We work hard to try and hide from God and others. But God removed their fig leaves and gave them better clothes, clothes from God. It is a foreshadow of the fact that God will provide for us in the midst of our sin and misery. He will one day remove our guilt and cover our shame.

———

RECAP

We have seen that sin is the cause of everything wrong with the world. We live in a world that is fallen and cursed. The world is filled with sin and misery. Sin has brought curses on the whole earth. The corruption, the sin we see everywhere, the influence of evil spirits, the inescapable presence and power of sin, suffering, and the moral complexity of life are all brought to us by sin. As humans, we have fallen far from how God has created us. As we realize our role to play in this fallen and cursed place and realize how it has affected us, we must mourn and look for God to save us. Our God hinted at the coming of a savior even from Genesis 3.

This is also a foreshadowing of the gospel, to which we turn in the next chapter. As the spiritual says, "If you want to find your way to God . . . the gospel highway must be trod."[9]

PART THREE
RESCUE'S STORY

CHAPTER 7
SEASON 3 FINALE

With the rise of streaming platforms, we are very familiar with the significance of a season finale. As you watch a show, you grow fond of certain characters and grow to despise others. You become invested in the conflict of the show as you cheer on your favorite side of the conflict. As the plot develops, so does your anticipation of the unknown and the mystery of what is to come in the big picture plot of the show. Excitement and interest flood your mind as you wonder what kind of thrilling action or surprises will be unveiled as you go along and wonder how the characters will change depending on the events of the plot.

At last, you come to the season finale. This is the climax of the season. This is the most exciting, drama-filled, action-filled part of the show. The finale is where we see the destinies of the characters, the outcome of conflict, the height of the action, and the future threats on the horizon. The finale is meant to bring strong emotions and jaw-dropping moments. We are supposed to be left in awe.

Did you know that you are in a season finale? The Bible has seasons, as we mentioned in chapter four. Season 1 is creation, and the season finale began on the sixth day of creation when God created humanity. Season 2 is de-creation, and the season finale began when the serpent entered the scene in Genesis 3. Season 3 is re-creation, and the season finale began when Jesus was born. The Bible calls the coming of Jesus and onward the "last days" (Acts 2:17; Hebrews 1:2). You are in the season 3 finale. In other words, we are in the last episode before eternity, which is season 4. Because of Jesus, we are seeing the climax of history – the destiny of the world, the outcome of the conflict between God and Satan, the height of kingdom action, and the future threats on the horizon in the book of Revelation.

As you behold the season finale, and even participate in it, I want you to stand in awe of Jesus and what he is doing.

WHERE WE ARE GOING

In a sentence, this chapter will show that Jesus is the climax of history, so stand in awe of him.

We are often exposed to a Christianity that doesn't give true hope. How? It doesn't make Jesus central. It doesn't see Jesus as the true solution to all of the world's problems and the true thing we have all been waiting for. God's season finale is not actually the finale in this version of Christianity. They talk about Jesus mostly when they are closing a sermon or when someone wants to become a Christian. Many churches are centered on politics, morality, cultural transformation, financial success, practical wisdom, emotional worship, social justice, and so forth. All of these things are *good*, but they are not *central* to the Bible. For these churches, Jesus merely becomes a name they use to simply talk about something else that is actually central to them. Jesus is the clothing to cover the body of what they actually want to talk about. Jesus is the icing to coat the cake of what is actually central to them.

I will show you that the Bible is really the story of how God is saving the world through Jesus. We are a part of an ongoing historical story where God is working a plan to save everyone and everything from all things horrible. The Bible is structured according to the covenants that God makes with his people, and these covenants reveal the story of how God is rescuing the world. We will look at each covenant to see how God 1) announces his plan of rescue 2) begins the rescue plan 3) prepares his people for rescue 4) appoints a ruler for rescue and 5) accomplishes rescue. Let's dive in.

———

HISTORY IS THE STORY OF GOD'S PURSUIT OF YOU

Every Bible book (like Jonah), every biblical event (like the liberation from Egypt), every biblical institution (like the temple), every biblical figure (like King David), and every biblical prophecy is about how Yahweh God is gloriously saving us through Jesus. The fact that Jesus is central means that Jesus is the most important thing in the Bible. Everything in the Bible, and everything in life, finds its importance and meaning in relation to him. It is not the other way around. For example, Jesus doesn't find his importance and meaning as he supports particular political agendas; a political agenda finds its importance and meaning in reference to Jesus.

Now, remember how earlier we said everything in the Bible is about covenants? God is rescuing the whole world from the wrath and curse of the covenant of life with another covenant — the covenant of grace. Adam and Eve had failed to do the good works of the covenant of life, and now they needed grace. Grace is God loving those who do not deserve it. In the covenant of grace, God set up an arrangement and a plan whereby he would graciously rescue the world through the offspring of the woman whom we mentioned at the end of the last chapter.

Let's do a quick overview of the covenants of the Bible. As we look at the Bible's covenants, we will see the story of God lovingly pursuing a renewed relationship with his people.

———

HUMANITY NEEDS RESCUE

Like a good TV show that grabs you in the first three minutes of the show, the Bible grabs us in the first three chapters, Genesis 1-3. We find out the main characters, the villain, the conflict that needs resolution, and the future hope of the main character's victory. We have already talked about these things in chapters 3-6. God is the main character. Satan is the enemy. The conflict is that Satan has captured humanity under sin and death, and God wants to do something about it.

GOD ANNOUNCES THE GRACE YOU NEED

Welcome to season 3, episode 1. We see the future hope of victory in Genesis 3:15 when God announces his plan to save the world by grace. He says, "And I will cause hostility between you and the woman, and between your offspring and her offspring. He will strike your head, and you will strike his heel" (Genesis 3:15).

In speaking to the serpent, God mentions 1) something God will do and 2) something that will happen. First, God will cause the serpent and the woman to be enemies, and, therefore, the children of the serpent will be enemies against the children of the woman. This is a gift from God since Eve and the serpent had just recently become friends in their rebellion against God. God, in some sense, wins back Eve by turning her against the serpent. Second, a child of the woman, "he," will strike the head of the serpent; also, the serpent will "strike his heel." Now you might be thinking, "Ok, duh. Snakes and people don't like each other, and snakes bite people while people step on them." This might seem like a poetic way of describing the relationship that humanity has with snakes, but the Bible interprets this more deeply. This is not a story explaining why humans are afraid of snakes; no, it's a prophecy. The Bible picks up on this prophecy. This is why the Bible traces the woman's offspring and the serpent's offspring.

Now, you may be wondering, "How can a person be the offspring of a serpent?" Well, to be someone's child is deeper than just sharing the same genes; it is also about sharing the same manner of life. All people are biologically children of Eve, "the mother of all living" (Genesis 3:20), but depending on their spiritual allegiance, they would be a child of the serpent or a child of the woman. The serpent's offspring would live against God and for the devil, and the woman's offspring would be those who live for God and who are like God. Throughout the Bible, God's people are looking for the "he," the child of the woman, that will crush the head of the serpent. This "he" is none other than Jesus.

There are several passages that pick up on this interpretation of Genesis 3:15. Let's look at one.

The Apostle John speaks about Cain (Adam and Eve's son who killed his brother Abel) as a child of the serpent:

> Whoever makes a practice of sinning is *of the devil*, for the devil has been sinning from the beginning. The reason the Son of God appeared was to destroy the works of the devil . . . By this it is evident who are the *children of God*, and who are the *children of the devil*: whoever does not practice righteousness is not of God, nor is the one who does not love his brother . . . We should not be like Cain, *who was of the evil one* and murdered his brother. And why did he murder him? Because his own deeds were evil and his brother's righteous. (1 John 3:8–12 ESV, emphasis added)

John refers to Cain as "of the devil" and "of the evil one" in the context of a passage that is about discerning the difference between the children of the devil and the children of God. To be "of" someone is a way to describe their parentage. Cain was a child of the devil, an offspring of the serpent, and his brother Abel was a child of God. Eve gave birth to two lines of children, one of the devil (the serpent) and one of God (the woman). Genesis 3:15 summarizes the plot of the whole Bible.

We already mentioned how we are under the covenant of life's curses in chapters five and six of this book, and we now must talk about the covenant of grace. In Genesis 3:15, God is announcing the covenant of grace. The covenant of grace undoes the curses of the covenant of life. The covenant of grace is God's arrangement with the chosen child of the woman. In the arrangement, the child of the woman will "destroy the works of the devil" (1 John 3:8). God makes several significant covenants with humans, and the whole point of every covenant is to point us toward the child of the woman, who will defeat the serpent. Like chocolate to a tootsie pop, at the core of every covenant in the Bible is the covenant of grace. The covenant of grace is God's rescue plan. Remember the parts of a covenant from the previous chapter? What are the promises, conditions, and parties? Let's look at the pieces of the covenant of grace:

- Parties: God and the coming child of the woman (spoiler alert: this is Jesus) are the parties. Included in the child's party are all who believe in him and are waiting for him to come (Romans 4:1-6).
- Blessings: God will undo all the works of Satan and bring the world to perfection.
- Conditions: The child of the woman must succeed where Adam failed. Whereas Adam sinned, the child of the woman must be totally righteous and trust God in all things. Whereas Adam didn't overcome Satan, the child must overcome Satan. This child must overcome Satan through death.
- Curses: If the child of the woman fails, the child will fall just like Adam, and the world will have no hope of restoration. The world can only have expectations of God's destruction.

Every covenant that is formed in the Bible is all about how to get people to believe and trust in the gospel, which is the coming child of the woman. Because of this, there is unity and continuity between the covenants. Like a relay race in track and field, each covenant in history grabs the baton of the covenant of grace from the previous covenant and runs it towards the finish line of history. Like a building project, each covenant builds upon the previous one, and each covenant sets up a foundation for the next one. Time fails us in looking at all of the significant covenants of the Bible, but let's look at a few of the ones frequently referenced in the Bible.

GOD PROMISES THE BLESSINGS YOU NEED

Welcome to season 3, episode 2! God begins the rescue plan by choosing a family for himself through which he will save the world. He chooses Abraham and his family. God gives the Abrahamic covenant so that he and his family will place their trust in the coming child of the woman (Galatians 3:6-9).

Let's do some background on who Abraham is. As people populate the earth after Adam and Eve, the world gets taken over by the children of the serpent. The only child of the woman left is Noah and his family. God destroys everyone in the world with a flood and repopulates the world through Noah. Despite the restart, spiritual corruption has not left humanity, and so the children of the serpent populate the earth again. Instead of destroying the earth again by a flood (which he promised in the Noahic covenant not to do again, Genesis 9:1-19), God decides to continue to further the offspring of the woman by picking a family. He picks Abram (aka Abraham) and Sarai (aka Sarah) as the chosen family by which he will bring rescue to the whole earth. The LORD gives many promises to Abraham and his offspring after him in Genesis 12:1-9, 15:1-21, 17:1-22. Let's look at Genesis 17:1-8:

When Abram was ninety-nine years old the LORD appeared to Abram and said to him, "I am God Almighty; walk before me, and be blameless, that *I may make my covenant* between me and you, and may multiply you greatly." Then Abram fell on his face. And God said to him, "Behold, my covenant is with you, and you shall be the father of a multitude of nations. No longer shall your name be called Abram, but your name shall be Abraham, for I have made you the father of a multitude of nations. I will make you exceedingly fruitful, and I will make you into nations, and kings shall come from you. And I will establish *my covenant between me and you and your offspring* after you throughout their generations for an everlasting covenant, to be God to you and to your offspring after you. And I will give *to you and to your offspring* after you the land of your sojournings, all the land of Canaan, for an everlasting possession, and I will be their God. (Genesis 17:1–8 ESV, emphasis added)

Let's analyze the above.

- Parties: God is the first party, and the second party is Abraham and his offspring.
- Blessings: As a part of this covenant, God promises at least four blessings. One, God will give Abraham many descendants. Two, God will give his presence to Abraham and his offspring. Three, God will give Abraham and his offspring the land of Canaan. Four, God will bless the whole world through Abraham (we find this promise in Genesis 12:3).
- Conditions: Abraham, as a condition, must follow the LORD sincerely. Although Abraham has a condition, it is essentially the bare minimum of commitments. This is why the Bible primarily views this covenant as kind of a one-sided covenant, where God is doing all of the giving and Abraham and his offspring are doing all of

the receiving (Galatians 3:18). It is promise-heavy and condition-light.

- Curses: As far as curses, only God himself takes on the curses of the covenant in Genesis 15. As God, in the form of a fire, walks through the pieces of dead animals in Genesis 15, he symbolizes that the curse is death if he fails to fulfill his promises to Abraham and his children.

The conflict remains in this episode. Abraham is as good as dead; Sarah's womb is dead (Romans 4:19); they are foreigners in a land that is supposed to be theirs (Hebrews 11:9); and they are surrounded by the serpent's offspring (Genesis 12:11-13). Each covenant has the people wondering, "When will we get the promised blessings?" We are getting excited about the season finale already. We can expect there to be numerous people in a beautiful place filled with God's presence, and God's blessings to flow to the whole earth. This covenant paints a picture of the world totally restored. In a world filled with sin, pain, and death, we not only want these blessings but also we need these blessings.

GOD SHOWS THE LIFESTYLE YOU NEED

Welcome to season 3, episode 3! In the Mosaic covenant, God further reveals the need for the covenant of grace. This covenant is also called "the old covenant." God gives the Mosaic covenant so that he and the Israelites will place their trust in the coming child of the woman (Galatians 3:6-9).

Let's look at some background. Abraham's family grows very large over generations. Eventually, those descended from Abraham's grandson named Jacob/Israel are enslaved in Egypt for 430 years. They are then freed by the LORD, who used Moses and Aaron as his instruments of deliverance. Now the children of Israel, aka Israelites, are newly freed and belong to the LORD. God made a covenant with Israel, with Moses as the mediator:

Then Moses climbed the mountain to appear before God. The LORD called to him from the mountain and said, "Give these instructions to the family of Jacob; announce it to the descendants of Israel: 'You have seen what I did to the Egyptians. You know how I carried you on eagles' wings and brought you to myself. Now if you will obey me and *keep my covenant,* you will be my own special treasure from among all the peoples on earth; for all the earth belongs to me. And you will be my kingdom of priests, my holy nation.' This is the message you must give to the people of Israel." So Moses returned from the mountain and called together the elders of the people and told them everything the LORD had commanded him. And all the people responded together, "We will do everything the LORD has commanded." So Moses brought the people's answer back to the LORD." (Exodus 19:3–8, emphasis added)

In this passage, the LORD establishes the old covenant through Moses. Let's look at the pieces of the covenant:

- Parties: God and Israel are the two parties.
- Blessings: The LORD will be their king if they promise to submit to him as their king. The promised blessing is flourishing under God's reign. They will have God's presence in God's place as God's people, who will bless the world; the blessings of this covenant reflect the blessings of the previous covenant (remember, they are unified!).
- Conditions: Israel would need to obey all of God's commands. This covenant is a condition-heavy covenant. The Bible often contrasts this one with the Abrahamic covenant. If the Abrahamic covenant was promise-heavy, then the Mosaic covenant was law-heavy (Galatians 3:10-18). The promised blessings were conditional upon the people's obedience to God's commands.

- Curses: The curse, which would fall upon the people if they disobeyed the LORD, was God's kingly anger and expulsion from the Promised Land, the kingly realm. They would lose God's presence and God's place, and they would cease to be God's people and a blessing to the world.

The conflict of the show remains in this episode. Just like Adam and Eve, Israel constantly fails to trust God. They sin against him and invite his judgment. They cannot fully enjoy God's presence and rule. How does this covenant make us look forward to the season finale? We are looking forward to a people totally renewed to be the image of God (remember this in chapter five?). We desperately want to be a part of a community that glorifies and enjoys God fully, a community that shines forth the glory of God in all that they do. We don't just need to know God's law; we need God's laws written on our hearts so that we can fully obey him.

GOD PROMISES THE RULER YOU NEED

Season 3, episode 4! In the Davidic covenant, God further reveals the need for the covenant of grace. God gives the Davidic covenant so that the kings and the Israelites will place their trust in the coming child of the woman. Let's look at the Davidic covenant.

After forming the Mosaic covenant, the Israelites inherited the Promised Land, and the golden years of their time in the Promised Land was under King David's rule. He was God's chosen king, and God gave him great promises: "You have said, 'I have made a covenant with my chosen one; I have sworn to David my servant: "I will *establish your offspring forever*, and build your throne for all generations."' Selah" (Psalm 89:3–4, emphasis added). 2 Samuel 7 provides a full explanation of this covenant. Let's look at the pieces:

- Parties: God and David's descendants are the two parties.
- Blessings: Essentially, God promised David that one of his descendants would always rule over Israel. The ruler would be God's son and would rule over the nation on God's behalf. God would richly bless Israel under the Davidic king. In other words, the Mosaic covenant's blessings would come under a king.
- Curses: If the kings abandoned Yahweh, God would discipline the kings. Also, while this covenant is happening, the Mosaic covenant is still in effect. If the king failed at leading the people into holiness, then the nation would experience the curses of the Mosaic covenant. Like the Abrahamic covenant, the Davidic covenant also is a promise-heavy covenant, meaning that there was little that humans could do to forfeit the blessings. Even when the LORD disciplines and dethrones the offspring of David during exile, God is still committed to seeing a descendant of David on the throne.

Again, the conflict remains. God had always wanted to rule the world through kings and queens (remember from chapter five?), but the kings failed at being the perfect reflection of God's rule, even the good ones. What blessings do we need to receive in the finale? We need a perfect king who can rule in such a way that brings all of God's goodness back to earth. Under this king's rule, the world can finally be restored.

————

JESUS MEETS EVERY NEED

We are now at the season 3 finale! Eventually, things get really bad for Israel. The kingdom splits as a result of the sins of David's son,

Solomon (1 Kings 12:31-33). The divided nation spirals downward into further transgression against the Mosaic covenant. This downward spiral happens because the Davidic covenant is being trampled; the kings refuse to submit to God as his son (2 Kings 21:10-15). As a result, the divided nation is exiled — no intact nation, no king, and no freedom in the land. They eventually return from exile, but things are still really bad. It looks as though all of the promises of the other covenants will never be fulfilled. In the conflict between God and Satan, it looks like God is losing. The works of the devil haven't been destroyed. His works are thriving. Have you been here in college? Have you felt like everything has gone bad and there is no hope?

But there is a plot twist, a big reveal in the finale! God rolls up his sleeves and says, "Let me do this myself." In a turn of events, God himself becomes a human to rescue Israel. How did he become human? The second person of the Trinity, the Son, becomes a human named Jesus. Jesus is the one with whom God created the covenant of grace. God brings the blessings of the covenant of grace by establishing a new covenant through the ministry of Jesus.

> The day is coming," says the LORD, "when I will make a new covenant with the people of Israel and Judah. This covenant will not be like the one I made with their ancestors when I took them by the hand and brought them out of the land of Egypt. They broke that covenant, though I loved them as a husband loves his wife," says the LORD. "But this is the new covenant I will make with the people of Israel after those days," says the LORD. "I will put my instructions deep within them, and I will write them on their hearts. I will be their God, and they will be my people. (Jeremiah 31:31–33)

The new covenant replaces the old covenant (the Mosaic covenant). The old covenant couldn't give the people the power to actually obey the covenant, but the new covenant will give people this power. The people will actually be able to enjoy their relation-ship with God and live into their purpose as God's people. Also, the new covenant is the covenant that will fulfill all the expecta-tions and/or shortcomings of the others.

JESUS IS YOUR BLESSING

In the new covenant, King Jesus brings the blessings of Abraham to all the nations (Acts 3:25-26), and because Jesus is bringing the blessings of Abraham to all nations, he is bringing it to your campus through you, Christian. The Holy Spirit has been poured out, bringing repentance to all. Like flowers planted into soil and growing into a fully blooming bush, the new covenant is the Abrahamic covenant fully blooming (Galatians 3:10-14).

Relatedly, because the new covenant is the Abrahamic covenant fully blooming, it is the covenant of grace fully bloom-ing. Allow me to explain. The Abrahamic covenant is the first formal establishment of the covenant of grace in history. While time fails us to go into detail, the Abrahamic covenant is essen-tially made with Jesus, the coming offspring of the woman. Look at the words of Apostle Paul: "God gave the promises to Abraham and his child. And notice that the Scripture doesn't say 'to his children,' as if it meant many descendants. Rather, it says 'to his child'—and that, of course, means Christ" (Galatians 3:16). Apostle Paul is saying that Christ is the offspring of Abraham. When God makes promises to Abraham, God makes the promises "to you and your offspring." Paul is saying "the offspring" is a reference not only to Abraham's children but also to Christ! And the way that you become one of the children of Abraham is uniting to the one true child of Abraham, and child of the woman, Jesus Christ. In other words, if "you belong to Christ, you are the true children of Abraham. You are his heirs, and God's promise to Abraham belongs to you" (Galatians 3:29).

JESUS IS YOUR OBEDIENCE AND SACRIFICE

In the new covenant, King Jesus succeeded in obeying the Mosaic law where the Israelites transgressed the Mosaic law. Jesus perfectly fulfilled every law. Also, Jesus abolished the Mosaic covenant because many of its ceremonial and dietary laws kept Israel separate from other nations. These laws were a barrier to the whole world experiencing God's blessings (Ephesians 2:13-16).

The Mosaic covenant was a temporary covenant that trained the people until the offspring of the woman came (Galatians 3:23-24). It taught them God's will (Romans 3:20-22), the depths of their sin and inability (Romans 7:7-9), and their desperate need for a savior (Romans 8:1-4). It also helped restrain the evil present among their society (1 Timothy 1:9). Lastly, it was designed to be a foreshadow of all that the offspring of the woman would be and do (Hebrews 10:1).

Not only did Jesus fulfill every law but also he took the punishment belonging to those who break the Mosaic laws. Jesus died on the cross in order to take the curses of the Mosaic covenant: "But Christ has rescued us from the curse pronounced by the law. When he was hung on the cross, he took upon himself the curse for our wrongdoing. For it is written in the scriptures, 'Cursed is everyone who is hung on a tree'" (Galatians 3:13). Jesus was "hung on a tree" when he was nailed to a cross of wood to die, and he did this so that we could receive blessings. He took our curses so that we could receive his blessings.

As stated above, Jesus is bringing these blessings to your college campus. As the name of Jesus spreads on your campus, people will know the freedom and beauty of embracing the one who lived perfectly for them and died for them. In a place that is known for its sin, Jesus will bring obedience to God's kingdom.

JESUS IS YOUR RULER

In the new covenant, King Jesus succeeded where the Davidic kings failed. Jesus is the King of kings whose kingdom is spreading to every nation. He brings flourishing that comes with being in God's kingdom. As students receive the good news about Jesus on your campus, people will know the joy of having a good ruler in a place where stress, hopelessness, and dysfunction so often go unchecked.

But where is the relation to the covenant of grace? The Davidic covenant narrows the search for the offspring of the woman to David's descendants. Also, this covenant further reveals that the primary role the child of the woman would play would be that of a king. Like the Abrahamic covenant, this covenant is both made with David and Jesus. Jesus is the offspring of David who would be the eternal king (Romans 1:1-4). When Jesus rose from the dead and ascended to power in heaven, he was fully taking on the Davidic throne and ruling over all things.

JESUS IS THE FINALE

Jesus is the second Adam who succeeded where Adam failed in the garden (1 Corinthians 15:45-47). Whereas Adam forfeited eternal life and gave death to all his children, Jesus earned eternal life and gives it to all his children. On top of that, something better than the garden of Eden, the new creation, is coming.

What is the relation to the covenant of grace? The new covenant is the covenant of grace in all its glory. The new covenant brings all of the promises of the covenant of grace to fruition. The new covenant is a fulfillment of the Abrahamic and Davidic covenants and a replacement for the Mosaic covenant. In the new covenant, Jesus accomplishes the rescue that was initially announced in Genesis 3:15.

What is unique about the new covenant? One, there is a new

kingship. God no longer rules over one nation in Palestine through a fallen king. God rules over the nations through an eternal king, Jesus. Under this new king, Israel has become multinational; people from all nations are a part of the kingdom. Two, there is a new priesthood. God no longer engages with people through the priesthood of Levi, who was the forefather of the tribe that served as priests. God engages with people through an eternal and heavenly priesthood after the pattern of Melchizedek (a priest in Genesis 14:18 greater than the Levitical priests), and the priest in this priesthood is Jesus himself. Three, there is a new prophet. Formerly, God spoke to the people through many different prophets who represented God, but now there is a prophet who is God himself, Jesus.

In the new covenant, Christ has and will accomplish the renewal of the whole universe. The new heaven and new earth with a renewed people, i.e. a new creation, is what Christ has done in the new covenant. We experience a foretaste of the new creation in the here and now, and we anticipate its fullness when Christ returns.

The fact that Jesus has created a new covenant is the greatest hope of your college career. In the midst of much bad news, you need really good news. In the midst of the ongoing story of college, you need to live within the finale.

MARIA STEWART AND THE AFRICAN FINALE

The African American story has been filled with oppression, slavery, and suffering. One of the biggest questions among African Americans is, "Where is our story going? Where is our happy ending?" You remember our friend Maria Stewart from chapter one? She has another lesson for us. She teaches us that Jesus is the finale to the story of African Americans. Jesus is and leads us to our happy ending. Look at the words of Stewart in "Religion and the Pure Principles of Morality, the Sure Foundation on Which We Must Build":

> I feel almost unable to address you; almost incompetent to perform the task; and, at times, I have felt ready to exclaim, O that my head were waters, and mine eyes a fountain of tears, that I might weep day and night, for the transgressions of the daughters of my people. Truly, my heart's desire and prayer is, that Ethiopia might stretch forth her hands unto God. But we have a great work to do. Never, no, never will the chains of slavery and ignorance burst till, we become united as one, and cultivate among ourselves the pure principles of piety, morality, and virtue.[1]

By quoting Jeremiah 9:1, a passage about the prophet Jeremiah grieving the sins of God's people, Stewart begins by telling us that she grieves the spiritual state of her fellow Africans in America. She then brings us to the inner places of her soul by quoting Psalm 68:31, which says, "Envoys will come out of Egypt; Ethiopia will quickly stretch out her hands to God" (Psalm 68:31 NASB). Psalm 68 celebrates how Yahweh delivered Israel from slavery in Israel and then led his people to his royal throne, which was his temple on Mt. Zion in Jerusalem. The author of the psalm declares that the kingdoms of Egypt and Ethiopia will come to see and worship God as he sits on his throne. Stewart shares that this is her "heart's desire and prayer." Why? Ethiopia was a common symbol for all of Africa during the times of Stewart. If it was in God's will for Ethiopia to stretch her hands to God, then what is preventing God from doing this to the modern day "Ethiopia" in America? Jesus is enthroned now (Ephesians 4:8), and is bringing all nations to worship God. Her deepest desire before God is to see her people worship and submit to Yahweh as King.

Often, we laugh at our forefathers and foremothers when they say Jesus is the answer to Africans' problems because it sounds like wishful thinking. However, nothing further can be the case. Stewart says, "But we have a great work to do." She gives a call to action and transformation. She declares that we will not be free and enlightened as a people until we commit ourselves to unity and submission to Yahweh. Only with the power and transformation that Jesus provides can we engage in the battle against oppression and the battle for African flourishing. Jesus meets our every need. We will revisit this more in chapter 11.

————

RECAP

The Bible is centrally about Jesus and how God is rescuing us through Jesus' ministry. The Bible is structured around the different covenants that God makes with humanity, and these covenants tell the story of history. The enemy (the serpent, Satan, the devil, and etc.) has ruined everything God created, and God is moving all of history toward the moment where a descendant of Eve will destroy the works of the serpent from the garden. God announces his plan in Genesis 3:15 to save us from the covenant of life's curses through a covenant of grace. God begins the rescue plan through Abraham's family. God gives several huge promises that God will fulfill throughout the rest of the Bible. God prepares and trains his people for the coming rescue through the Mosaic covenant. He teaches them his ways, retrains their evil, and shows them their need for a savior. God then gives his people a ruler that will bring God's blessings to the people. Ultimately, the promised blessings from all of these covenants reach us through the new covenant that Jesus forms with us. This is the season 3 finale, and it is glorious.

The rest of this book will be explaining what it means to enjoy the season 3 finale of history. The last chapter of this book will explain season 4.

To the person and work of Jesus we now turn.

CHAPTER 8

DOUBLE MAJOR, AIN'T NOTHING MINOR

love hearing student introductions at Howard University. The formula is this, "Hey, my name is _____. I am a [classification/year], [insert majors], and [insert minors] from [insert place of origin]." I have heard amazing Howard intros! "Hey, I am Travis. I am a freshman psychology and Africana studies double major with a vocal performance minor from Chicago!" Howard introductions orient people to who a student is, their dreams, their course work, their social circles, their culture, and their level of ambition.

Many students have an intentionally unique combination of majors and minors to prepare them for a future occupation. "I am a chemistry major because I want to go to med school, but I am also doing Africana studies because I want to start medical clinics in Eastern Africa." The double major uniquely prepares them to enter into their purpose and to accomplish their goals. If you are a double major, you are one person with two majors. Are you 100% a chemistry major? Yes. Are you 100% an africana studies major? Yes.

What if I told you that Jesus was a double major? He is a God major and a human major. These two majors work together to make the one person, Jesus, uniquely equipped to accomplish his role as redeemer, i.e someone who pays a price to gain something (in Jesus' case, you!).

WHERE WE ARE GOING

In a sentence, this chapter teaches that Jesus is the only one who is uniquely qualified to save you, so place your trust only in him.

Christians have often been those who worship Jesus exclusively. This means that Christians do not worship anyone except Jesus. People can accuse Christians of being closed minded, especially those who embrace the polytheism that comes with systems like Yoruba religion. However, Christians are not closed minded; we simply believe that Jesus is the only person who fits the profile of the one we need to be saved from all that is wrong with us.

For a redeemer, you need someone who is both God and human at the same time. If Jesus was a human but not God, there would be no hope for you. If Jesus was God but not a human, there would be no hope for you. It is only because of the dual nature of who Jesus is that he can redeem you. Who Jesus is, is just as important as what Jesus did. We will talk about 1) the importance and work of a redeemer 2) how Jesus is both God and human 3) why it's important that Jesus was humbled and 4) why it is important that Jesus was exalted.

―――――

OVERVIEW OF THE ESSENTIALS

Before we get into the details of Jesus' Godhood and humanity, let's do a quick overview of a few things that could get easily lost.

Here are the major events in the life of Jesus in chronological order:

- Jesus was born.
- Jesus grew up as a child and into adulthood.

- Jesus was baptized at the age of 30 years old.
- Jesus served people by teaching them, healing them, and casting evil spirits out of them alongside his disciples (a fancy word for students).
- Jesus was captured by his enemies and was crucified, which was a form of capital punishment.
- Jesus died on the cross.
- Jesus was buried in a tomb.
- Jesus rose again on the third day of his death.
- Jesus appeared to his disciples after his resurrection.
- Jesus ascended into heaven to reign over all things.

Here is why Jesus was a "God major":

- God wanted to reveal himself to you in HD (High Definition) as a human. To see and know Jesus was to see and know God.
- God wanted to succeed where we will always fail. It took God himself to do the monumental task of being our Savior. A human couldn't.

Here is why Jesus was a "humanity major":

- God wanted to perfectly obey his own law on our behalf. Where all of humanity failed, he wanted to succeed. He had to be a human to represent us in this.
- God wanted to die on our behalf for our sins. He took the curses of the covenants so that we can receive the blessings. He had to be a human to represent us in his death.
- God wanted to rise and ascend to power on our behalf. Where humanity should have reigned from the beginning (remember chapter five?), he now reigns as a human. He had to be a human to represent us in his reign.

- God wanted to relate to our trials and sufferings. Jesus can relate to our sufferings and relate to us gently day by day because he experienced all the same things himself, except without sin.

Again, Jesus needed and wanted to be a double major in order to take on the job of our Redeemer. In the next chapter we will look more specifically at how Jesus functioned as our Redeemer, but let's look briefly at the role of a redeemer.

———

JESUS' JOB IS TO REDEEM YOU

The goal of every covenant throughout biblical history was deliverance. Deliverance is another word for rescue or salvation Humanity has gotten itself in trouble by our own sin and rebellion, and we need something or someone to save us from the sin and misery we are in. We see the reality of deliverance in everyday life – a lifeguard delivering a drowning person, a firefighter delivering someone from a burning building, a surgeon saving someone from certain death. God himself, as we have already seen, is the one who delivers us from this sin and misery, and he does this through the offspring of the woman. If the offspring of the woman is the instrument of God to deliver us from our sin and misery, then what must this person be like in order to complete such a tall task? This person primarily functions as a redeemer.

YOU NEED A REDEEMER

What is a redeemer? A redeemer is someone who buys something or someone from another and brings the item or person into their own possession. It is an economic term. Although you may not have realized it before, you redeem things all the time. You redeem things whenever you purchase almost anything – clothes, shoes, food, a phone, a computer, and so forth. Yet the irony is that we ourselves need to be bought from the sin and misery that we undergo and be taken into the possession of God, who will bless us richly.

Redemption is a common theme in the Bible. Among Israel, people would redeem all kinds of things — everything from houses to people (Leviticus 27:15). The concept is seen prominently in several places and different ways in the Old Testament. We see it in Israel's redemption from Egypt (Deuteronomy 7:7-8); the redemption of firstborns (Exodus 13:14-16; Numbers 3:45, 18:15); and kinsman-redeemers (Leviticus 25:48-49). A redemption-price was also paid for on behalf of all different kinds of situations among the people. The root of the vast majority, if not all, of the Old Testament sacrifices was the reality of redemption. Humans can only approach God when something is offered as a payment for the debt that is their fallen condition. Whether offered for a sin or for giving thanks or for uncleanliness, the sacrifices were payments that brought sinful people closer to God.

JESUS IS OUR REDEEMER

Again, God's plan in the covenant of grace is to bring us his grace through a redeemer. The work of salvation, from beginning to end, can be summed up in the word "redemption" (Luke 1:68, 2::38). The Redeemer of the covenant of grace is Jesus, "who gave himself for us to *redeem* us from all lawlessness and to purify for himself a people for his own possession who are zealous for good works" (Titus 2:14 ESV, emphasis added). His redeeming work redeems us at the beginning of our Christian walk (Romans 3:24), all the way to the end, when we will experience "the redemption of our bodies" (Romans 8:23 ESV) at Jesus' return.

Let's look at several things about Jesus' role as Redeemer.

JESUS IS THE ONLY REDEEMER

There is no other place where you can find grace and rescue from everything that is fallen in your life. Jesus, the Redeemer, is the only Redeemer, for "God has given no other name under heaven by which we must be saved" (Acts 4:12). The scriptures tell us again that God has appointed one person to be the Redeemer: "For there is one God, and there is *one mediator* between God and men, the man Christ Jesus, who gave himself as a *ransom for all*" (1 Timothy 2:5–6 ESV, emphasis added). This passage mentions a mediator and a ransom. A mediator is a go-between for two different parties in an arrangement. A ransom is a payment to release someone. These two concepts define Jesus' role as a redeemer. A mediator + a ransom = a redeemer.

Jesus paid a ransom in order to bring you to God as the middle-man between you and God. Also, the above passage tells us that there is "one" mediator. There is only one because Jesus is the only one equipped to be your mediator and ransomer. Imagine that you have a rare, but fatal, injury. You need surgery to save your life, but there is only one surgeon who has studied this particular injury. Just as a specially qualified surgeon is the only person who can do a new and cutting edge procedure to heal you, Jesus is the only one with the proper skill set to heal you from your spiritual condition.

———

ATHANASIUS, THE CHAMPION OF JESUS' DIVINITY

Our old friend in this chapter is Athanasius of Alexandria. He teaches us how important it is that Jesus is both God and human. Athanasius was an Egyptian bishop who spent much of his life fighting for the truth that Jesus was God. He is a monumental shaper of Christian beliefs, a fierce warrior for truth, a brilliant theologian, and a key figure in Christian history. It is significant that this hero in the Christian faith was called "the black dwarf" by his opponents. He was, by our modern standards, a Black man. This fact pushes against the conceptions of Christianity as a White man's religion.

Athanasius[1] was born around 296 AD as a Copt in Alexandria, Egypt. He spent much of his early life living through intense Christian persecution at the order of Roman emperors from 303-311 AD. After his early years, the bishop of Alexandria, Alexander, began to mentor Athanasius, and Athanasius eventually became a deacon, which was like a bishop's assistant. During this time, a false teaching was spreading that God the Father created God the Son, and therefore God the Son was not God in the same way as God the Father (remember chapter three?). Alexander, with Athanasius at his side, fought against this teaching at the Council of Nicaea in 325 AD. Although Arius' teachings were condemned, they would not die. Athanasius eventually became bishop of Alexandria and spent the rest of his life fighting against Arius' teachings, even at a great cost to himself. Athanasius died in 373 AD still fighting for the truth.

Why did Athanasius fight for God the Son's full Godhood? Well, if God the Son was created, then God the Son was not eternal and was not one with God in the ways we talked about in chapter three. God the Son, at best, becomes a god. If this god became Jesus, then this meant that Jesus was not God and that God himself did not become flesh. If Jesus was not God, then Jesus could not save us. To summarize, if God the Son was created, then there would be no salvation. For Athanasius, a Black African Christian in Egypt well acquainted with suffering, Jesus being God was everything. These theological debates are not just for elite White scholars, as these debates are so often characterized. You might be asking, "But why was Jesus being God so important?" We will see this as we go throughout this chapter and the next chapter. We will lean on Athanasius' insights from his famous book, *On the Incarnation,* to see how important it is that God became a human.

———

GOD THE SON BECAME A HUMAN TO REACH YOU

As we look at who Jesus is, remember the flow of the biblical story – creation, de-creation, re-creation, new creation. All of who Jesus is was designed so that God can recreate you. Just as a baby in the womb is attached to its mother through an umbilical cord, when you are saved, you become one with Jesus. And just as all that belongs to the mother's blood stream belongs to the baby, all that belongs to Jesus belongs to you. We will look at this more in chapters 10-12, but I will highlight some ways that Jesus is amazing news to us.

The Bible is clear, as we saw in chapter three, that Jesus is the second person of the Trinity who became a human. Jesus is God the Son. What does it mean to be the Son of God? The picture of a father and son describe several aspects of Jesus' relationship with the Father and as Redeemer, but we will look at one.

The Son metaphor governs Jesus' relationship with the Father from eternity past. John 1:14 refers to Jesus as "the *only Son* from the Father" (John 1:14 ESV, emphasis added), and John 1:18 refers to him as "the *only begotten* God who is in the bosom of the Father" (John 1:18 NASB, emphasis added). John also refers to him as "the Word" in that same passage. Like a Navy SEAL or other special operation forces, God the Son went to earth on a mission to do battle against Satan. Satan was the "ruler of this world," (John 12:31) and the earth was under Satan's grip. God went to earth in order to invade Satan's realm, which he stole from Adam and Eve, in order to destroy Satan's reign from the inside out. God the Father and God the Son (aka the Word) were in agreement that God the Son would go to earth in order to fulfill the covenant of grace. It is only in union with Jesus the Son that you become a child of God. He shares his child-status with you.

Athanasius tells us that "the renewal of creation has been wrought by the Self-same Word Who made it in the beginning."[2] In other words, the same Word that created all things (remember from chapter three?) is the same Word that became human to re-create all things. God sent because he loved us: "It was our sorry case that caused the Word to come down, our transgression that called out His love for us, so that He made haste to help us and to appear among us."[3] God saw how miserable we were, and it was his love that moved him to send his Son!

How did the Son of God become a human?

GOD CAME TO BE LIKE YOU

First, Jesus was born like you. Jesus didn't teleport to the earth as a grown man. No, the eternal Son of God was born as a baby like you (Matthew 1:23-2:1). Jesus also had to grow up just as other humans did. Jesus grew physically, went through puberty, had to learn, and was a part of a family as a child (Luke 2:40-41). He did all of this so that he can relate to you when you go through troubles and struggles in every stage of life as a human (Hebrews 2:17). Why is all of this good news? It is only because Jesus was born that we can be reborn.

Second, Jesus became *truly* human. Just as a human, Adam, represented humanity before God and failed, we need a human to represent humanity before God to save us (Romans 5:15-17; 2 Corinthians 5:14-15). Jesus could only represent us if he was truly human, truly one of us.

Athanasius tells us, "He took to himself a body, a human body even as our own . . . He took *our* body."[4] He didn't have some sort of humanity that was altered by his Godhood into something that wasn't truly human. He was human, just like us, except without sin. Jesus had a body that became tired (John 4:6), needed to eat and drink (Luke 4:2; John 19:28), needed to rest (Mark 4:38), and could bleed and die (Mark 15:37). Jesus also had a human soul: he had emotions (John 11:35), had a human mind with limited knowledge (Matthew 24:36), made decisions in the midst of temptation (Luke 4:1-2), and had a spiritual life with the Father through prayer (Luke 11:1). The author of Hebrews tells us that Jesus did this so that he could accomplish salvation on our behalf: "Because God's children are human beings—made of flesh and blood—the Son also became flesh and blood. For only as a human being could he die, and only by dying could he break the power of the devil, who had the power of death" (Hebrews 2:14). Again, the author of Hebrews says,

> We also know that the Son did not come to help angels; he came to help the descendants of Abraham. Therefore, it was necessary for him to be made in every respect like us, his brothers and sisters, so that he could be our merciful and faithful High Priest before God. Then he could offer a sacrifice that would take away the sins of the people. (Hebrews 2:16–17)

If Jesus were to save angels, he would need to be like angels. However, Jesus came to save you, so he needed to be human. Jesus became *truly* human so that he could *truly* relate to you; *truly* die for you; *truly* rise for you, destroying the power of death; and *truly* relate to you day by day as he helps you through your struggles. Why is this good news? It is only by being united to Jesus the true human that we are restored to being fully human.

GOD CAME TO BE UNLIKE YOU

Second, Jesus was born sinless unlike you, and this is good news. Just as basketball teammates rejoice when they receive a star player who has a different skill-level than all the other players, so humanity rejoices that we have received someone different. We were born sinful, with original sin (remember this from chapter six?), but Jesus was born without sin. It is essential for our rescue that Jesus is a sinless human. Why? If he was sinful, he wouldn't be able to set an example for us. Also, if he was sinful, he couldn't die for our sins. When he died, he would've faced death as the curse for his own sins. You can only die for someone else's sins when you don't have to die for your own. Also, you can only give another person blessings that you yourself have earned. Jesus earned the blessings of the covenant of grace by his perfect obedience and gives them to us when we receive them by faith.

How was his birth different? The Bible is clear that Jesus was born of Mary, who was a virgin, unlike you. How was Jesus conceived? Jesus' conception was a miracle done by the Holy Spirit. A part of this miracle is that Jesus does not have original sin (remember this from chapter six?). Jesus was the first human born sinless since Adam. Luke tells us, "The angel replied, 'The Holy Spirit will come upon you, and the power of the Most High will overshadow you. So the baby to be born will be holy, and he will be called the Son of God'" (Luke 1:35). And this Holy Spirit-conceived baby was sinless: "For God made Christ, *who never sinned*, to be the offering for our sin, so that we could be made right with God through Christ" (2 Corinthians 5:21, emphasis added). John tells us, "You know that he appeared in order to take away sins, and *in him there is no sin*" (1 John 3:5 ESV, emphasis added). We are all born corrupted and sinful because we had an ordinary birth, but Jesus did not. Athanasius tells us, "Not even His birth from a virgin, therefore, changed Him in any way, nor was He defiled by being in the body. Rather, He sanctified the body by being in it."[5] Why is this good news? It is only because we are united to the sinless one that we sinners can move towards perfection.

Fourth, Jesus is a human with a particular family tree (Matthew 1:1). The Bible is careful to highlight that he is descended from Adam, Abraham, Israel, and David. He had to be such in order to be the offspring/seed/child/descendants who received the covenant promises discussed in the previous chapter. Just like the children of a monarch receive the throne and its royal titles, the children of the covenant party-leaders received the promises and all that came with them. Jesus is the offspring of all of these covenants, therefore Jesus is the offspring who will receive the blessings of all of those covenants. He receives those blessings so that he can give them to us! He is an offspring of the woman, coming to destroy the works of the devil (Luke 3:23-38). He is an offspring of Abraham, the promised child who will bring the blessings of God to every family of the earth (Abrahamic covenant). He is also a son of Israel who will fulfill the law of God on your behalf (Mosaic covenant). And lastly, he is an offspring of David, the king bringing God's everlasting kingdom (Davidic covenant). The good news is that Jesus is, in every way, the child of the woman for those of us who have become the children of the serpent, and, in union with Jesus, we are brought back into the covenant family.

Also, Jesus operated as a human even though he was God. In other words, Jesus obeyed God the Father and performed miracles just like an ordinary human would. This is amazing because Jesus can be a real example of human life to us who are authentically human. We can sometimes think of Jesus as a super-human like Superman or Luke Cage or in the category of things like Yoruba religion's orishas, but Jesus was a legitimate human. He did extraordinary things by the power of the Holy Spirit and depending on God the Father just like a human would (John 5:19; Hebrews 9:14).

What does this humanness actually look like? We can look at Jesus' wilderness temptations in Matthew 4:1-11. When he fought temptation, he fought it like we would and experienced the draining effects (v. 11). However, because he is God, it was impossible for him to actually sin. Another example is his miracles. He does works that the prophets of old did, like mass feedings (2 Kings 4:42-44) and defying the ordinary rules of physics (2 Kings 6:6). God gave the prophets the power to do these works by the Spirit, and Jesus also did them by the Spirit's power. However, God the Father did miraculous works through Jesus to a greater degree to show that Jesus was God in the flesh, not merely a prophet (John 10:34-39).

Lastly, did you know that Jesus is a human even now? Jesus is both God and human forever. After Jesus rose from the dead, he was truly human, not a ghost (John 20:27); ascended into heaven as a human (Acts 1:11); is laboring in heaven as a human (Hebrews 7:24-25); and will come back as a human (Acts 1:11). Even though Jesus is in heaven, he still relates to you with a human touch. How amazing!

We have talked about Jesus' humanity, and now let's talk about what this means alongside his divinity.

––––––

JESUS WAS ONE PERSON WITH TWO NATURES

Let's talk more about Jesus' double major.

GOD REMAINED HIMSELF TO BRING US TO HIMSELF

The Son of God became human while still being God. Jesus did not become a human by giving up his Godhood (aka his divine nature), which he had before he became a human. No, he became a human by taking on a human body, while keeping his divine nature. Like putting on a suit jacket can bring someone from casual to business casual, God putting on humanity brought him from God to God-human. The Apostle Paul describes this when he says, "Though he was in the form of God, did not count equality with God a thing to be grasped, but emptied himself, by taking the form of a servant, being born in the likeness of men" (Philippians 2:6–7 ESV). The phrase "emptied himself" refers to the fact that God the Son gave up something in order to be like us. He went from "the form of God" to the "form of a servant . . . the likeness of men." God gave up the outward display of his heavenly glory as God. In exchange, he took the appearance of a human. This is why no one knew that Jesus was God before his public ministry unless someone pointed it out (Matthew 13:54-58; John 1:29-34). Jesus was one person. These two natures were united in the one person of Jesus. But what does this dual nature mean?

There are a few errors we must avoid when we consider that one person has two natures. First, these two natures do not change each other. We might think, "Can someone be truly God if they are also human? And can someone be truly human if they are also God?" It's not as if his human nature makes him not authentically God or his divine nature makes him not authentically human. Second, the two natures don't mix with each other to form a new, third nature. It's not like colors. Blue and red make purple, but divine and human don't make some different, third thing. Christ is still blue and red. Third, they cannot separate or divide the person of Christ into two different people in one body. There wasn't a divine Jesus and then a human Jesus living in one body. There is one Jesus.

What does the fact that he is one person with two natures mean for how we talk about Jesus?

This leads us to say beautiful things about Jesus' ministry. For example, this is why Paul can say that God obtained his people "with his own blood" (Acts 20:28). Jesus underwent death because he has a human nature, though he is God, because of his divine nature. On the cross, God died! How beautiful it is that God died for you.

Also, it is because of the fact that the two natures are united in one person that Jesus perfectly represents God. God teaches you about himself through a human body. Athanasius tells us, "he became Himself an object for the senses, so that those who were seeking God in sensible things might apprehend the Father through the works which He, the Word of God, did in the body."[6] In Jesus, "the fullness of God was pleased to dwell" (Colossians 1:19 ESV); "in him the whole fullness of deity dwells bodily"

(Colossians 2:9 ESV); and in relation to God, Jesus is "the exact imprint of his nature" (Hebrews 1:3 ESV). When you look at Jesus, you look at God; to know Jesus is to know God; and to receive Jesus' love is to receive God's love.

It is because of the two natures in one person that Jesus is frequently referred to with the divine name (Mark 1:2-3; John 18:4-6) and is worshiped (Mark 14:33; Matthew 28:17), though he is human. Jesus is truly human and truly God, one-hundred percent God and one-hundred percent human – all the time and everywhere – united in one person.

Let's take a moment to look at the stages of Jesus' life as the God-human.

JESUS WAS A HUMBLE AND EXALTED REDEEMER

First, the unique qualities of Jesus express themselves in the stages of his life. The Bible generally views Jesus' own life in two distinct stages — his humiliation and his exaltation. Paul describes these two stages in Philippians 2: "When he appeared in human form, he *humbled* himself in obedience to God and died a criminal's death on a cross. Therefore, God *elevated* him to the place of highest honor and gave him the name above all other names," (Philippians 2:7–9, emphasis added). Another passage that describes both stages of his life is Isaiah 52:13-53:12. His humiliation was becoming a human, living as a human, dying, and being buried. In his exaltation, Jesus was raised from the dead, ascended into heaven, seated at the right hand of the Father to rule, and will come again to judge all things.

JESUS WAS A HUMBLE REDEEMER

When I say "humiliation," I mean that Christ humbled himself. Like a carnival ride that drops you from hundreds of feet in the air, Jesus descended from heaven to be with us. Being a human is not humble for a human, but it is humble for God because he created humans.

Jesus humbled himself by being born. And this birth was a humble birth even when compared to other human births. He was born in an animal feeding bin. Though it was humble, we shouldn't underestimate its importance. That humble birth meant salvation for the world. With our Christian African ancestors we sing, "Down in a lonely manger, The humble Christ was born, And God sent us salvation, That blessed Christmas morn."[7]

Not only did Jesus become a human, he was not rich and there "was nothing beautiful or majestic about his appearance, nothing to attract us to him. He was despised and rejected— a man of sorrows, acquainted with deepest grief. We turned our backs on him and looked the other way. He was despised, and we did not care" (Isaiah 53:2–3). His life was a humble life even by human standards.

At the end of his life, he died and was buried: "He had done no wrong and had never deceived anyone. But he was buried like a criminal; he was put in a rich man's grave" (Isaiah 53:9). Jesus died a humiliating death as a naked convict hanging on a piece of wood for unjust charges against him. Jesus' humiliation characterizes everything that happened in Jesus' life before his resurrection.

Why is Jesus' humiliation good news? He can relate to our sorrows and trials, especially those who are abused, oppressed, and marginalized. We will see this in a minute.

JESUS IS AN EXALTED REDEEMER

But also, Philippians 2:7-9 speaks about God giving Jesus a name above every name. Jesus' rising from the dead; his ascension into heaven; his reign at the right hand of the Father; and his future judgment of the world, are all ways that God has, is, and will exalt Jesus. This passage summarizes exaltation:

> [God] raised Christ from the dead and seated him in the place of honor at God's right hand in the heavenly realms. Now he is far above any ruler or authority or power or leader or anything else— not only in this world but also in the world to come. God has put all things under the authority of Christ and has made him head over all things for the benefit of the church. (Ephesians 1:20–22)

Isaiah 53:12 speaks of Jesus' exaltation as well: "I will give him the honors of a victorious soldier, because he exposed himself to death. He was counted among the rebels. He bore the sins of many and interceded for rebels" (Isaiah 53:12). His exaltation is everything that happened during and after his resurrection.

Let's circle back and look at what Jesus' humiliation means for the lowly and marginalized all over the world.

———

THE HUMBLE JESUS RELATES TO THE OPPRESSED, PERSECUTED, AND MARGINALIZED

It is important to highlight the fact that Jesus came not only as a human but also as a lowly human because it is a statement about the world and God's relation to it. In Jesus' humanity, he shows us that God is near, literally near, to the poor and lowly. He was born of modest means. For example, his family was ideally required to offer a lamb when Jesus was born, but they offered a pigeon. Why? They couldn't afford a lamb (Leviticus 12:8). A pigeon was the sacrifice of the lowly because pigeons were so common and, therefore, cheap. Jesus grew up in Nazareth, a place where someone said, "Can anything good come from Nazareth?" (John 1:45). He centered his ministry in Capernaum, not Jerusalem (the royal city), and he ministered mostly to the lowly, hungry masses of northern Palestine (Mark 8:3; Matthew 15:32). Jesus was unjustly captured by corrupt powers and received the death penalty unjustly. The manner of his death was cruel and for only the lowliest of criminals. Jesus, therefore, can relate to the state of all those who are lowly, especially Black folks all over the globe. The fact that God himself became a human and could identify with our suffering is a comfort to those suffering and a reason to trust God in the midst of our suffering.

JESUS USES THE WEAK AND FOOLISH IN THE EYES OF THE WORLD

Throughout the Bible, God chooses the weak and foolish things in the eyes of the world (i.e. humble things) to shame and destroy the strong and wise things in the world. Jesus' life is an example of this. Paul highlights this biblical pattern in the salvation of the Christians in Corinth:

> For consider your calling, brothers: not many of you were wise according to worldly standards, not many were powerful, not many were of noble birth. But God chose what is foolish in the world to shame the wise; God chose what is weak in the world to shame the strong; God chose what is low and despised in the world, even things that are not, to bring to nothing things that are, so that no human being might boast in the presence of God. (1 Corinthians 1:26–29 ESV)

God loves to choose the underdog, the stranger, the outcast, the weakest, the enslaved, the morally scandalous, the poor, and the afflicted of the world in order to shame and bring to nothing the rulers, the insiders, the strong, the oppressor, the hypocrite, the rich, and the wealthy of this world. Think about how Abram, Isaac, Jacob, Joseph, Moses, Rahab, Gideon, David, Daniel, and more, all started off as the underdog. He takes the lowly and then exalts them over and against the present evil powers. Why? So that when God works in the world, no human can boast in themselves. God gets all the glory. Isn't this good news as a lowly college student struggling to stay encouraged through school? You compare yourself to your peers and feel like the underdog. The good news is that God can use anybody, and he can use you!

Also, God prefers to use the lowly because those who are powerful and rich so often love "this present evil age" (Galatians 1:4 ESV). Kings, rulers, and merchants are often highlighted as those tied to the corruption of this present age. For example, in describing the anti-God city of the world empire (Revelation 17:4-7), the Bible says that the "kings of the world have committed adultery with her. Because of her desires for extravagant luxury, the merchants of the world have grown rich" (Revelation 18:3). When Babylon is destroyed, it says the "merchants of the world will weep and mourn for her, for there is no one left to buy their goods" (Revelation 18:11). While the rulers, merchants, and traders are mourning, the Christians, who she opposed, are called to rejoice: "Rejoice over her fate, O heaven and people of God and apostles and prophets! For at last God has judged her for your sakes" (Revelation 18:20). This is a challenge that you shouldn't pass over as college students. We so often go to college to succeed and fulfill our ambitions, but we must realize that some professions can cause us to compromise, to be comfortable participants in "the present evil age."

In fact, to be a disciple, one must embrace the lowliness that Jesus embraced. Those who follow the humble and afflicted one find themselves becoming humble and afflicted. "Foxes have holes, and birds of the air have nests, but the Son of Man has nowhere to lay his head," says Jesus (Luke 9:58 ESV). Jesus calls his disciples his "little ones" (Matthew 10:42), invites them to embrace a life of lowly affliction (Matthew 10:38-39), and warns them that the powerful will abuse them (Matthew 10:16-18). Indeed, this is why Jesus so closely identifies himself with the afflicted, the hungry, the thirsty, the naked, the sick, the imprisoned, and the vulnerable (Matthew 25:35-40). Jesus himself was afflicted, and his disciples will find themselves at some point one of these things in their service to Jesus (Matthew 10:16-23).

JESUS GIVES THE RICH AND POWERFUL A NEW PATH

The rich can be saved (Luke 18:27), but they are given strict warnings and a new path forward for their life in the kingdom (1 Timothy 6:8-10, 17–19 ESV). As Jesus instructed us, they are to store "treasures in heaven, where neither moth nor rust destroys and where thieves do not break in and steal" (Matthew 6:20 ESV). As you graduate college, you must remember that money and prestige isn't everything. With a love of money comes many temptations. As you seek to be successful, remember that this world isn't all that there is.

All of the above things are why Black Christians have delighted to identify with Jesus. We have been despised and persecuted in the world in our fight against the evil that is White oppression, which comes from the "ruler of this world," Satan (John 16:11).

Let's also look at what Jesus' exaltation means for the lowly and marginalized all over the globe.

THE EXALTED JESUS' SALVATION IS HOLISTIC

The salvation that Jesus the exalted one brings is holistic, meaning, he saves the whole person. As the exalted one, Jesus delivers us from the oppression of Satan, who seeks to crush whole people both inwardly and outwardly. Jesus is destroying "the world," which is the outward manifestation of Satan's kingdom, which seeks to aggravate the cursed condition of the world. As Satan's kingdom is destroyed, the poor, the captive, the blind, and the oppressed can rejoice (Luke 4:16-21). Because the exalted Jesus has disarmed the evil demonic powers that govern this world under the direction of Satan, the effects of their reign are being undone (Daniel 10:13-21, 20; Ephesians 1:21, 6:12; Revelation 12:7-12). Even sicknesses are undone as Satan's rule is undone (Acts 10:38; James 5:14-15). The witness and works of God's people undo all of Satan's kingdom, and we are the conduits of this holistic salvation.

The fact that Jesus is exalted brings hope to the marginalized. They realized they could be blessed in their poverty, lowliness, and mourning because the lowly Jesus would bring a reversal of their condition, both in this life and the life to come (Matthew 5:1-12). His exaltation brings hope in the face of a world filled with death: "The cold grave could not hold Him nor death's cold iron band, And the Lord will bear my spirit home."[8]

Salvation is not merely a narrow term referring to only individual soul-renewal, according to the Bible. Salvation is broad because God saves us from everything in creation that flows from the covenant of life's curse. Because the curse of the covenant of life affects all of life, the blessing of the covenant of grace spreads to all of life. Because of this, the scriptures use the word "salvation" to refer to many different situations (Exodus 14:30; Numbers 10:9; 1 Chronicles 16:35; Matthew 8:25; Luke 7:50; Acts 2:40; 2 Corinthians 1:10; Galatians 1:4). This Jesus, who brings holistic salvation, pushes his church into good works that brings his kingdom to bear in the world.

JESUS BRINGS LIBERATION

Because of the reality of Christ's holistic salvation, we can agree with the Christian activists that liberation is something that God is working in the world through his people. Because the kingship of Jesus covers the whole universe, his kingdom is and will invade every segment of the universe. The coming of God's kingdom means the destruction of all things that rear their head to oppose God, including oppressive governments, powers, and societies. His wrath is revealed and manifested against them from heaven in this life and the next (Romans 1:18).

Black Christians might disagree about the ways that God brings liberation; the methods that Christians ought to use for liberation; the boundaries of the mission of the church as an institution; and what we can expect God to do on this side of eternity. However, we are in large agreement that liberation from all the dominion of Satan is a powerful theme in the Bible and in God's work in the world.

LIBERATION IN THIS LIFE IS NOT THE DOMINANT BIBLICAL THEME

There are a couple things we must briefly say about liberation as a biblical theme. Liberation fails us as the central theme of the Bible for a few reasons (remember chapter seven?).

Although external liberation from the sin of others is an important theme in the Bible, Jesus came primarily to renovate our inner lives and to transform our hearts. Only through a people who are transformed from the inside can God's kingdom wholeness truly manifest itself outwardly. Though outward conformity to God's justice and righteousness should happen whether or not someone or a society has changed inwardly, that outward change will not last unless there is an inward change.

Poverty and oppression are not the sole markers of those who God favors. The poor and oppressed who do not follow Christ are not aligned with God in the same way as those who do. Yes, the scriptures teach that God's heart and justice lean towards the poor and afflicted. Solomon tells us, "One who is gracious to a poor man lends to the LORD, And He will repay him for his good deed" (Proverbs 19:17 NASB), and Matthew 25:31-46 shows his posture towards the afflicted. Yes, the scriptures put an emphasis on the fact that the poor and afflicted should be defended from the abuse and oppression by the hands of the rich and powerful. And yes, we see in the Gospel Accounts that the lowly, afflicted, and marginalized are often much more likely to understand the kingdom as good news than the insider and the powerful in Israel. However, it is possible to be poor and afflicted and yet to be enemies of God. For example, Luke 17:11-19 tells us about ten leprous men. When you had leprosy, God demanded that you were quarantined from the rest of society (Leviticus 13:45-46), so they were outcasts because of their leprosy. Jesus heals ten outcasts, but only the Samaritan one comes back to glorify God and give thanks to Jesus. Among the community of the afflicted who were healed, only one developed a faith in God. It is possible to receive God's mercy outwardly yet not inwardly.

Related to the above, the poor are not poor solely because of the oppression of others. It is possible for poverty to come upon a person because of their own negligence and sin. The scriptures tell us, "Poor is he who works with a negligent hand, But the hand of the diligent makes rich" (Proverbs 10:4 NASB) and, "He who loves pleasure will become a poor man; He who loves wine and oil will not become rich" (Proverbs 21:17 NASB). The scriptures teach that people have a personal responsibility in their social situation.

Also, liberation of the poor and oppressed from adverse situations *in this life* isn't the main point of the scriptures. If we are honest, many of us wish the Bible were more radical on certain issues. We are disappointed when God tells an abused, enslaved Egyptian woman named Hagar to go back to Sarai, her harsh mistress (Genesis 16:9); when God permits slavery, though it is not a part of his ideal will for the world (Exodus 21:1-8); when God tells Christians to persevere under unjust suffering (1 Peter 2:18-20); when Jesus encourages non-violent means against violence (Matthew 5:38-42); when the Bible's authors aren't more outspoken against slavemasters (Ephesians 6:5-9); when the Bible applauds Christians for joyfully accepting injustice (Hebrews 10:34); and more. God can disappoint our view of liberation if we only see liberation as something that must happen in its fullness in this life right now.

God's kingdom, and therefore liberation, is also a future reality that will eventually destroy all the works of Satan in this world. Though Christian good works oppose evil in this life, we acknowledge that we cannot totally eradicate it. Our mode of resistance against evil in the here and now is deeply shaped by the fact that this world is passing away and that a new one is coming. The reign of God is coming in full, so a part of our posture in the midst of evil is both resistance and patiently waiting at the same time. This is how Paul can say something like,

> Each one should remain in the condition in which he was called. Were you a bondservant when called? Do not be concerned about it. (But if you can gain your freedom, avail yourself of the opportunity.) For he who was called in the Lord as a bondservant is a freedman of the Lord. Likewise he who was free when called is a bondservant of Christ. You were bought with a price; do not become bondservants of men. So, brothers, in whatever condition each was called, there let him remain with God . . . This is what I mean, brothers: the appointed time has grown very short. From now on, let those who have wives live as though they had none, and those who mourn as though they were not mourning, and those who rejoice as though they were not rejoicing, and those who buy as though they had no goods, and those who deal with the world as though they had no dealings with it. For the present form of this world is passing away." (1 Corinthians 7:20-24, 29–31 ESV)

How can Paul tell a slave[9] (aka a "bondservant," someone bound to service without being paid), on the one hand, to not worry about being a slave but, on the other hand, encourage that person to get their freedom and not to become slaves of men because they are slaves to Jesus? We live in the complexity of wanting to change this world but also realizing the next world is coming. The future kingdom shapes our resistance now (i.e. don't be slaves because you belong to Jesus. Get your freedom) but also allows us to have patience in anticipation of the coming kingdom (i.e. if you can't get your freedom, don't worry. The best is yet to come. Obey your master). We might be thinking, "Can Paul make up his mind?! Is Paul going to be radical or not?!" However, Paul and the rest of the biblical authors realize that we live with one foot in this world (enslaved) and another foot in the next (free). And our current standing now is shaped by each world in which we have a foot.

———

RECAP

We have explored how Christ was a double major, both God and human. These two majors qualify him to fulfill the role of our Redeemer. God the Son became a human just like us except without sin. He became a human in order to represent us before God the Father. Jesus lived the life we should've lived, died the death we deserved, and rose again for our own life. He became a human in order to take the covenant curses upon himself so that he could give all of the covenant blessings to us. In the one person of Jesus the two natures of God exist. The fact that Jesus is both God and human allows him to reveal God to us and for God to save us as a human. Jesus, as one who was humbled, can relate to the lowly and oppressed. Jesus, as one who was exalted, can bring blessings wherever the curses are found and can bring life wherever death is found.

CHRIST'S OFFICES

The Redeemer saves us by being a prophet, a priest, and a king. In the scriptures, there is a lot of overlap between the roles of these three offices; however, they were distinct. There were prophets, priests, and kings among the people of God throughout biblical history, but they all failed at their jobs, even the good ones. Where everyone else failed, Jesus would succeed at being a prophet, a priest, and a king.

Now, Let's look at each office.

CHAPTER 9
CAN HE GET THE JOB DONE?

ésumés are important when applying for a job. Jobs have a unique role to fill, so they send out an announcement. They are looking for someone with the right skill set to do the job. How do they find this out? They request a résumé from applicants. A résumé describes someone's skill set and what they have done in the past. It typically includes numbers and stats that display that person's ability.

Whether you know it or not, there is a job opening in your life, a necessary one. You need a savior to turn your life around, and you need someone who can get this job done. In experiencing this need, we look for saviors in all the wrong places. We look to our grades, relationships, money, popularity, our appearance, our parent's approval, and more, to save us from all that is wrong in life. At the end of the day, these things will always fail you. Though there are many different competitors for the job, I want to give you Jesus' résumé. Jesus has always had one job: Redeemer. This job had three primary roles: a prophet, a priest, and a king. Allow me to walk you through Jesus' résumé. I hope you will see that his skill set perfectly qualifies him to be your savior and fulfill the job description of prophet, priest, and king. You need a prophet to guide you, a priest to connect you to God's presence, and a king to give you victory.

WHERE WE ARE GOING

In a sentence, this chapter drives home this point: Jesus is the perfect savior for you, so trust in him.

When in college, we often see Jesus as little more than a get-into-heaven ticket, a clutch prayer answerer, and a moral guide. We think something along the lines of, "He died for my sins so that I can get into heaven." That's true, but if Jesus only gets us into heaven, then why do I need him now as a college student when I feel like I have so much of my life ahead of me? And if he is just good for answering clutch prayers, then why do I need to devote my whole life to him? If he is only a moral guide, then I will just try "my best," which often means that you will be a good person as long as it doesn't cost you much. Given all these views of Jesus, some college students figure that they will have their fun in college and then devote their lives to Jesus after college. Because, after all, what has Jesus done for you, and what is he doing in the here and now?

I want to convince you that Jesus has done and is doing so much for his people that your mind will be blown. His ministry as your Redeemer will radically change your life for the better. Why would you wait until after college to follow him? In this chapter, we will look at some of the key things that Jesus does for us as our Redeemer. We will look at how Jesus 1) gives us guidance about how to live the good-life 2) ushers us into the presence of God and 3) leads us into victory. Jesus did these things during his earthly ministry and is still doing them right now while he is in heaven.

———

ATHANASIUS CONNECTS WHO GOD IS TO WHAT HE DOES

As we transition from the previous chapter to this one, we must see the connection between who God is and what God does. Athanasius understood that Jesus' person is connected to Jesus' work. In other words, who Jesus is, is connected to what he does.

In his book, *On the Incarnation*, Athanasius describes humanity's fallen condition. First, he talks about how humanity is sinful and corrupt. We need someone to help us stop sinning and fix our corrupted inner selves. Second, humanity has lost the knowledge of who God is. If that wasn't enough, third, God told us that we would die for our sin (Genesis 2:15-17). Who could remove the death penalty over us, reteach us about God, and renovate our inner selves? Who could get such a job done? Athanasius gives us an answer: "What – or rather *Who* was it that was needed for such grace and such recall as we required? Who, save the Word of God himself, Who also in the beginning had made all things out of nothing? His part it was, and His alone."[1] Throughout his book, *On the Incarnation*, Athanasius declares that it is only Jesus who can die for us, reveal God to us, and renew us. Jesus gets the job done. Let's look at how Jesus does all these things through his offices.

———

JESUS GUIDES US INTO THE GOOD-LIFE

How does Jesus lead us into the good-life? Jesus does this as a prophet. There is so much confusion about how to truly enjoy life in college. There are so many different voices and paths. In the midst of the confusion, Jesus grabs our hand and guides us by his word and Spirit (aka the Holy Spirit). Let's explore how Jesus functions as our prophet.

A PROPHET REPRESENTS GOD TO THE PEOPLE

What is a prophet? A prophet was someone who communicated on behalf of God to the people. They called the people back to faithfulness to the covenant they made with God. Remember, the covenants brought God's blessings to the people when the people were faithful to the covenant. So, when the people listened to the prophets, they experienced God's blessings, in other words, the good-life.

All of the prophets throughout biblical history ultimately failed to truly turn God's people back to God. Though there were generally good prophets, like Moses and Elijah, none of the prophets were able to perfectly lead the people into the good-life. The prophets began to worship other gods, prophesy lies on behalf of God, align themselves with evil power, and oppress instead of serve the people. But there was a foreshadowing of a future prophet who would come to succeed where the others failed. Moses foretold a day when a prophet would come in the pattern of his own ministry, except better (Deuteronomy 18:15-20). The people during Jesus' day were looking for this ultimate prophet who would come.

JESUS IS THE GREATEST PROPHET

Jesus perfectly represents God and leads you into wholeness. Acts 3:22-26 tells us that Jesus is "the Prophet." As both God and human, he was the perfect prophet. Why? He represented and revealed God with his very being. Jesus himself was God's prophetic message to us. Hebrews 1:1-2 tells us, "Long ago, at many times and in many ways, God spoke to our fathers by the prophets, but in these last days he has spoken to us by his Son" (Hebrews 1:1–2 ESV). God has spoken singularly and decisively in the Son. Jesus, as God himself, represented God perfectly in everything he did. He did not bring a message about God; no, he *was* the message about God. Because Jesus was the message, Jesus' message was ultimately about himself. Following Jesus was the key to being faithful to God's covenant and experiencing the good-life.

JESUS GIVES HIS PROPHETIC MESSAGE

Jesus' prophetic ministry redeems us from the ways we are lost and need guidance.

Let's look at his prophetic ministry from his birth to ascension. First, Jesus' birth was a prophetic act. Given the fact that Jesus was God in the flesh, whenever Jesus did anything, he prophetically represented God to the people perfectly:

> Anyone who has seen me has seen the Father! So why are you asking me to show him to you? Don't you believe that I am in the Father and the Father is in me? The words I speak are not my own, but my Father who lives in me does his work through me. Just believe that I am in the Father and the Father is in me. (John 14:9–11)

Second, Jesus' entire ministry was prophetic. Jesus carried forward the message of the previous prophets before him, but with more insight and authority (John 1:18). He also did the same works of the prophets before him, but with more power (John 9:29-34). Third of all, Jesus received opposition that came with being a prophet. People slandered him, tried to physically harm him, repeatedly tested him, and attempted to kill him (Luke 4:28-30). In his ministry, Jesus' prophetic ministry received opposition because the people were far away from God. He received so much opposition that it eventually led him to being murdered on a cross. Murder was a common experience of the prophets since their messages were hard to swallow for sinful people. Fourth, even in his death, Jesus was prophetic: Mark, one of the gospel writers, tells us, "When the Roman officer who stood facing him saw how he had died, he exclaimed, 'This man truly was the Son of God!'" (Mark 15:39). In his death, Jesus was prophetically revealing himself as the Son of God and, therefore, revealing God himself.

Jesus rose again and ascended to power in heaven, communicating to us prophetically that he was God's righteous one, worthy of life, though the world said, "Guilty and worthy of death." At every point, Jesus was leading us to God so that he could lead us to the good-life.

JESUS SPREADS HIS PROPHETIC MESSAGE

Jesus continues his prophetic ministry in heaven. How? He sent his Spirit to give his word to the apostles and prophets. He told the apostles, "But you will receive power when the Holy Spirit comes upon you. And you will be my witnesses, telling people about me everywhere—in Jerusalem, throughout Judea, in Samaria, and to the ends of the earth" (Acts 1:8). Do you see that the apostles' job is to simply witness about Jesus' earthly ministry? His prophetic ministry from heaven is to make sure that people understand the significance of all that he did and said when he was on earth. Jesus' prophetic ministry on earth is the foundation for Jesus' prophetic ministry from heaven. Jesus exercised his prophetic ministry through the apostles by the power of his Spirit, and the New Testament prophets worked alongside the apostles.

The Bible is where we have Jesus' words to us. Eventually, the apostles and prophets formed the Bible's New Testament writings, which were documents filled with Jesus' words that he gave when he was on earth and the words that he gave through his apostles and prophets. Even in the Old Testament, Jesus' Spirit was giving prophetic words through the prophets. When speaking about the Old Testament prophets, Apostle Peter tells us that they "wondered what time or situation the Spirit of Christ within them was talking about when he told them in advance about Christ's suffering and his great glory afterward" (1 Peter

1:10–11). Did you catch that? It was the Spirit of Christ that was giving the Old Testament authors their words. Christ has given us the whole Bible, both the Old and New Testament. Though he is in heaven, Jesus continues to lead us into the good-life whenever the Bible is read, preached, discussed, prayed, sung, and the like. And his word in the Bible transforms us as the Spirit gives us the ability to receive it, understand it, and live it out.

———

JESUS BRINGS US INTO GOD'S PRESENCE

How do we live in the presence of God? In college, there is confusion about who God is and if we are actually close to him. Is God with me in my young adult experiences? Does he hear me? Is he with me? Does he live in me? If you belong to Jesus, God is with you; God hears you; and God lives in you because of Jesus' priestly ministry. Let's explore how Jesus is a priest to us.

A PRIEST REPRESENTS THE PEOPLE TO GOD

What is a priest? As a summary, a priest labored in the presence of God to bring others into the presence of God. In other words, a priest paved the path into the presence of God. The priest's most prominent duty in the scriptures was to offer sacrifices for the people. There were burnt offerings, grain offerings, peace offerings, sin offerings, guilt offerings, and more, but the most important function of the sacrifices was that they made reparations to God for people's sins. The Bible tells us, "Every high priest is a man chosen to represent other people in their dealings with God. He presents their gifts to God and offers sacrifices for their sins" (Hebrews 5:1). They symbolically took away the people's sin and made God favorable towards them. The sacrifices reconciled the people to God and, thereby, brought people more deeply into the presence of God.

In general, priests throughout Old Testament history failed. They were sinful — they needed to offer sacrifices for themselves. The priests were mortal — they died and needed to be replaced repeatedly. The priesthood was weak — they offered sacrifices over and over again. The priest's sacrifices were unable to actually deal with the people's sins:

> The old system under the law of Moses was only a shadow, a dim preview of the good things to come, not the good things themselves. The sacrifices under that system were repeated again and again, year after year, but they *were never able to provide perfect cleansing for those who came to worship.* If they could have provided perfect cleansing, the sacrifices would have stopped, for the worshipers would have been purified once for all time, and their feelings of guilt would have disappeared. But instead, those sacrifices actually reminded them of their sins year after year. *For it is not possible for the blood of bulls and goats to take away sins.* (Hebrews 10:1–4, emphasis added)

The sacrifices merely pointed the people to their need for a true and better sacrifice that would actually take away their sins and cleanse their guilty conscience. Also, the priests were supposed to help the judges make fair decisions, but they failed. The biggest failure they had was sentencing Jesus to death. These priests were from the Israelite tribe of Levi (the levitical priesthood), and their priesthood was never meant to last because it failed to give us full access to God's presence.

JESUS BRINGS A NEW PRIESTHOOD

Jesus is our new priest. Because of the failure of the levitical priesthood, God raises up another priesthood, one modeled after Melchizedek's priesthood (Genesis 14:18; Hebrews 5:8–10). Jesus is the new priest in this new priesthood. As a priest of a new and better order, he successfully brings us into the presence of God.

How is he better than the priests in the Old Testament? Jesus is perfectly holy and sinless; therefore, he does not need to offer sacrifices for himself. In fact, Jesus himself was a sacrifice on our behalf. Jesus "offered for all time a single sacrifice for sins"; therefore, he accomplishes forgiveness once and for all (Hebrews 10:11-14 ESV). Hebrews tells us about Jesus' sacrifice, saying, "Unlike those other high priests, he does not need to offer sacrifices every day. They did this for their own sins first and then for the sins of the people. But Jesus did this once for all when he offered himself as the sacrifice for the people's sins" (Hebrews 7:27). As a sacrificial lamb, he "was led like a sheep to the slaughter. And as a lamb is silent before the shearers, he did not open his mouth" (Acts 8:32). Jesus rose again and lives forever in heaven; therefore, he can make sure we have access to God's presence forever (Hebrews 7).

JESUS PAVED THE PATH TO GOD'S PRESENCE

Let's look at his priestly ministry from his birth to ascension. One, Jesus' birth was a priestly act. Jesus was born as a human so that he could serve us sympathetically as our priest. He can relate to us as a priest because he is human like us (Hebrews 4:14-16). Jesus was also born in order to die as the sacrifice we needed to free us from sin. Two, Jesus' ministry was priestly. Just like the priests in the Old Testament era, Jesus regularly taught the people, dealt with their wounds and uncleanliness, and helped to decide disputes between people. Three, Jesus' death was priestly. He eventually died as a sacrifice for their sins. Just like the sacrifices of the Old Testament era, Jesus died in the place of those who deserved death for their sins. He died on their behalf, in their place so they would not have to die. Athanasius tells us, "He accepted death at the hands of men, thereby completely to destroy it in His own body."[2] Jesus used death to destroy death.

The scriptures have beautiful passages that highlight Christ's priestly death. Jesus purchased us "from the futile ways inherited from your forefathers, not with perishable things such as silver or gold, but with the precious blood of Christ" (1 Peter 1:18–19 ESV). Like the redemption in the Old Testament, Jesus purchased us, except he did so with his very own life. Jesus "came not to be served but to serve others and to give his life as a ransom for many" (Matthew 20:28). Jesus gave his life to deliver us. Jesus died for humanity, and his death "redeems them from the transgressions committed under the first covenant" (Hebrews 9:15 ESV). By his death, he has made us reconciled to God: "You were his enemies, separated from him by your evil thoughts and actions. Yet now he has reconciled you to himself through the death of Christ in his physical body" (Colossians 1:21–22). How powerful a sacrifice! One person's death could free all of humanity from the sin and misery that defines this earth. Jesus died for us, so we sing, "I know it was the blood, I know it was the blood, I know it was the blood for me. One day that I was lost, Jesus died up on the cross. I know it was the blood for me."[3]

Jesus rose and ascended into heaven as our exalted priest. Because we are united with him, we are seated with him in heaven (Ephesians 2:6). Where he is, we are. Therefore, we are always in God's presence even though we are physically on earth.

BUT DOESN'T THE CROSS GIVE SUPPORT TO ABUSE AND OPPRESSION?

There are some who reject Jesus because they believe his death gives support to abuse and oppression. When we look at Jesus' sacrificial death, some take issue with the fact that this was the way God wanted to rescue us. Why did God have to let his Son go through death in that way? If Jesus' oppression and abuse are a part of God's divine plan, some believe it gives some people a reason to speak about oppression and abuse as under divine approval. Also, there are some who hate the fact that Jesus' body was a substitute for our own, which, they say, gives divine approval to people's bodies being used for the benefit of others.

They are referring to the abuse of bodies that happened throughout history in oppressive societies, particularly the bodies of Black women.

We must first be clear that we strongly oppose anyone who has used the teaching about Christ's substitutionary death to justify the oppression and suffering of those whose bodies and lives have been expended for the benefit of another. This is a clear abuse of the teaching about Christ being a substitute for us. The cross is actually the place where we see divine disapproval of oppression. It is the place where oppression and abuse are shown for what it truly is — anti-God in every way. God came to the earth, and where did he end up? Hanging on a piece of wood to slowly die. The oppression and abuse happening is literally anti-God, and in Acts 2:23, 36, judgment is pronounced over these murderers. They must repent for murdering Jesus. Also, Jesus displays unity with the oppressed and abused by actually becoming oppressed and abused. God's answer to this suffering is to enter into it himself to give hope to those who go through it. As he walks with the downtrodden in this world, he can relate and sympathize (Hebrews 2:17, 4:15). With the spiritual, we sing, "Nobody knows the trouble I've seen, Nobody knows but Jesus. Nobody knows the trouble I've seen, Glory Hallelujah!"[4]

Though God hates the oppression and abuse of the cross, he is big and good enough to bring good out of the darkest moment in human history (remember chapter four?). Evil people killed Jesus, not God (Acts 2:23). However, it was God's "definite plan and foreknowledge" to use this for the deliverance of humanity (Acts 2:23, ESV). God turned a murder into a sacrificial death, a wrongful death into an atoning death, a homicide into a whole burnt offering. God and Christ permitted this evil to happen so that good might happen (remember, permissive decrees from chapter four?). Even still, God's disgust rests on the evil of the cross.

Some argue that the teaching about good coming out of Christ's murder is unbiblical and makes light of suffering.

However, many places in the scriptures speak of the fact that Christ willingly endured evil so that good might happen. Peter tells us, "For Christ also suffered once for sins, the righteous for the unrighteous, that he might bring us to God" (1 Peter 3:18 ESV). Earlier in his first letter, Peter speaks about Christ suffering under oppression, "He himself bore our sins in his body on the tree, that we might die to sin and live to righteousness. By his wounds you have been healed. For you were straying like sheep, but have now returned to the Shepherd and Overseer of your souls" (1 Peter 2:24–25 ESV). John the Baptist tells us that Jesus is "the Lamb of God, who takes away the sin of the world!" (John 1:29 ESV). Paul tells us that Jesus is the one "who gave himself as a ransom for all," (1 Timothy 2:6 ESV) and the one "who gave himself for us to redeem us from all lawlessness and to purify for himself a people for his own possession who are zealous for good works" (Titus 2:14 ESV). John says, "He is the atoning sacrifice for our sins, and not only for ours but also for the sins of the whole world" (1 John 2:2 NIV). God does not make light of suffering in Christ's death; in fact, we are supposed to stand in horror at it. In fact, at noon during Christ's death, the sun ceased to give its light. This was a sign of several things, but one was God's wrath and judgment on those who caused Christ to suffer (Luke 23:44; Isaiah 13:9-11).

Even further, Christ's death is an example for us as Christians. Peter tells us, "For God called you to do good, even if it means suffering, just as Christ suffered for you. He is your example, and you must follow in his steps" (1 Peter 2:21). Christ not only suffered to take away our sins, but he suffered to give us an example of resisting evil. Because of Christ's suffering and sacrifice, we can endure suffering. Again, this does not mean that God approves of the evil that causes the suffering, but it does mean that Christ is our model as we suffer under oppression. Let's look at a couple passages.

After the apostles were beaten for doing good, they were "*rejoicing* that they were counted worthy to suffer dishonor for the name" (Acts 5:41 ESV, emphasis added). Furthermore, Paul tells us that for believers "it has been *granted to you* that for the sake of Christ you should not only believe in him but also suffer for his sake, engaged in the same conflict that you saw I had and now hear that I still have" (Philippians 1:29–30 ESV, emphasis added). As Christians resist evil and survive under the grips of unjust powers, suffering will come. We do not seek suffering nor is suffering itself a part of God's vision for a perfect world, however, we joyfully endure suffering for the sake of Christ.

There are some who would say that the cross is nothing more than evil overcoming good, and, therefore, the resurrection is the main place where God gains victory over evil. However, God gains victory not only in the resurrection but also in the crucifixion! This is why immediately after Christ's death, "many godly men and women who had died were raised from the dead" (Matthew 27:52). In the cross itself, Jesus had gained victory over the powers of Satan, just like he did in his resurrection. We fail to see victory in the cross because the cross is foolish to those who only see victory as a display of power or a display of something that makes human-sense. However, God is clear that he intentionally made the cross weak and foolish, and with this, he would put to shame the powerful and wise of this world (1 Corinthians 1:20–23). The cross was an explosively powerful moment in every realm of the universe because of its atoning nature (Hebrews 9:11-12, 23-24).

JESUS IS BRINGS AND KEEPS US IN GOD'S PRESENCE

Jesus now serves in the heavenly realms as the only one who victoriously can serve the needs of his people in power. Jesus is the way that we have access to God's presence every day, every hour, every second. Jesus is the "go between"for everything in our relationship with God.

What does it look like for Jesus to be our "go between?" One,

Jesus is in the heavenly realms conversing with the Father about our needs: "Therefore he is able, once and forever, to save those who come to God through him. He lives forever to intercede with God on their behalf" (Hebrews 7:25). It's not as if Jesus is trying to convince an irritated God the Father to help us. No, Jesus doesn't need to convince the Father to love us (John 16:26-27). The Father delights in the fact that the Son brings the needs of his children before him. They partner together to help us. Two, Jesus himself, as a human priest, is sympathetic, so he is able to care for us as a priest in a compassionate and relatable manner (Hebrews 4:14-16). Because of this, we are encouraged to "approach God's throne of grace with confidence, so that we may receive mercy and find grace to help us in our time of need" (Hebrews 4:16 NIV).

JESUS LEADS US INTO VICTORY

How does Jesus lead us into victory? There are so many things that are frustrating in college. Sin and bad habits oppose us. Depression and anxiety oppose us. Suffering opposes us. Shady people oppose us. How do we gain victory in all of these situations? Jesus has conquered them all as our king. Let's explore how Jesus functions as our king.

A KING WAS THE LEADER OF GOD'S PEOPLE

What is a king? I am sure you, like I, have many pictures of what it means to be a king. Maybe you picture King T'Challa, Simba, King Tut, or perhaps a scene from your favorite warrior movie. Like our favorite movies, the Bible also gives us pictures of a king. It might seem foreign to us now in our secular United States context, but during most of biblical history, the kingdom of Israel was God's chosen nation, and God was the king. But though God was king, he exercised his reign over Israel through a human king who ruled on his behalf.

Let's look at some of the functions of a king. First, a king is a warrior, which is someone who fights in wars. The king led Israel in battle to assure peace from their enemies. Second, a king is a judge. A judge is a person who applies God's wisdom to his people's disputes, teaching the people between right and wrong. The source of this wisdom is the word of God. Third, a king is an administrative leader. The king manages the kingdom's time, energy, and resources to accomplish God's purposes – like building new buildings, managing the food supplies, or appointing royal officials. Lastly, a king is the spiritual leader of God's people. The king's job is to ensure the people are following the LORD's commands and worshiping the LORD exclusively. The king's role was so important that he was one of the few who had a copy of God's law (Deuteronomy 17:18) along with the priests and the elders (Deuteronomy 31:9), and on this law, he was required to meditate day and night (Deuteronomy 17:19; Joshua 1:8; Psalm 1:2).

In general, the kings of biblical history failed to be proper warriors, judges, administrative leaders, and spiritual leaders. Though there were generally good kings, they were all imperfect, collectively leading the people into a downward spiral of oppression and suffering.

JESUS IS OUR KING

Jesus himself was the king who would come to bring God's reign to manifest itself on the earth perfectly. As we have already seen, Jesus is the king in the line of David, who comes to bring wholeness. Jesus is the perfect warrior, judge, administrator, and spiritual leader — all on our behalf. It is because of Jesus' kingship that we can sing with Black African Christians from long ago, "When Israel was in Egypt's land, Let my people go, Oppressed so hard they could not stand, Let my people go. Go down, Moses, Way down in Egypt's land, Tell old Pharaoh, Let my people go."[5] We know that Jesus is a king who will destroy the works of the "pharaohs" of the world, who Satan uses to oppose God's people. On top of this, Jesus has broken Satan's grip over our spirits. If you belong to Jesus, the kingdom of Satan no longer has any power over you. You have been transferred into a new kingdom.

JESUS' VICTORY IS WON

Let's look at Jesus' kingly ministry from his birth to ascension.

One, Jesus' birth was kingly. People recognized the fact that Jesus' birth meant that all of God's enemies would be defeated (Luke 1:68-75).

Two, Jesus' baptism was kingly. In Mark 1:9-11, we are told of Jesus' baptism and that the Spirit descended upon him there. Many things are happening here, but one of them is that King Jesus declares war by the power of the Spirit. The Spirit is clothing Jesus with power, becoming the engine for Jesus, the war machine against evil. After being baptized, the Spirit directs Jesus into the wilderness to be tempted by Satan. After the Spirit equips Jesus for battle, the Spirit sends Jesus to start fighting, and he is victorious over the devil's temptations. From here on out in the Gospel Accounts, Jesus will start exercising his authority over the demons. Why? Mark 3:22-30 teaches us that Jesus could command demons and cast them out because he has tied up the strongman. Jesus has broken into Satan's palace, tied him up, and, therefore, can now release people from demonic oppression and possession. This is the beginning of the end for the devil.

Three, Jesus' earthly ministry was kingly. Throughout his ministry, Jesus does the administrative work of a king by feeding people, appointing leadership over the church, and giving instructions to his followers on their mission to advance his kingdom.

Four, Jesus had a kingly death. Jesus' death on the cross is the king dying in order to forgive his people for their offenses against the crown and free them from the kingdom of the devil, who was then "the ruler of this world" (John 12:30).

In Jesus' resurrection, ascension, and reign, Jesus sits on the throne that Adam and Eve should've had and that the devil had. As king, he defeats those who sentenced him to death, defeats death itself, and defeats Satan. Athanasius tells us, "The supreme object of His coming was to bring about the resurrection of the body. This was to be the monument to His victory over death." Again, Athanasius tells us, "Death has become like a tyrant who has been completely conquered by the legitimate monarch; bound hand and foot as he now is, the passers-by jeer at him, hitting him and abusing him, no longer afraid of his cruelty and rage because of the king who conquered him."[6]

JESUS SPREADS HIS VICTORY INTO OUR LIVES

After Jesus gained victory, he then began to spread his kingdom. Jesus commissions his apostles to spread his kingdom all over the earth: "I have been given all authority in heaven and on earth. Therefore, go and make disciples of all the nations," (Matthew 28:18–19). On the day of Pentecost, which was a Jewish festival in Jerusalem, he poured out his Spirit on the apostles. Pentecost is Jesus giving his weapons and power to the church so that they can continue to wage the war against evil here on earth. Eventually, Jesus will return to judge the world, destroying all evil and renewing all who belong to him. This is the day when "the Son of Man will come with his angels in the glory of his Father and will judge all people according to their deeds" (Matthew 16:27). Because of the power of Jesus, we sing, "Ride on, King Jesus, No man can a hinder me, Ride on, King Jesus ride on, No man can a hinder me."[7]

As his kingdom-people, humanity is meant to work alongside Jesus in establishing his kingdom. When you receive Jesus as your King, you are rescued "from the kingdom of darkness and transferred us into the Kingdom of his dear Son, who purchased our freedom and forgave our sins" (Colossians 1:13–14). His victory comes into our lives. Now that we are in the kingdom, we join the fight against darkness. Our weapons are his word and works, and as we labor we sing the words of the spiritual, "I am on the battle-field for my Lord."[8] We sing, "My God, He's a mighty man o' war, Sinner, please don't let this harvest pass. I know that my God, He will save you, If you trust Him."[9]

———

RECAP

Jesus, as our prophet, speaks on behalf of God to humanity, letting us know how we can live the good life. Jesus, as our priest, gives himself as a sacrifice and even now is the middle man between God and us so that we can live in God's presence. Jesus, as our king, rules over us and fights all of our battles. Jesus — in his birth, life, death, ascension, and current reign — is continuously operating as our prophet, priest, and king.

Let's look at how the Spirit brings to us some of the benefits of redemption.

PART FOUR
RESCUE'S EFFECT

CHAPTER 10
SPECIAL DELIVERY!

Online shopping is very popular now. I actually remember when shopping at brick-and-mortar stores was actually preferred over online shopping! In a way, I believe online shopping helps us understand redemption.

There are at least three things that happen when someone buys something online. One, a buyer pays the price. Two, the things that they paid for come into their possession. Three, the new owner's plan and purposes now govern the possession. Notice this: when you buy online, you purchase something before it comes into your possession. You own it in many ways, but you do not yet have it, control it, or benefit from it. There is a difference between purchasing something and actually possessing something. When the package gets to your doorstep, you finally possess the thing you purchased. You are able to enjoy that thing, and that thing is able to enjoy being a part of your life.

Family, a Christian is like a package from Amazon. When Christ died for Christians 2,000 years ago, he purchased them with his own blood. Though he purchased them 2,000 years ago, they were not yet in his possession. There is a difference between paying for something and possessing something. In other words, there is a difference between redeeming something and applying redemption to something. Before you came to Jesus, Jesus had already purchased you but did not yet *have* you. But when someone places their trust in Jesus, Christ comes to possess what he has already purchased. You are able to enjoy belonging to Jesus. You are able to enjoy the application of his redemption. In other words, all of the redeeming work that was done 2,000 years ago has an effect on you now when you come into his possession. This all happens by the Spirit of God.

WHERE WE ARE GOING

In a sentence, this chapter wants to drive home the point that you must be saved, so trust in Jesus.

Black people are very religious and spiritual people. Often it is a standard part of our culture to practice some form of spirituality. For example, though I have recently heard of actual Black atheists, I don't know if I have ever met one. This leads us to gladly accept the name "Christian" if we have even some minor type of association with church or the Bible, which many of us do have. We often talk about "being saved" or being "Christian," but we don't actually know how that happens or when that happens. What does it mean to "get saved?"

I want to convince you that coming into the possession of Jesus is the most glorious and delightful thing for you. I want God to save you into the loving and powerful embrace of Jesus. We are going to talk about what it means to be saved or, in other words, to be converted to Christ.

Here is the thing: you can only enjoy Jesus once you get into his possession. So how do we get into his possession? And what are the plans and purposes he has for us as his new possession? We will talk about 1) how the Spirit brings us into connection with Jesus through faith and the new birth and 2) how we chose God because he first chose us. Let's dive in.

———

THE SPIRIT SAVES US

When we think about salvation, we often think about Jesus, but the Spirit is often the unsung hero of salvation. When we think about real space and time, who actually saves us? Jesus is physically in heaven. Does he literally come down to save us, to live in us? No. It is the third person of the Trinity, the Spirit that moves upon us, lives in us, and rescues us on behalf of the Father and Son. Unlike a crime boss, who orders a hit on someone's life to kill them, Jesus orders a hit on your life to bring you to life. His muscle is the Spirit. The Spirit goes and does the work of salvation on Christ's behalf.

WE ARE SAVED WHEN THE SPIRIT BRINGS REDEMPTION TO US

Christ comes to possess us by the Spirit of God. The Spirit is the one to bring all of the benefits of his redemption to bear on our personal lives. Like swallowing a vitamin capsule filled with nutrients, the Holy Spirit is the capsule that brings all of the nutrients of redemption. Like an intravenous device (an IV) connects your blood system to vital hydration, nutrients, and medicine, the Spirit brings all of the living water of redemption into your inner being. Like applying lotion to ashy skin, the Spirit takes redemption and applies it to you so that you are transformed.

At the Last Supper, Jesus teaches the disciples how he is connected with them through the Holy Spirit: "And I will ask the Father, and he will give you another Advocate, who will never leave you. He is the Holy Spirit, who leads into all truth . . . No, I will not abandon you as orphans—I will come to you" (John 14:16–18). We talked a little bit about this in chapter three when we talked about the Trinity. Jesus was at that time their current

Advocate (i.e. Helper), but Jesus, in his own absence, would send another. This other Advocate would live within the disciples, and because this Spirit would live in the disciples, Jesus would live in the disciples. And in this spiritual connection with his disciples, Jesus applies his work of redemption. The Apostle Paul highlights this when he says, "He washed away our sins, giving us a new birth and new life through the Holy Spirit. He generously poured out the Spirit upon us through Jesus Christ our Savior" (Titus 3:5–6).

In many other places, the Bible highlights the connection between the saving work of Christ and the Spirit. Jesus' work in redeeming us and the Spirit's work are so closely tied together that Paul calls the Lord Jesus, "the Spirit": "So all of us who have had that veil removed can see and reflect the glory of the Lord. And *the Lord—who is the Spirit—makes us more and more like him* as we are changed into his glorious image" (2 Corinthians 3:18, emphasis added). If we think on the Trinity's level, the Spirit and the Lord are distinct persons. But if we think of how God works in the life of a Christian, the Spirit is Christ working in our lives. The Spirit of Christ is Christ in that sense. It is almost like a lady calling a handy man named Trey to come fix her air conditioning. Trey comes with his nephew, Mike, who is in training. Although Mike did most of the work on behalf of Trey's company, the lady tells all her friends, "Trey came over and fixed my air conditioning." As people, they are different, but their work is so closely connected that to refer to one is to refer to the other. In another place, Paul says, "The scriptures tell us, 'The first man, Adam, became a living person.' *But the last Adam—that is, Christ—is a life-giving Spirit* . . . Earthly people are like the earthly man, and heavenly people are like the heavenly man. Just as we are now like the earthly man, we will someday be like the heavenly man" (1 Corinthians 15:45, 48–49, emphasis added). Paul calls Jesus a life-giving Spirit. Again, Christ isn't the Spirit, but their work is so closely tied together that he can be said to be the Spirit. And the work of the Spirit makes us more like Christ.

What happens as Christ possesses us through the Spirit of God? How does that process look?

WE ARE SAVED WHEN THE SPIRIT GIVES US FAITH

Christ possesses us as we exercise faith in him. Spirit grants us faith, and this faith unites us to Christ. John 3:1-21 shows us this. Verses 1-12 talks about how the Spirit is necessary for salvation, and verses 13-21 talk about the necessity of faith (i.e. belief) for salvation. The Spirit's work and our faith go together. They are two sides of the same coin.

What is faith? "Now faith is confidence in what we hope for and assurance about what we do not see" (Hebrews 11:1 NIV). In other words, there are realities that are not yet present and that we cannot see. Faith allows us to operate in life as if we already have the things we are hoping for and as if we can actually see the things that we do not see.

Faith, in the Bible, is not something we just do with our minds. No, faith is something that we do with our whole beings. Therefore, faith is something that concerns and shapes all of our lives and every ounce of our beings. This is why in Hebrews chapter 11, the people were described as "living by faith" (Hebrews 11:13 NIV). Living by faith looks like,

- connecting our whole lives with unseen realities
- clinging to the promises of God in the deepest places of our being (i.e., hope)
- receiving the promised blessings of God.

These three things have everything to do with Christ. Faith,

- sees Christ "though you have never seen him" (1 Peter 1:8)

- clings to the promise of salvation in Christ (Hebrews 11:1)
- receives the promised blessings that come from Christ's redemption (Ephesians 2:8).

This faith unites us to Christ.

Faith is something that both the Spirit, and we do. As I place a pencil in my daughter's hand and then put my hand over hers to help her write, who is writing? She or I? Both. In the same way, the Spirit gives us the ability to do something that we do. The Spirit grants it to us, and we exercise faith as the Spirit grants it to us. With this faith, we cry out to Jesus to save us. At this moment, Christians are united to Christ. Paul describes this faith, aka "belief," in Romans 10:13-14 "'Everyone who calls on the name of the LORD will be saved.' But how can they call on him to save them unless they believe in him? And how can they believe in him if they have never heard about him?" (Romans 10:13–14). Like jumper cables connecting one car's battery to another's, faith and the Spirit are the two major cables that connect us to Christ. The Spirit works faith in us, which unites us to Christ in deep ways.

Doing campus ministry can be unpredictable because you are doing ministry in a setting that isn't your own. You often don't know if a classroom will have the devices or technology you need in order to use the projector or screen. Given such, I often carry an HDMI cable whenever I go somewhere to help the students lead Bible studies.

An HDMI cable connects two different devices. It transfers high-definition audio and/or visuals from one device to another. Without an HDMI cable, what was on the computer screen could not be placed onto the bigger screen in the room so that the students could see the presentation. Without an HDMI, the students could not benefit from the presentation.

Jesus has so many amazing things about himself that he wants to show off. He wants you to present his visuals so the world can see his glory. He also wants you to present his audio so that you can proclaim him to a hopeless world. He is going to reveal himself through you. However, you and Jesus are two different devices. He cannot present himself through you unless there is a connection between you. The Spirit and faith are the HDMI cable that connects him to you. All that belongs to him comes to you through the Spirit and faith.

CHRISTIANS HAVE A DEEP UNION WITH JESUS

The scriptures describe the union with Christ as a deep spiritual fellowship. Being united to Christ is like being a branch on a grape tree: "Yes, I am the vine; you are the branches. Those who remain in me, and I in them, will produce much fruit. For apart from me you can do nothing" (John 15:5). There is an organic unity. Another picture Jesus uses to describe this unity is a home: "I pray that out of his glorious riches he may strengthen you with power through his Spirit in your inner being, so that Christ *may dwell in your hearts* through faith" (Ephesians 3:16–17 NIV, emphasis added).

How does Christ dwell in our hearts? Through the Spirit (remember chapter three?). Jesus grants us wonderful blessings from God through his Spirit. Even further, Jesus is with us through his Spirit being in us. It is because of the Spirit that we can sing, "I want Jesus to walk with me, I want Jesus to walk with me, All along my pilgrim journey, I want Jesus to walk with me. In my trials, Lord walk with me . . . In my sorrows, Lord walk with me . . . In my troubles, Lord walk with me."[1]

———

THE SPIRIT RENOVATES US FROM THE INSIDE OUT

How do we come to first exercise this faith in Christ? The Spirit must first deeply renovate us. Remember how sin works? Sin has touched every single part of us so that nothing is left intact how God made it. We are spiritually dead and wandering in the dark regarding God. Remember, we instinctively rebel against God because of the fall of Adam and Eve. How does it come to be that we, who are spiritually dead, actually choose God and embrace Jesus? Again, the Spirit. The Spirit must renovate us from the inside out.

THE SPIRIT BRINGS A LIVING FAITH

It is entirely possible for someone to be dead within but exercise an outward form of faith. The Bible calls this faith a dead faith (James 2:17, 2:26). How does someone get a dead faith?

The word of God goes out to everyone, inviting them to believe in Jesus. Christ explains different kinds of responses in the parable of the sower in Matthew 13:3-9, 18-23, where Jesus illustrates four different ways that people respond to God's word. We will only consider three of them for our purposes. Two of them involve dead faith and one involves living faith. The first example of dead faith explains that some people receive the word gladly but abandon Jesus when they face hostility because of what they believe. The second details others who receive the word, but are too concerned about wealth and the world in order for their lives to change. Lastly, Jesus illustrates living faith as people receive the word and experience deep change that spills over to change the lives of others. Though many people (and even demons! James 2:19) respond to the word of God with some form of faith (John 2:23-25), a smaller number are actually united to Christ with true faith.

Those who are united to Christ with a living faith experience an "effectual calling." Effectual is another word for effective, productive, or powerful. Effectual calling happens when God calls someone to Jesus, and that calling results in a living faith. Like a phone call that goes through to the other phone, an effectual call is when God's call is received and picked up. An ineffectual call is when God calls someone, but that call is either totally rejected or results in a dead faith. What is the difference between those who are and who are not effectually called? The work of God's Spirit. The Spirit gives a living faith, but without the Spirit, someone will only have a dead faith.

It might seem strange that the Spirit is responsible for everything that happens in our salvation, but the Bible clearly teaches this. Those who are effectually called are born again: "Jesus answered him, 'Truly, truly, I say to you, unless one is born again he cannot see the kingdom of God' . . . Do not marvel that I said to you, 'You must be born again.' The wind blows where it wishes, and you hear its sound, but you do not know where it comes from or where it goes. So it is with everyone who is born of the Spirit" (John 3:3, 7–8 ESV). The whole process whereby the Spirit effectually calls us is the new birth because the Spirit is giving life. The Spirit must do this because people "can reproduce only human life, but the Holy Spirit gives birth to spiritual life" (John 3:6). Thus, by the spirit, we are born again.

THE SPIRIT BRINGS NEW BIRTH

How does this process of being born again happen?

One, the Spirit convicts us of our sin. The Spirit convinces the world that it is sinful: "When he comes, he will prove the world to be in the wrong about sin and righteousness and judgment: about sin, because people do not believe in me;" (John 16:8–9 NIV). It is only through the Spirit's work that we know our guilt before God.

Two, the Spirit teaches us about Christ. 1st Corinthians 2 explains that the Spirit helps us understand and believe the things given to us by God: "But it was to us that God revealed these things by his Spirit . . . And we have received God's Spirit (not the world's spirit), so we can know the wonderful things God has freely given us" (1 Corinthians 2:10–12). The believer both under-stands and receives the things of God because God has given the believer his own Spirit, who gives understanding in all things.

Three, the Spirit renews our decision making (i.e. our wills). One of the promises of the new covenant is that the Spirit will give us the ability actually to be able to obey God. Ezekiel, the prophet, speaks of this amazing work of the Spirit: "And I will give you a new heart, and I will put a new spirit in you. I will take out your stony, stubborn heart and give you a tender, responsive heart. And I will put my Spirit in you so that you will follow my decrees and be careful to obey my regulations" (Ezekiel 36:26–27). By the power of the Spirit, our inner selves are renewed so that we can actually obey God.

Four, the Spirit persuades people to come to God. If someone is even interested in Christ, it is because God himself is drawing them. After all, Christ says, "For no one can come to me unless the Father who sent me draws them to me" (John 6:44). It is because of the Spirit that we can sing with the spiritual, "Sweet Jesus, sweet Jesus, He's the Lily of the Valley, He's the Bright and Morning Star."[2] It is the Spirit who gives people the actual power to come to God after they are persuaded. Again, Luke, the author of Acts, tells us this when Lydia was interested in hearing about God, "As she listened to us, the Lord opened her heart, and she accepted what Paul was saying" (Acts 16:14). It was only because the Lord first opened her heart that she was able to receive the good news about Christ.

THE SPIRIT DOES HIS WORK AS WE SPREAD THE GOOD NEWS

Praise the Holy Spirit! He is the one who is active from beginning to end as we are drawn to God. When and where does the Spirit unite us to Christ? He does it wherever Christians tell others about Jesus and invite them to believe in Jesus. Jesus is literally in heaven, but he comes near to us, so to speak, when we are presented with the message of the gospel, the good news (Ephesians 2:17). And when we have faith in Christ, we sing with our Christian ancestors, "Glory, glory, hallelujah! Since I laid my burden down, Glory, glory, hallelujah! Since I laid my burden down. I feel better, so much better, Since I laid my burden down, I feel better, so much better, since I laid my burden down."[3]

This is why it is so important that we tell our friends about Jesus and invite them into Christian community, where they will hear about Jesus over and over. God is going to use those moments to bring people new life! That is when the Spirit works, and that is when people have faith in Christ.

———

GOD CHOOSES

In the previous section, we saw that rescue from the sin and misery of the curse happens by the Spirit, from beginning to end. God's initiative and action through the Spirit is the cause of salvation. How does God choose who will be born again and who won't? This is where we come to what the Bible calls "election." An election, simply put, is a choice made by someone. God is the one who chooses who will be saved and who will not be saved.

GOD UNCONDITIONALLY LOVES HIS PEOPLE

It is important to emphasize that God does not choose us because something in us earned his election or attracted us to him. When God moves towards people in salvation, it is not because of anything that they have done. Moses tells the Israelites this as they are about to enter the Promised Land:

It is not because you are so good or have such integrity that you are about to occupy their land. The LORD your God will drive these nations out ahead of you only because of their wickedness, and to fulfill the oath he swore to your ancestors Abraham, Isaac, and Jacob. You must recognize that the LORD your God is not giving you this good land because you are good, for you are not— you are a stubborn people. (Deuteronomy 9:5–6)

God is telling the Israelites that they are a stubborn people, so they should not get it twisted! It is only because of God's gracious faithfulness to his promises that God is bringing them into the land. Though they are stubborn, Moses also tells them, "For you are a holy people, who belong to the LORD your God. Of all the people on earth, the LORD your God has chosen you to be his own special treasure" (Deuteronomy 7:6). They are both stubborn yet holy, rebellious yet chosen, frustrating yet a special treasure. They are such not because of their worthiness but because of God's work for them and in them.

Because of this reality, God's election kills any pride in us. Some claim that the doctrine of election is used to prop up the prejudice and racism of particular people groups. How? They claim that a people can justify their dominion over another people group by claiming they are chosen by God. Indeed, this doctrine can be twisted for such purposes. However, God's election, being unconditional, actually reminds us of our humble beginnings and has us stand in awe of God's grace! We were not chosen because we were great but because God himself has a great love. All boasting in ourselves and pride is nonsense. The doctrine of election creates in us humility and a desire to move toward others with the same grace and love we received in election.

GOD TAKES THE INITIATIVE IN LOVE

Paul explains, at length, election in Romans 9. Time fails us to go into depth, but let's look at a couple of things. Paul uses Abraham's family to illustrate how effectual calling relates to election. Abraham had two sons, Isaac and Ishmael. Though both were children of Abraham, only one was a spiritual child of Abraham, and the other was only "fleshly." In other words, as we mentioned earlier, one was a child of the woman and another the child of the serpent. Paul says, "No, for not all who are born into the nation of Israel are truly members of God's people! Being descendants of Abraham doesn't make them truly Abraham's children. For the scriptures say, 'Isaac is the son through whom your descendants will be counted,' though Abraham had other children, too" (Romans 9:6–7). In other words, many are called to be a part of God's people, but only some are effectually called.

Paul then shifts to the next generation of Abraham's family to illustrate election — Isaac's family. Isaac had a wife named Rebekah, and she had two sons named Jacob (aka Israel) and Esau. Pauls says:

> When he married Rebekah, she gave birth to twins. But before they were born, before they had done anything good or bad, she received a message from God. (This message shows that God chooses people according to his own purposes; he calls people, but not according to their good or bad works.) She was told, "Your older son will serve your younger son." In the words of the scriptures, "I loved Jacob, but I rejected Esau." (Romans 9:10–13)

When Rebekah was pregnant with Jacob and Esau, God told Rebekah that the younger, Jacob, would be chosen as God's own, but Esau would not. In other words, Jacob would be a child of the woman, and Esau would be a child of the serpent. God did this before they had even been born, before they had done anything! God sent Rebekah this message because he had chosen and would call Jacob, but not Esau. It is God's active choosing and rejecting that determines their effectual calling.

Now two questions naturally arise. The first is, "Is there injustice on God's part?" (Romans 9:14 ESV). And Paul's answer is,

"By no means!" (Romans 9:14 ESV). Since we are all sinners, God does not owe us grace or mercy. In fact, we all deserve God's wrath and curse because of our sin (remember chapter six?). God goes above and beyond when he chooses to have mercy on anyone. Paul illustrates this from Exodus 33:19, which is what Yahweh said when he chose to renew his covenant with a people who had just committed a huge sin, which was worshiping a golden calf. Since this was idolatry, the people deserved to be destroyed for what they did. However, God chose to renew his relationship with his people based purely on mercy! Paul then brings up the pharaoh who enslaved the Israelites in Egypt in Exodus chapters 1-14. God raised up a wicked pharaoh to have an occasion to display his power and make himself known by saving Israel and judging the Egyptians. From these two Exodus narratives, Paul's two conclusions are that "it depends not on human will or exertion, but on God, who has mercy" (Romans 9:16 ESV) and that "he has mercy on whomever he wills, and he hardens whomever he wills" (Romans 9:18 ESV).

The second question is, "Why does he still find fault? For who can resist his will?" (Romans 9:19 ESV). In response to this question, Paul says, "But who are you, O man, to answer back to God? Will what is molded say to its molder, 'Why have you made me like this?' Has the potter no right over the clay, to make out of the same lump one vessel for honorable use and another for dishonorable use?" (Romans 9:20–21 ESV). Essentially, Paul tells us that God is God, and we do not have the knowledge nor the right to question why God chooses to save some and not others. As Paul says later on in this same line of thought, "Oh, how great are God's riches and wisdom and knowledge! How impossible it is for us to understand his decisions and his ways!" (Romans 11:33). God elects who he will save and elects who he will judge, and we will never wrap our heads around why. All we know is that God is merciful and gracious while people are rebellious and lost.

WE MUST CHOOSE TO LOVE GOD

But don't humans have free will and reject God? Isn't this why God doesn't save people? The answer is yes. It is both true that God doesn't save some because he chooses to *and* that people are not saved because they have rejected God. Later, in explaining why so many of God's people were not chosen, Paul says,

> But the people of Israel, who tried so hard to get right with God by keeping the law, never succeeded. Why not? Because they were trying to get right with God by keeping the law instead of by trusting in him. They stumbled over the great rock in their path . . . For they don't understand God's way of making people right with himself. Refusing to accept God's way, they cling to their own way of getting right with God by trying to keep the law. (Romans 9:31–32; 10:3)

They are under God's judgment because they decided, with their free will, to reject the good news of Jesus. It is both God's election and our election, so to speak. And it is only God's election that can overcome our election to reject him and turn it into an election to embrace him. As Jesus told his disciples, "You didn't choose me. I chose you. I appointed you to go and produce lasting fruit, so that the Father will give you whatever you ask for, using my name" (John 15:16).

GOD LIKES TO LOVE YOU

So if God's election to save and reject people is not based upon anything good or bad that we have done, then what is the reason why God moves to save humanity from their own horrible decisions?

God did it "out of his mere good pleasure" as Westminster Shorter Catechism Question 20 tells us. Pleasure has a sexual connotation in our day, but do not think about it in this way.

Think about the connotation that comes with the word "delight" or "happy." The foundational reason for all God does on humanity's behalf is that it delights him! He likes to love you. And this reason does not have any other rival reasons. God saves not because it would delight him *and* he owed it to us. God saves not because it would excite him *and* he could not survive without us. No, God did it solely because it would thrill him. And he made this choice from eternity past, and we know this because "before he made the world, God loved us and chose us in Christ to be holy and without fault in his eyes. God decided in advance to adopt us into his own family by bringing us to himself through Jesus Christ. This is what he wanted to do, and it gave *him great pleasure*" (Ephesians 1:4–5, emphasis added). Out of his own delight, God chooses those who will be saved.

Your salvation did not begin when you decided to follow Jesus. No, your salvation began in the eternal decrees of God. Throughout the scriptures, we are told about God's sovereignty in salvation. As people throughout history have heard the word of God, "all who were chosen for eternal life became believers" (Acts 13:48). If you believe in Jesus, it is because "God chose you" (2 Thessalonians 2:13). Elsewhere, Paul also highlights God's eternal decree:

> And we know that for those who love God all things work together for good, for those who are called according to his purpose. For those whom he foreknew he also predestined to be conformed to the image of his Son, in order that he might be the firstborn among many brothers. And those whom he predestined he also called, and those whom he called he also justified, and those whom he justified he also glorified. (Romans 8:28–30 ESV)

The question arises, "Does God take pleasure in destroying the wicked?" And the answer is both yes and no. Yes, God takes pleasure in restoring order and wholeness to his world, which will happen when he purges evil from the world and all who insist on practicing it. However, the scriptures are clear that God is merciful. He hates destroying those who refuse him and lay waste to his world. He delays the day of judgment because "he is being patient for your sake. He does not want anyone to be destroyed, but wants everyone to repent" (2 Peter 3:9). Indeed, God "wants everyone to be saved and to understand the truth" (1 Timothy 2:4).

If you are confused, that is normal! Again, we can apprehend things about God, but we can never comprehend him. There will always be mystery surrounding him regarding how he operates. Again, we shout with Paul in worship-filled wonder, "Oh, how great are God's riches and wisdom and knowledge! How impossible it is for us to understand his decisions and his ways!" (Romans 11:33).

————

KNOWING THE JOY OF SALVATION WITH AUGUSTINE

Remember our old friend, Augustine? In chapter three, he taught us about how to find rest in God alone. Now we will learn how Augustine teaches us about the joys of salvation.

Augustine has what is likely the most famous conversion to Christianity in world history, other than the Apostle Paul. He writes about it in his famous and groundbreaking prayer-memoir *Confessions*. Century after century, people have been inspired by our African forefather's conversion. For years, Augustine wrestled within his heart to find God, and when he finally placed his faith in Jesus, his life was changed. Augustine breaks out into prayerful, poetic praise as he reflects on his salvation. Reflecting upon why he didn't choose God sooner, he says,

> But, during all those years, where was my free will? What was the hidden, secret place from which it was summoned in a moment,

so that I might bend my neck to your easy yoke and take your light burden on my shoulders, Christ Jesus, my Helper and my Redeemer? How sweet all at once it was for me to be rid of those fruitless joys which I had once feared to lose and was now glad to reject! You drove them from me, you who are the true, the sovereign joy. You drove them from me and took their place, you who are sweeter than all pleasure . . . At last my mind was free from the gnawing anxieties of ambition and gain, from wallowing in filth and scratching the itching sore of lust. I began to talk to you freely, O Lord my God, my Light, my Wealth, and my Salvation.[4]

Augustine realizes that Jesus is the greatest joy in the world. How could he be so crazy not to center his whole life on him?! Augustine confesses that he did not accept the greatest joy because he was clinging to empty joys. These joys were worldly success, selfish fame, a greed for money, and lust. He was obsessed with these and was afraid to let them go so that he could grasp onto God. Though he thought these things gave him life, they actually crushed him. He made them his god. The hand clinging to false joys is not open to receive something better. Jesus, by his grace, stripped those crushing joys and placed his own light and easy Lordship upon Augustine.

It is my prayer that you realize that God is the greatest joy. Why are you waiting to give yourself to him? Embrace him as your Lord today.

———

RECAP

In this chapter, we talked about being saved and the necessity of being saved. The Spirit brings redemption to us and saves us when the Spirit gives us the power to have faith. The Spirit and faith bring us into a deep union with Christ, and in this union,

Jesus gives us all the blessings of redemption. The only way we can have this faith in Christ is from the renovation of the Spirit within us from the inside out. The Spirit restores us and renews us so that we can actually choose Christ. This new life reaches us when we hear the good news about Jesus. Behind the scenes, it is God who initiates the Spirit's work in our lives by choosing us from eternity past. If we choose God, it is because he first chooses us.

Let's now transition to talk about the amazing blessings God gives to those who are born again in Christ.

CHAPTER 11

BLESSINGS ON BLESSINGS

t amazes me how the rapper Drake has been consistently putting out hits for over a decade. One of his biggest hits in the past few years is the song "God's Plan." The song is about how God's plan was for him to be blessed and to bless others despite people wishing bad things on him. In the song, he talks about the bad wishes coming toward him. There's a sense that while he is trying to be successful, there are people, often unknown and unseen, who hope bad things happen to him. Despite these bad wishes, he is blessed and is blessing others. The song rejoices in the fact that he is carefree, has achieved financial wealth and success, and can use it to help others. In the music video, he gives out money to a bunch of random people. For Drake, overcoming the bad with the good is God's plan. Drake feels his success was in some way planned by God, meaning it was bound to overcome the bad things people wished on him.

Many of us can resonate with this song. We sense that God's plan is somehow and some way behind the good that happens to us. We also have a sense of anxiety when we know how "dangerous" the world can be and how it can be against our thriving. Humans are hardwired to be aware of the invisible spiritual workings "behind the scenes" of the world, so we intuitively know that there is good vs. evil. We want to believe that God has planned our good to happen in the face of bad. We desire for God's plan to bless us and for it to overcome the world's plan to curse us.

WHERE WE ARE GOING

In a sentence, the main point of this chapter is that God blesses you through Jesus, so enjoy these blessings.

Unfortunately, we are often exposed to a Christianity that does not draw us in. We are given all the facts about Jesus, but we wonder, "What does this mean for my life? What do I get out of this?"

In this chapter, we will examine how God blesses us in Christ and how it was always a part of God's plan. Amid the curse on this world, Jesus brings blessing. Jesus has accomplished many beautiful blessings for you, and so much is in store for you! We will look at how 1) God has given you unconditional love 2) pardoned and accepted you 3) given you a new place in his family 3) changed you into a new you 4) sustained you in every area of life and 5) given you a glorious future. Let's dive in.

———

JUSTIFICATION

God justifies those who are born again.

In Christ, we are justified. The word "justify" is courtroom language. It means to declare someone or something as righteous or right. As sinners, we stand before God guilty and worthy of his just condemnation. However, God has provided a way of deliverance from our guilt and condemnation. What does God do when he justifies us?

JUSTIFICATION IS PARDON AND ACCEPTANCE

First, God justifies us not because of anything we have done but because he is gracious! Romans 3:24, and many other places in the Bible, teach that we "are justified by his grace as a gift, through the redemption that is in Christ Jesus," (Rom 3:24 ESV). It is God who sent Christ to redeem us, God who sent his Spirit to unite us to Christ, and God who justifies us. God has not done any of this in response to some kind of worthiness within us. No, as we have already said, it is because of his "mere pleasure."

Second, in justifying us, God forgives us. Our sins are forgiven in the courtroom of God the Judge (Romans 4:6-8). This is an amazing truth! So often we are haunted by the guilt of the things that we have done in the past, but God has forgiven us. In our justification, all our sins – past, present, and future – are forgiven. If this is true, then why do we ask for forgiveness? Our ongoing sin breaks our closeness and fellowship with God. When we sin as Christians, we feel this distance and want to close it. Confession is restoring our fellowship with God, knowing that he will always draw near to us because of the reality of justification. There are numerous places in Scripture that beautifully speak about forgiveness. Psalm 103 speaks about how powerful the LORD's forgiveness is:

> The LORD is compassionate and merciful,
> slow to get angry and filled with unfailing love.
> He will not constantly accuse us,
> nor remain angry forever.
> He does not punish us for all our sins;
> he does not deal harshly with us, as we deserve.
> For his unfailing love toward those who fear him
> is as great as the height of the heavens above the earth.
> He has removed our sins as far from us
> as the east is from the west. (Psalm 103:8–12)

God doesn't just halfway forgive you. He fully forgives you! The psalmist describes the forgiveness God bestows on you by using distance, saying your sins are as far from you as "east is from the west." How far is this? Infinitely far! When you are justified, your past sins are nowhere to be found in God's courtroom and are therefore totally forgiven.

Psalm 32 speaks about the joy that comes with being forgiven by God:

> Oh, what joy for those
> whose disobedience is forgiven,
> whose sin is put out of sight!
> Yes, what joy for those
> whose record the LORD has cleared of guilt,
> whose lives are lived in complete honesty! (Psalm 32:1–2)

Guilt can cause us to go through deep and lasting pain, both physically and spiritually. However, God invites us to receive the joy of forgiveness. In the midst of a sinful world, God blesses us with forgiveness.

Third, in justifying us, God accepts us as righteous. To be righteous is to measure up to a moral standard. In other words, it is to perfectly follow God's law. Not only is our sin removed when we are pardoned, but righteousness is given in its place. The Bible emphasizes that God accepts us as righteous, not because of any merit within us: "For what does the Scripture say? 'Abraham believed God, and it was counted to him as righteousness.' Now to the one who works, his wages are not counted as a gift but as his due. And to the one who does not work but believes in him who justifies the ungodly, his faith is counted as righteousness" (Romans 4:3–5 ESV). The Apostle Paul is using Abraham as an example of one who was accepted as righteous not as wages in response to their good works but as a gift. Abraham received this gift by faith (remember chapter ten?). From where did this righteousness come? It came from God. God grants us his own righteousness. Paul expresses this as he shares how he wants to be found in Christ: "and be found in him, not having a righteousness of my own that comes from the law, but that which comes through faith in Christ, the righteousness from God that depends on faith" (Philippians 3:9 ESV). This righteousness from God is the righteousness of Christ himself, the perfect righteousness he had as the God-human: "And because of him you are in Christ Jesus, who became to us wisdom from God, *righteousness* and sanctification and redemption," (1 Corinthians 1:30 ESV, emphasis). Being united to him, his death is our death, and his righteousness is our righteousness.

How does justification relate to our union with Christ? We only are counted as righteous in God's sight because we are united with the righteous one, Christ himself. Our sins are only considered as punished because we are united with the punished one, Christ, who was punished on the cross. We are only accepted as righteous because we are united with the Christ who was accepted as righteous in his resurrection. The Bible captures the two-fold truth in Romans 4:25: "He was handed over to die because of our sins, and he was raised to life to make us right with God" (Romans 4:25). Christ's resurrection was God justifying him before every one who had counted him as a sinner and criminal in his death on the cross. At the cross, the world said, "Sinner!" but at the empty tomb, God said, "My righteous Son!" This same reality is true of us. The world screams at Christians, "Wrong!" But God sings over Christians, "My righteous children!" Because of our justification, we know that God is for us and not against us in the day-to-day struggles of life.

A PICTURE OF JUSTIFICATION

Imagine that you have received an invitation to a dinner party from God. As you open the beautiful, handwritten letter, you are so excited, and you read: "You are cordially invited to the greatest banquet that ever existed." You are now jumping up and down, and you are so happy. But as you read further, you see the words, "Dress to impress, or no admission." Your heart falls down in your chest because you know God demands perfection. If you don't show up with the most fabulous dress or tuxedo in the universe, you are sure that God will not let you in.

So you visit every store in a 30 mile radius. And after searching far and wide, you finally find the most extravagant outfit you have ever seen. Wanting to be accepted into the party, you spend every dime you have to buy the outfit. On the night of the party, you rent a limo and pull up to God's house with your outfit on, looking fly.

You walk up to the front door with your invitation and say to God, "Thank you so much for inviting me! I tried my best to dress to impress. I'm sure you'll let me."

And God then says, "Thank you for coming! But did you read the rest of the invitation?"

You lift the letter, and you look at the bottom. In bold print, it reads, "I will provide the attire."

God laughs and pulls out an incredibly marvelous outfit that nearly blinds you with its glory. He says, "Take off that trash that you are wearing. You knew I was a strict God who requires perfection, and that's true! But I wish you also knew that I am a providing God who also loves to give that perfection. There are no outfits in the world that I like except my own. All the others are like feces to me. Put this outfit on. Then you will be properly dressed for my party. I love you." And you enter the party with God and all of His other saints dressed in the same glorious clothes.

Family, that is what it is like to come to God trying to be accepted with our own righteousness. It will always be trash in his eyes, no matter how pretty it is to us. And he is so loving that he gives us the righteousness of Jesus to cover us. That exchange is what happens at the moment we first have faith. This is a picture of justification.

———

ADOPTION

God adopts those who are born again.

In Christ, we are adopted. Humanity was and is designed to be kin to God, but we were disowned because of Adam and Eve's sin. In our redemption, we are adopted back into the household of God. "God decided in advance to adopt us into his own family by bringing us to himself through Jesus Christ. This is what he wanted to do, and it gave him great pleasure" (Ephesians 1:5). As sons of God, we receive many beautiful gifts. It is hard to create a distinct list of blessings that belong to adoption and not to other categories since a foundational metaphor for God is a father, and a foundational metaphor for Christ is a son. As those united to Christ, we are sons and God is our Father. In some sense, we can say every blessing of redemption has something to do with adoption.

IS ADOPTION AS SONS INCLUSIVE?

Now, the ladies might be wondering, "Why does the Bible often say 'sons of God' when many Christians are women?" When using the metaphor "son of God," the Bible has in mind both men and women. The image of a "son of God" oftentimes is very intentional on behalf of the biblical authors. During the biblical days, the firstborn son, as the heir, was the one who had the highest privileges in the household of the father. Applying the son of God metaphor to both men and women teaches that both sexes have the status of the firstborn son. Both men and women are heirs. The label "son of God" is a beautiful metaphor for many reasons, one of which is that it fully includes women and men equally into the blessings of God. The Bible does not exclude women from its vision of adoption, and the Old Testament displays this in passages where it includes "daughter" language explicitly alongside "son" language (Deuteronomy 32:19; Isaiah 43:6). The New Testament also displays this when it translates the Old Testament's "son" language into "sons and daughters" language, which Paul does in 2 Corinthians 6:18 (a NT passage). 2 Samuel 7:14 (an OT passage) uses the word "son," but Paul translates it as "sons and daughters." The Bible authors are noticing how "son" language is meant to be a metaphor for both men and women.

Let's look at a few things about adoption.

ADOPTION IS GRACIOUS

Adoption is an act of God's grace. "But to all who believed him and accepted him, he gave the right to become children of God. They are reborn—not with a physical birth resulting from human passion or plan, but a birth that comes from God" (John 1:12–13). As we have already seen with the doctrine of election, becoming a child of God is not something we can do. Becoming a child of God is an act of God on us. He is the one who births us again and brings us new life.

ADOPTION CHANGES YOUR LIFE

As a result of this new birth, we are being transformed to be like God. Remember that we are kin to God as God's image-bearers. As his children, we are to be a picture of him and be like him in all we do. Also, remember that the image of God cannot fully be realized as individuals. We are to be children of God together as a human family, and only then can we bear forth the image of God to the world. We are a family meant to display our Father's glory and goodness.

As sons of God, we are under the Father's daily care and provisions. Jesus teaches:

> Ask, and it will be given to you; seek, and you will find; knock, and it will be opened to you. For everyone who asks receives, and

the one who seeks finds, and to the one who knocks it will be opened. Or which one of you, if his son asks him for bread, will give him a stone? Or if he asks for a fish, will give him a serpent? If you then, who are evil, know how to give good gifts to your children, how much more will your Father who is in heaven give good things to those who ask him! (Matthew 7:7–11 ESV)

Human parents give their children food and clothing, and they are fallen. God, who is not fallen but perfect, will give so much more than earthly parents. Why should we ever doubt God's provision when we rarely doubt the provision of imperfect parents for their children?

ADOPTION GIVES YOU ACCESS TO PRAYER

Related to this, we have a right to pray to him for these provisions and to expect him to deliver on these requests. Of course, God gives according to his own will, so we will find that our greed is not honored by the Lord in prayer. James teaches this when he says, "You ask and do not receive, because you ask wrongly, to spend it on your passions" (James 4:3 ESV). However, the LORD is good and will meet our needs. As with our children, the Lord is tender. "The LORD is like a father to his children, tender and compassionate to those who fear him" (Psalm 103:13). God is warm and intimately near to us as a parent.

ADOPTION BRINGS DISCIPLINE

Though a warm and generous parent, God also disciplines us because he loves us: "Think about it: Just as a parent disciplines a child, the LORD your God disciplines you for your own good" (Deuteronomy 8:5). Often suffering or trials are the ways that God disciplines us when we are running away from him. He wants us to wake up again to a life of close fellowship with him.

ADOPTION BRINGS A ROYAL STATUS

As sons of God, we will reign with Christ and will be glorified with Christ in this life. Because we are united to the Royal-Son, we too will be royal members of the household who reign with Christ. "You are worthy to take the scroll and break its seals and open it. For you were slaughtered, and your blood has ransomed people for God from every tribe and language and people and nation. And you have *caused them to become a Kingdom of priests* for our God. And *they will reign on the earth*" (Revelation 5:9–10, emphasis added). Throughout the scriptures, we are told that we exercise power and authority over the earth with Christ even now. In this life, our reign is not yet fully realized, so we often endure opposition from God's enemies and suffering. Thus, Paul says, "If we endure hardship, we will reign with him. If we deny him, he will deny us" (2 Timothy 2:12).

ADOPTION BRINGS COMFORT IN SUFFERING

As sons of God, we are strengthened in the midst of suffering and oppression. Dr. Howard Thurman – Howard's first dean of the chapel and well known African American pastor and theologian – notes this when he says, "The awareness of being a child of God tends to stabilize the ego and results in a new courage, fearless-ness, and power. I have seen it happen again and again." [1] To be a child of God is to know that your Heavenly Father is for you and with you when evil people surround you and seek to persecute you. Not only this but also God's Fatherly care and provision carry us in the midst of suffering.

ADOPTION GIVES YOU A NEW FAMILY

As sons of God, Christians have a new relationship with each other, which has profound implications for how we engage each other in community. In Paul's letter to Philemon, he displays how a slave's relationship with his master must change now that they are both in Christ. "For this perhaps is why he was parted from you for a while, that you might have him back forever, no longer as a bondservant but more than a bondservant, as a beloved brother—especially to me, but how much more to you, both in the flesh and in the Lord" (Philemon 1:15–16 ESV). The fact that they are both sons of God and brothers in Christ alters their relationship as master and slave. Paul would urge slaves to gain their freedom if they are able anyway (1 Corinthians 7:21) and would also condemn enslavers (1 Timothy 1:10), but the message of Christ does something even deeper. It puts slaves and their masters on equal footing in Christ. Remember how we talked about the "already-not yet" of the kingdom in the first chapter? Their new creation relationship (siblings) alters the way they engage their present age realities (master and slave). Adoption restructures the relationships between Christians.

Like justification, our adoption flows from our union with Christ. We are called sons of God because we are united to the ultimate Son of God.

———

SANCTIFICATION

God sanctifies those who are born again.

WHAT IS SANCTIFICATION?

In Christ, we are sanctified. To be sanctified is another way of saying to be holy. The process of sanctification happens through union with Christ. As we are sanctified, we experience both the realities of Christ's cross and Christ's resurrection. In other words, the old us dies, and the new us is raised to life.

Sanctification is the process of becoming holy. What does it mean to be holy? Holiness is a relational term. Things are holy when they are connected to God, who alone is holy as the "Holy One of Israel" (Isaiah 5:19). To be holy is to be set apart for a special use to God, to be devoted or dedicated to God. Holiness is different from righteousness. Whereas holiness is about relationships primarily, righteousness is about morality. This is why objects in the Bible are called "holy," but they are not called "righteous." Objects can't make moral decisions, but they can be connected to the Holy One as they are set apart for God's use.

Sanctification, or becoming holy, is an essential part of salvation: "But we ought always to thank God for you, brothers and sisters loved by the Lord, because God chose you as firstfruits to be saved through the *sanctifying work of the Spirit* and through belief in the truth" (2 Thessalonians 2:13 NIV, emphasis added). We are only saved because the Spirit sanctifies us. Indeed, the Spirit is saving us from the power of sin as he sanctifies us.

YOU ARE SANCTIFIED INTO A NEW POSITION AND PRACTICE

The Bible uses the term "sanctification" in two different yet organically unified ways.

One, it is the act in which we are initially set apart for a special use to God, the act in which we become holy. This is why all Christians are called saints, or "holy ones." We are all positionally holy before the LORD. We are in the position of being connected to the Holy One. In other words, we are in the position of being holy even if we are not practicing holiness yet. We are sanctified at the moment of salvation.

The second way is the act in which we are increasingly set apart for a special use to God. In other words, we practically become more holy. Holiness is something that describes a person's position in relation to God and describes the qualities of something. For example, when someone first becomes a Christian, they are a saint, which means they are positionally holy. However, they still have all kinds of habits that show they still need to grow. In their life, they don't reflect God's character yet. This is why the Bible can simultaneously call us "holy ones" and then command us "to be holy." Because we are holy, we must live holy: "For God did not call us to be impure, but to live a holy life" (1 Thessalonians 4:7 NIV). Holiness is primarily about being connected to God; it is secondarily about morality. You become holy first, and then you start to live a holy lifestyle second. In Christian circles, we typically describe someone as holy who is upstanding in their moral character because moral excellence is required if someone is set apart for special use to God. All those who are set apart to God will seek to display upstanding moral character as a part of their devotion to him.

Along with moral character being connected to holiness, holiness also means to be whole, perfect, or complete. Sanctification is the process by which God makes you complete or whole. This is why a person was not allowed to present to God an animal that was wounded or blemished at the temple. This is why Jesus remixes Leviticus 11:45, which says "you must be holy because I am holy," to the version, "But you are to be perfect, even as your Father in heaven is perfect" (Matthew 5:48). "Perfect" is another word for "whole." Jesus was likely using holy and perfect interchangeably. If something was to be set apart for use to God, it needed to be complete or whole.

SANCTIFICATION MAKES YOU LIKE GOD

Since God is holy, sanctification is a term used to describe the process by which God makes us look more and more like him. This ties together all of the things we have previously mentioned: being set apart to God, living morally upstanding lives, and being brought into wholeness. Remember how we were designed to be images of God? In sanctification, God is restoring us so we can function more fully as image-bearers — kin, kings and queens, and clergy. This process is described as both death and resurrection.

Romans 6:6 describes this dying process: "We know that our old sinful selves were crucified with Christ so that sin might lose its power in our lives. We are no longer slaves to sin. For when we died with Christ we were set free from the power of sin" (Romans 6:6–7). As a Christian, you experience the cross. When you have faith in Christ, the old you that was a slave to sin dies. Therefore, you must not sin. To sin as a Christian is to pretend to be something you are not — a slave to sin.

And while we experience the cross in our sanctification, we experience the resurrection:

> Since we have been united with him in his death, we will also be raised to life as he was . . . When he died, he died once to break the power of sin. But now that he lives, he lives for the glory of God. So you also should consider yourselves to be dead to the power of sin and alive to God through Christ Jesus. (Romans 6:5, 10-11)

Christ was raised from the dead, and if you are united to Christ, you too have been raised from the dead.

In the process of sanctification, you are constantly living out of the reality that you have died, so you must "put to death the sinful, earthly things lurking within you" (Colossians 3:5). In the process of sanctification, you are constantly living out of the reality that you are alive, so you must "live to righteousness" (1 Peter 2:24).

CHANGING CLOTHES

When I was in college from 2009-2013, I went to the University of Virginia. It was a predominantly White institution (PWI), so the Black community was tightly knit. A few things brought what seemed like all of the Black community together: probates and fashion shows.

I remember the fashion shows were fun. The models would

walk out, flaunt their stuff, and then there would be a wardrobe change. One part might be formal wear, the next business casual, and the next casual. And the models would have fun performing and entertaining the crowd, and the crowd would have fun cheering on their friends who were modeling.

What if I told you that life is like one big fashion show? You are created to be models for God's fashion show. He created you to be in his image and made you to show off his clothing line — love, joy, peace, patience, kindness, goodness, faithfulness, meekness, and self-control (Galatians 5:22-23). As you walk on the runway of life, you are made to have fun flaunting God's glory in you, and others are made to cheer you on while you do it.

As the scriptures talk about sanctification, it can use "clothing" language to talk about the image of God:

> But that is not the way you learned Christ!— assuming that you have heard about him and were taught in him, as the truth is in Jesus, to *put off your old self*, which belongs to your former manner of life and is corrupt through deceitful desires, and to be renewed in the spirit of your minds, and to *put on the new self, created after the likeness of God* in true righteousness and holiness. (Ephesians 4:20–24 ESV)

This passage combines clothing language and image of God language. "Put off" and "put on" is clothing language, and "likeness of God" is image of God language (Genesis 1:26). To combine these two things, God is calling you to put off the way of life that was not in harmony with God's image, and he is calling you to put on a new way of life that is in harmony with God's image. Humanity was created to be a model for God. We were designed to demonstrate who he is to the world, imitating him (Ephesians 5:1). However, instead of modeling for God, we often choose to model for the devil.

To trust in Jesus as your Savior but to model for the devil is like having a new set of clothes but wanting to always wear the old torn up ones. Jesus' goal in your life is to convince you, day in and day out, to wear the beautiful new clothes he's given you and not the ones the devil had you wearing at one point.

SANCTIFICATION HAPPENS BY GOD'S GRACE

Like justification and adoption, sanctification flows from God's grace, as it says in Philippians 2:13, "For God is working in you, giving you the desire and the power to do what pleases him" (Philippians 2:13). God himself, the gracious God, will take the initiative so that he might "sanctify you entirely" (1 Thessalonians 5:23 NASB). Yet, God will only bring us there as we strive towards it: "let us work toward complete holiness because we fear God" (2 Corinthians 7:1). It is both God and us who work in the process of sanctification. Yet still, sanctification is God's grace through and through. In the process of sanctification, the Christian knows that because of Jesus "There is a balm in Gilead, To make the wounded whole, There is a balm in Gilead, To heal the sin-sick soul."[2]

YOU ARE SANCTIFIED FOR A PURPOSE

Sanctification does not only have ourselves as the focus. God wants to sanctify his people so they can be a light to the nations, just as Christ was a light shining in the midst of darkness. We sing, "This little light of mine, I'm going to let it shine, Oh, this little light of mine, I'm going to let it shine, Hallelujah . . . All in my heart . . . All in my house . . . Everywhere I go . . . Out in the dark."[3] as we rejoice in the fact that we are sanctified so that we can be a blessing to a dark world.

Are you afraid of the dark? Fear of the dark is one of the most common fears. In the dark, we are separated from one of our most valuable senses – sight. We can not see danger, and we are completely vulnerable and exposed. But I also want to ask you another question: Do you love the dark? While fear of the dark is something we have all experienced, love of the dark is also something we have all experienced. And we love it for the opposite reason we fear it: in the dark, we are immune to other people's strongest sense– sight. In the dark, we are hidden from the gaze of other people. In the dark, we feel more comfortable doing things we should not do, being the type of person for which we feel ashamed.

The same is true of spiritual darkness. Spiritual darkness is the absence of the knowledge and presence of God. The scriptures call those who have rejected God, darkness, and the way of life that they live, darkness.

We both fear and love the spiritual darkness. We fear spiritual darkness because there we find guilt, shame, fear, and sin. We do not have our spiritual sight intact, so we are wide open to the destructive powers of sin – sin from ourselves and sin from others. Yet, at the same time, do we not love spiritual darkness? We get ourselves into dark situations because our hearts want the darkness. We want to be in that destructive relationship that we know will leave us empty. We want to over-book our schedules even though it will leave us burnt out. We want to get drunk or do that drug even though we know it will leave us worse than it found us. We want to cling to that familiar thing in our life, which we know we ought to let go.

It's because our hearts desire the power, approval, comfort, or security that these things promise, but these things always over-promise and under-deliver. You can only find fulfillment in God, who is light.

———

SANCTIFICATION FOR AFRICAN UPLIFT WITH MARIA STEWART

It is also true that our Christian African ancestors saw in Black people's sanctification our people's uplift. Many believed that slavery and ignorance among Black Africans would not be destroyed until we participated with God heartily in our sanctification as a people. Maria Stewart, who will again help us in this chapter, finds herself among their number.

I sometimes struggle when our Black Christian ancestors offer points of correction and strong calls to rise up to Black people. Why? I think my generation of Black people can often cringe at the thought that we are where we are as a people due to some failure of our own. I have had to push myself to let my Black Christian ancestors challenge me in this. Though they very plainly and truthfully highlighted the evil of White racism, they also highlighted Black people's own failure to unite against oppression and invest in themselves as a people. I need to do the same. We must *empower* and *improve* ourselves along with highlighting the wrongs done against us.

I believe the primary way that Black Africans will embrace wholeness and flourishing as a people today is by embracing God's work of sanctification. Not only must the downward, crushing pressure of oppression be lifted but also the people oppressed must sanctify themselves so that they can lift up and press against the crushing pressure. As we so often see in the aftermath of formal oppression, Africans are tempted to repeat the abuses of the oppressors and function within the same structures and systems left behind. As Black historians have noted, Black folks can repeat towards each other the same injustices they experienced under White oppression. We can become our own oppressors if we are not sanctified.

It has often been the conviction of our Black African Christian ancestors that devoting ourselves to sanctification for our own uplift was the path forward. Stewart calls us Africans to arise:

> I am of a strong opinion, that the day on which we unite, heart and soul, turn our attention to knowledge and improvement, that day the hissing and reproach among the nations of the earth against us will cease. And even those who now point at us with the finger of scorn, will aid and befriend us. It is of no use for us to

sit with our hands folded, hanging our heads like bulrushes, lamenting our wretched condition; but let us make a mighty effort, and arise; and if no one will promote or respect us let us promote and respect ourselves.[4]

Stewart urges Africans to rise up and develop themselves, even if no one else will come to our aid. She expresses a, perhaps misplaced, hope that the world will cease to have scorn for Africans once we develop ourselves. Though today we are not as optimistic as Stewart regarding the world recognizing us, we can acknowledge that God's work in and among us will bring shine forth God's glory, whether or not people have the eyes to see it.

Nowadays, we would mistakenly name this call to improvement and holiness "respectability politics." However, our Christian ancestors knew that a free people must be a godly and, therefore, strong people. To be truly free, we must be free from oppression *and* submit ourselves to the rule of God. To be free from one is to be bound to another.

In the hopes that Africans would embrace God and therefore flourishing, Stewart prays,

Quicken thy professing children. Grant that the young may be constrained to believe that there is a reality in religion, and a beauty in the fear of the Lord. Have mercy on the benighted sons and daughters of Africa. Grant that we may soon become so distinguished for our moral and religious improvements, that the nations of the earth may take knowledge of us; and grant that our cries may come up before the throne like holy incense . . . Clothe us with humility of soul, and give us a becoming dignity of manners: may we imitate the character of the meek and lowly Jesus; and do grant that Ethiopia may soon stretch forth her hands unto thee.[5]

The error of respectability politics is that it urges Black folks to conform to the dominant culture's standards so that they may accept us. However, this is not what Stewart is saying here. She is praying that Black Africans would conform to *Jesus'* standards, regardless of the dominant culture's standards. The focus is Jesus, not White acceptance. The focus is Black empowerment for God's glory, not being liked. And in conforming to the image of Christ, it is our hope that the world will glorify our Father in heaven and stand in awe of the glory of God shining in and through us.

Respectability politics also, at times, implies that our oppression is our fault. It places the burden on Africans to earn justice from White people. This is not what I am saying. Injustice should not happen no matter who it happens to. What I am saying, and many of our Christian ancestors have said, is that Black folks have agency and power and, therefore, a role to play in our uplift or our demise. Though it is a good thing when other ethnic or racial groups collectively help, Black people can't wait for some other people group to take ownership of our destiny. By the power and grace of God, we must rise against the evil done towards us and repair our people in the aftermath through love, justice, and good works.

———

OTHER BLESSINGS IN THIS LIFE

There are too many blessings that we receive from Christ's redemption to count, but I want just to mention a few more that I believe are particularly important for you to know.

JESUS GIVES ASSURANCE THAT YOU BELONG TO GOD

We are assured of God's love. Because of our justification, adoption, and sanctification, we increasingly grow more and more confident that God loves us. We have been disappointed so often in this life by people who offered us their word that they would do something for us but never came through. We must ask the question, "Can we trust God?" Can we trust that if we believe in Christ, we will be saved? Paul addresses this question in Romans: "And this hope will not lead to disappointment. For we know how dearly God loves us, because he has given us the Holy Spirit to fill our hearts with his love" (Romans 5:5). "This hope" is the hope that God will bring us to eternal glory. But how do we know God won't abandon us? In the next several verses, he gives us reasons why God will not abandon us. As I paraphrase, he says, "If Christ saved us and loved us when we were unrighteous, sinners, and enemies, how much more now that we have been saved and reconciled to him by faith? If God loved you as an enemy, he will definitely love you and never let you down as a friend." As we behold all of the beautiful things Christ has done for us in our redemption, we grow in our maturity (Romans 5:3) and, therefore, grow more confident that God will never leave us.

JESUS EASES A TROUBLED CONSCIENCE

We are given peace of conscience. Formerly our conscience would always bother us because of our horrible actions against God and our fellow humans. The scriptures tell us that Christ, through his death on the cross, has cleaned our dirty conscience. The author of Hebrews acknowledges this: "Just think how much more the blood of Christ will purify our consciences from sinful deeds so that we can worship the living God" (Hebrews 9:14). The death of Christ shows us that we are forgiven, so our consciences should stop condemning us where Christ is not condemning us.

THE HOLY SPIRIT GIVES JOY

We are given joy from the Spirit. The Christian life is described over and over again as one of joy, which is partially what this whole book is about – enjoying God. In the church in Rome, they had conflict over what kind of meat to eat, but Paul reminds them that "the Kingdom of God is not a matter of what we eat or drink, but of living a life of goodness and peace and *joy in the Holy Spirit*" (Romans 14:17, emphasis added). As the Spirit of God transforms us, we increasingly experience the joy that he gives us.

GOD IS BRINGING YOU TO SPIRITUAL MATURITY

We are growing in grace, meaning God is increasingly pouring out his grace on us so that we may grow in spiritual maturity. As Christians, it is so easy for our faith to be shaken when we are still spiritually young, but to remain firm in your faith, "you must grow in the grace and knowledge of our Lord and Savior Jesus Christ" (2 Peter 3:18). Like the older kid on the basketball court, the more you grow, the harder it is for the opponent to move you.

GOD IS PRESERVING YOU

We are preserved by God to persevere in our faith. First, let's look at God's preservation. Jesus tells an audience, "However, those the Father has given me will come to me, and I will never reject them. For I have come down from heaven to do the will of God who sent me, not to do my own will. And this is the will of God, that *I should not lose even one of all those he has given me, but that I should raise them up at the last day.*" (John 6:37–39, emphasis added). Jesus tells another audience, "My sheep listen to my voice; I know them, and they follow me. I give them eternal life, and *they will never perish. No one can snatch them away from me,* for my Father has given them to me, and he is more powerful than anyone else. No one can snatch them from the Father's hand" (John 10:27–29, emphasis added). We know that if we truly belong to God's elect that we will never lose our salvation. God will preserve you "who are protected by the power of God through faith for a salvation ready to be revealed in the last time" (1 Peter 1:5 NASB).

GOD GIVES YOU THE ABILITY TO PERSEVERE

Second, because God is preserving us, we will persevere. Only because God's power and grace preserves us can we persevere through the difficulties of the Christian life. God carries us from beginning to end.

As we discussed earlier, many people are called to faith by the gospel, some of these folks responding positively, but "many are called, but few are chosen" (Matthew 22:14). Those who are not chosen evidence this by walking away from God permanently, and those who are chosen evidence this by persevering to the end. In the parable of the sower (Matthew 13:1-9, 18-23), we see that there are those who will believe but will eventually fall away because their faith was not alive and rooted. The faith that these people exercised was not a genuine faith in God, but a dead faith (James 2:17). John said, in referring to people who had recently left the church, "They went out from us, but they did not really belong to us. For if they had belonged to us, they would have remained with us; but their going showed that none of them belonged to us" (1 John 2:19 NIV). These people who left had joined the church, yet they were not true believers. They belonged to the church without *belonging* to the church as God's elect. These are the folks who are the weeds that grew among the crops, according to Jesus' parable of the wheat and the tares (Matthew 13:24-30).

How do we know that we belong to God's elect and will therefore persevere? We evidence this by our lives: "No one who is born of God will continue to sin, because God's seed remains in them; they cannot go on sinning, because they have been born of God" (1 John 3:9 NIV). The phrase "continue to sin" refers to a lifestyle of sin. John acknowledges that the believer will not be perfect but will lead a changed life. Indeed, the believer will often have many dark moments and moments where they are not even sure themselves if they still want to follow God, but he "who began the good work within you, will continue his work until it is finally finished on the day when Christ Jesus returns" (Philippians 1:6).

So far, we have talked about the benefits of redemption in this life, but let's now talk about what happens when and after we die.

———

RECAP

We discussed what God's blessings are in the midst of a world of curses. God has justified us, which means he pardons our sins and accepts us as righteous. God adopts us. He reclaims us as his children by bringing us to new life. He cares and provides for us as his children; transforms us; disciplines us; supports us in suffering; and unites Christians as a family. As children, we have a future hope. Also, God changes us. He makes us holy by bringing us to himself, transforming us, and making us whole. Our holiness makes us a light to the nations, and as holiness is what Black Africans need in order to resist oppression and its devastating effects. Along with justification, adoption, and sanctification, we are given assurance, peace, joy, growth, preservation, and perseverance.

Let's now turn to our last chapter, which is on God's blessings to us at and after death.

CHAPTER 12

HEY, LET ME GET YOUR PASSWORD

Many of you are familiar with subscription plans. Some companies provide a good or service, and you cannot take advantage of it until you become a subscriber. You usually pay them a monthly fee; in return, they give you some type of good or service. When you sign up for Disney+, Netflix, Apple Music, or Amazon Prime, you get all kinds of benefits and perks. For example, I have Amazon Prime. The benefit that I most enjoy is the free one and two-day shipping. It is amazing that you can buy something on the computer and have it at your house the next day!

Though being a subscriber is great, there is a problem. There are often benefits of which I am unaware; therefore, I don't take advantage of them. Amazon emails me at times to remind me of benefits I am not using. One email's subject line says, "Prime member: You have an unused Prime benefit." Amazon told me, "We noticed that you weren't taking full advantage of your Prime Membership. As a Prime Member, you get access to Amazon Music, an ad-free music streaming service at no additional cost." I am a subscriber, but I am not fully enjoying my benefits. Because I am not fully enjoying my benefits, I am not enjoying Amazon.

If you have placed your trust in Jesus, you are a subscriber to the kingdom of God. Jesus has paid your subscription fee with his very own life. You are signing into his account with his permission: "Hey Jesus, let me get your password." You now have full access to the top-tier subscription in the kingdom. However, there is a problem. As kingdom subscribers, we often don't take advantage of the benefits. In fact, we often do not know the benefits that come with being a believer!

I want to outline the benefits of being a believer at death and after death.

WHERE WE ARE GOING

In a sentence, this chapter will show you that Jesus brings blessings when death comes, so face death boldly.

Death will come to us all. Death is the great fear and enduring enemy of life. During your college years, you are young, but you are not invincible. Even during some of your youngest and most hopeful years, death can come to find you. What is our comfort as we face the reality of death? Jesus.

Though death is a part of the curse over this world, Jesus brings blessings at and after death. Jesus melts away the fear of death and even allows us to welcome it. If we do not realize the fact that Jesus awaits to bless us at death, we will allow the fear of death to consume us and drown out our hope in life. However, receiving the good news about Jesus means that you can live without fear and live with a powerful hope. We will see that 1) Christians will be with Jesus right after they die 2) we will be waiting for our bodies 3) Jesus will come again to resurrect us and judge us 4) at this judgment Jesus will reward us and destroy all things contrary to him 5) eternity will be perfect 6) the knowledge of the future causes us to change our present situations and 7) dying well is a skill we must attain.

———

WHAT HAPPENS WHEN WE DIE?

Not only does union with Christ bring benefits in this life (see previous chapter), but we will receive benefits at death and in the next life. In eternity, all of the beautiful benefits that we experience in this life will be brought to completion in the next life.

BELIEVERS WILL BE WITH JESUS

What happens at our death? In Christ, though death is still a part of the curse that rests upon humanity because we broke the covenant of life, we no longer fear death. In Christ, we cry out with the Apostle Paul, "O death, where is your victory? O death, where is your sting?" (1 Corinthians 15:55). We know that death brings us into a deeper enjoyment of our redemption.

Death brings believers to Christ and into his holy dwelling. Jesus is the central feature of heaven, and with the spiritual, we sing, "Oh when I come to die, Oh, when I come to die, Oh, when I come to die, Give me Jesus. Give me Jesus, Give me Jesus, You may have all this world, Give me Jesus."[1] Because of the work of Christ, in heaven, our sanctification is brought to completion in our spirits. We become the "spirits of the righteous ones in heaven who have *now been made perfect*" (Hebrews 12:23, emphasis added). There is no in-between stage between life and heaven. Believers immediately pass into heaven, just like Jesus told the fellow convict who was dying with him, "I assure you, today you will be with me in paradise" (Luke 23:43). And indeed, the Bible teaches us that it is better after death because we know that we will be with the Lord: "Yes, we are fully confident, and we would rather be away from these earthly bodies, for then we will be at home with the Lord" (2 Corinthians 5:8). In Philippians 1:23, Paul states that he desires to die because he wants to be with Christ, which is far better than being here on earth.

However, those who rejected Christ in this life do not have heaven awaiting them but a place of torment. The realm of the dead, which the Bible calls several different names (e.g. "Sheol" and "Hades"), has a different place for those who belong to Christ and for those who do not. For example, Luke 16:19-31 tells us about how a rich man, who was merciless in his life, was tormented in Hades while being able to see Lazarus in heavenly comfort. In the realm of the dead, there are both those in bliss and those in torture.

WE WILL WAIT ON OUR BODIES

Though we are brought to perfect holiness in heaven, we are still waiting to have our bodies made perfect, which are still buried on earth. Though decaying, these dead bodies are still significant because they are still considered a part of ourselves. God does not see us as spirits living in dispensable bodies. God sees us as a complex combination of both body and spirit. You are a spirit-body. Even though we are in heaven in spirit, we are also asleep on earth (1 Thessalonians 4:13-14). The dead are simultaneously asleep in the earthly realms while being conscious as spirits in the heavenly realms. This is why the Bible writers identify dead bodies with the spirits now in heaven. For example, Daniel refers to the dead as those "who sleep in the dust of the earth" (Daniel 12:2 NIV), and Jesus even refers to the dead as "all who are in their graves" (John 5:28). We are simultaneously in our graves but also heaven.

The separation of our spirit and body is why it is good news that Jesus rose again. Because he rose again, our own bodies will rise again, being united to our spirits. When describing the return of Christ, Paul says, "First, the believers who have died will rise from their graves" (1 Thessalonians 4:16). The final destination of the Christian life actually is not heaven. The final destination of the Christian life is the new heavens and new earth. In the heavenly realms,[2] some will be with Jesus, and others will be in torment, all awaiting the day of resurrection.

THE PLACE OF DEATH IN THE CHRISTIAN AFRICAN'S SPIRITUAL LIFE

For the oppressed Christian, death is more commonly on the mind. In their spirituality, death is a result of the curse but also something that transports them from the crushing situation of this world into the presence of Jesus. For those who are comfortable in this life, death is not something that is thought of often, and the thought of being in heaven might be unwelcome as it separates you from your current hopes for life in this world. However, because of their oppression and Christian persecution, many of our African Christian ancestors often did not place any hope in this world. When singing about death, they sang, "Oh, freedom! Oh, freedom! Oh, freedom over me! And before I'd be a slave, I'll be buried in my grave, And go home to my Lord and be free ... No more mourning over me . . . There'll be singing over me . . . There'll be shouting over me . . . There'll be praying over me."[3]

––––––

WHAT HAPPENS WHEN WE RISE?

What happens on the day of resurrection? Christ himself will return. All people will rise from their graves, for God "will raise both the righteous and the unrighteous" (Acts 24:15).

JESUS WILL JUDGE US

Everyone will stand before the judgment seat of God to be judged. The dead will be resurrected and the living assembled to stand before him. Paul tells us that "we must all stand before Christ to be judged. We will each receive whatever we deserve for the good or evil we have done in this earthly body" (2 Corinthians 5:10). Jesus shall judge us because, in his words, "the Father judges no one. Instead, he has given the Son absolute authority to judge, so that everyone will honor the Son, just as they honor the Father" (John 5:22–23). Jesus, as a just Judge, will judge us according to what we have done. Even Christians will be judged based upon how they lived the Christian life.

This judgment happens when Jesus returns on the day of resurrection: "Don't be so surprised! Indeed, the time is coming when all the dead in their graves will hear the voice of God's Son, and they will rise again. Those who have done good will rise to experience eternal life, and those who have continued in evil will rise to experience judgment" (John 5:28–29). What will be the distinction between the righteous and the unrighteous? The righteous are those who are united to Christ, and the unrighteous are those who reject God and Christ. Those who rejected Christ lived lives apart from his transforming power and, therefore, lived empty lives. Those who received Christ lived lives under his transforming power and, thus, lives full of meaning and goodness. Because of the two different lives they lived, each will experience different judgments. In that day, "You'll hear the trumpet sound . . . You'll hear the sinner mourn . . . You'll hear the Christian shout, To wake the nations underground, Looking to my God's right hand, When the stars begin to fall."[4]

Those who belong to Christ will be acknowledged and acquitted, hearing the words from God, "Well done, my good and faithful servant" (Matthew 25:21), and those who do not belong to Christ will experience his wrath.

Jesus teaches this in his parables of the sheep and the goat:

All the nations will be gathered in his presence, and he will separate the people as a shepherd separates the sheep from the goats. He will place the sheep at his right hand and the goats at his left . . . . Then the King will say to those on his right, "Come, you who are blessed by my Father, inherit the Kingdom prepared for you from the creation of the world . . . Then the King will turn to those on the left and say, "Away with you, you cursed ones, into the eternal fire prepared for the devil and his demons." (Matthew 25:32–33, 34, 41)

In this parable, there are two kinds of people. Those whose lives were pleasing to Jesus because they were filled with mercy and service to others, and those whose lives were unpleasant to Jesus because they were lacking in mercy and service to others. Those who are unrighteous will face eternal judgment, but those who are righteous will face eternity with God. Regarding believers, Paul says, "First, the believers who have died will rise from their graves. Then, together with them, we who are still alive and remain on the earth will be caught up in the clouds to meet the Lord in the air. Then we will be with the Lord forever" (1 Thessalonians 4:16–17). After the resurrection of the dead, an eternity with God awaits believers.

WE WILL RECEIVE OUR BLESSINGS IN FULL

In Christ, believers will receive the full manifestation of all things that belong to them. All the benefits of redemption will be fully manifested.

Redemption will be fully manifested in our bodies, for we will receive the "redemption of our bodies" (Romans 8:23 NIV), and these bodies will be perfect, glorious bodies (1 Corinthians 15:42-43).

Our justification will be fully manifested. Remember justification in the previous chapter? As believers, we enjoy justification in the here and now, but there will be a day when God will literally justify us as we stand before his throne. Just as Jesus was justified (i.e., vindicated) by his resurrection, we will be justified when we are resurrected from the dead. Our resurrection of glory itself is God justifying us, showing the world that we are righteous before him. On the day of the resurrected, the believers will be openly and verbally acknowledged and acquitted before God and the unrighteous. The acknowledgment and acquittal in judgment is our literal justification; God verbally declares us as just.

Our adoption will be fully manifested. As sons of God, our ultimate adoption will happen when Christ returns. "And not only the creation, but we ourselves, who have the first-fruits of the Spirit, groan inwardly as we wait eagerly for adoption as sons, the redemption of our bodies" (Romans 8:23 ESV). Though we have been adopted now in Christ, there is still a part of our adoption that has yet to be realized. When Christ returns, we will be given new bodies, and then God will fully give all of the privileges of being his children to us.

As sons of God, we are heirs to the wonderful inheritance of God, which is the new heavens and the new earth. "And because we are his children, God has sent the Spirit of his Son into our hearts, prompting us to call out, 'Abba, Father.' Now you are no longer a slave but God's own child. And since you are his child, God has made you his heir" (Galatians 4:6–7). An heir was someone who received a double portion of the family's possession when the head of the household died. As a child lived in the household, they lived in anticipation of a future much different than the present. For us, God will never die, but we will receive an amazing inheritance from him when Christ returns. "All praise to God, the Father of our Lord Jesus Christ. It is by his great mercy that we have been born again, because God raised Jesus Christ from the dead. Now we live with great expectation, and we have *a priceless inheritance—an inheritance* that is kept in heaven for you, pure and undefiled, beyond the reach of change and decay" (1 Peter 1:3–4, emphasis added).

Our inheritance as children will have everything to do with the Holy Spirit. When speaking of our inheritance elsewhere, the Bible uses the economic term of a guarantee, which is like a deposit or downpayment. It is money given that lets someone know that the rest is coming later. "*The Spirit is God's guarantee* that he will give us the inheritance he promised and that he has purchased us to be his own people. He did this so we would praise and glorify him" (Ephesians 1:14). If the Spirit is the guarantee, then the rest of the payment must be a full measure of the Holy Spirit. For example, we will receive spiritual bodies when our adoption is fully manifested (1 Corinthians 15:44). It is hard to tell exactly what this is, but we can assume that our bodies will be glorified by being saturated with the Spirit. We have the "guarantee" now for our bodies and will receive the "full payment" later.

Our sanctification will be fully manifested, being perfectly holy living in a universe that is God's holy temple itself. When Jesus comes back, we will be just like him because we will see him. The return of Jesus is the completion of what he began when we were first saved. John speaks of this when he says, "Beloved, we are God's children now, and what we will be has not yet appeared; but we know that when he appears we shall be like him, because we shall see him as he is. And everyone who thus hopes in him purifies himself as he is pure" (1 John 3:2–3 ESV). We purify, i.e. sanctify, ourselves in the here and now in anticipation of our future and total transformation into the image of God. In this hope, we sing with our ancestors, "I want to be ready, I want to be ready, I want to be ready to walk in Jerusalem just like John."[5] We will sing of this new Jerusalem, "Oh! What a beautiful city, Oh! What a beautiful city, Oh! What a beautiful city."[6] Our future sanctification is a motivation to pursue present sanctification.

God will fully manifest our victory over our enemies:

Then the devil, who had deceived them, was thrown into the fiery lake of burning sulfur . . . Then death and the grave were thrown into the lake of fire . . . But cowards, unbelievers, the corrupt, murderers, the immoral, those who practice witchcraft, idol worshipers, and all liars—their fate is in the fiery lake of burning sulfur. (Revelation 20:10, 14; 21:8)

Those who seek to oppose God's people will be no more. We will receive the presence of God in full because in eternity "God's dwelling place is now among the people, and he will dwell with them. They will be his people, and God himself will be with them and be their God" (Revelation 21:3 NIV). And we — as those who are restored kin, kings and queens, and clergy — will receive new dominion over a new earth, for "No longer will there be any curse. The throne of God and of the Lamb will be in the city, and his servants will serve him. They will see his face, and his name will be on their foreheads. There will be no more night. They will not need the light of a lamp or the light of the sun, for the Lord God will give them light. And they will reign for ever and ever" (Revelation 22:3–5 NIV).

THE HOPE OF THE FUTURE AFFECTS OUR PRESENT

The hope of the return of Christ and the resurrection of the dead has always been central for African Christians as those who have suffered. They knew that this world was actually not our home, but they sang, "Deep river, my home is over Jordan, Deep river, Lord, I want to cross over into camp ground. Oh, don't you want to go to that gospel feast, That promised land where all is peace? O don't you want to go to that promised land, that land where all is peace?"[7]

DOES HEAVEN MAKE BLACK PEOPLE PASSIVE?

Some have wrongly assumed that Christ's benefits to us at our death and at his return make African Christians docile, or compliant. They say heaven is a teaching from White folks that convinces Black people to receive hell now because of a future heaven.

The afterlife, however, does not make people docile; it energizes us in the here and now! The future hope of a new creation leads us to seek change in the old creation. Indeed, Black Christians have seen the future as an inspiration to change the present. Paul, at the end of a long chapter on the resurrection of Christ and the resurrection of the dead, says, "So, my dear brothers and sisters, be strong and immovable. Always work enthusiastically for the Lord, for you know that nothing you do for the Lord is ever useless" (1 Corinthians 15:58). When we know that Jesus will overcome all things and that we will be with him for eternity, we know suffering for him and serving his kingdom now is not in vain. A vision of our future with Jesus inspires us to advance his kingdom in the present.

Though the end makes us active, not passive, the sole focus of the scriptures is not the present fight for liberation. The scriptures heavily emphasize looking to the future, and the present is merely what we do while we await that future. Waiting is a powerful theme in the scriptures. Hebrews 4:1-10 teaches us that the goal of all things is the future rest we will experience, and we obey God now in anticipation of this rest. Hebrews 11 acknowledges that the faithful do not receive the full measure of God's promises in this life, but we live faithfully in the present as we wait. James 5:7-11 urges us to live for God as we await the coming of the Lord.

WE FIGHT FOR CHANGE WHILE WAITING FOR CHANGE

To go even further, because the focus is on the future, the fight to change this world is not all that we have. Paul tells the Corinthians,

> This is what I mean, brothers: the appointed time has grown very short. From now on, let those who have wives live as though they had none, and those who mourn as though they were not mourning, and those who rejoice as though they were not rejoicing, and those who buy as though they had no goods, and those who deal with the world as though they had no dealings with it. For the

present form of this world is passing away. (1 Corinthians 7:29–31 ESV)

He poetically encourages them not to place all their hopes in the fact that this world will fulfill them.

We change the world, but our struggle is tempered by knowing that this world is already passing away. This is why Paul can say,

Each one should remain in the condition in which he was called. Were you a bondservant when called? Do not be concerned about it. (But if you can gain your freedom, avail yourself of the opportunity.) For he who was called in the Lord as a bondservant is a freedman of the Lord. Likewise he who was free when called is a bondservant of Christ. You were bought with a price; do not become bondservants of men. So, brothers, in whatever condition each was called, there let him remain with God. (1 Corinthians 7:20–24 ESV)

Liberation from slavery is a good thing and should be pursued. However, if you are not able to be liberated from slavery, it is ok because this world is not the focus. The focus is on the future world, the new creation. And because that future world has already broken into the present, you are already free even though, in this present age, you are in bondage. A Christian lives with these two things in tension: 1) an interest in changing the world, while knowing this world is already passing away and 2) knowing that we are already participants in another world.

———

LEARNING HOW TO DIE WITH MONICA

Our final old friend is Monica, who is the mother of Augustine. In many ways, she is the hero's hero. Augustine is a hero of a theologian, but Monica is the one who raised him and prayed him into the Christian faith. Augustine says of her, "In the flesh she brought me to birth in this world: in her heart she brought me to birth in your eternal light."[8] The love and prayers of Monica were the engine behind Augustine's journey to Jesus. Also, she was an African Christian in the early days of Christianity, when Christianity was widespread in North Africa.

AUGUSTINE PRAISES MONICA

Augustine, in *Confessions,* tells us about the final days he had with Monica. She embodied the words of the scriptures when it says, "For to me to live is Christ, and to die is gain. If I am to live in the flesh, that means fruitful labor for me. Yet which I shall choose I cannot tell. I am hard pressed between the two. My desire is to depart and be with Christ, for that is far better" (Philippians 1:21–23 ESV). Monica knew that living was living for Christ, and dying was profitable because it brought her closer to Christ. It is with this conviction that she faced death with joy.

MONICA'S LIFE IS FILLED WITH GODLINESS

Monica was a North African native. She grew up in a Christian home where she learned the Christian faith primarily from a Christian household servant who raised her. Monica was patient, wise, and tough. She was fundamentally a peacemaker at heart. Even more, she was a constant servant of other Christians, winning their admiration for herself and for the Lord. Monica was a fierce prayer warrior, and she would pray passionately and persistently with tears that her son, Augustine, would become a Christian. Her constant ministry to him is legendary. Augustine shares all this with us in *Confessions* as he praises his mother.

During the last days of her life, she and Augustine were having a spiritual conversation in Ostia, Italy, a sea's journey away from their home in Africa. Monica tells Augustine,

My son, for my part I find no further pleasure in this life. What I am still to do or why I am here in the world, I do not know, for I have no more to hope for on this earth. There was one reason, and one alone, why I wished to remain a little longer in this life, and that was to see you a Catholic Christian before I died. God has granted my wish and more besides, for I now see you as his servant, spurning such happiness as the world can give. What is left for me to do in this world?[9]

Like the Apostle Paul in Philippians 1:21-23, Monica had been ready to die to go see Jesus, but the only reason she wanted to stay was to see her son become a "Catholic Christian," which is an older way of simply saying "a Christian." Now that she had seen Jesus bring her son to himself, she was ready to go see Jesus. Her life was about Jesus, and her death was all about Jesus. Whether in life or death, she was centered on Jesus. Because of her faith in Jesus, the one who has defeated death, she was able to face death with courage.

And even in death, her hope was the resurrection of the dead. When they talked with her about the potential of being buried so far from Africa, she said, "Nothing is far from God, and I need have no fear that he will not know where to find me when he comes to raise me to life at the end of the world."[10] At the end of the day, her only hope was seeing Jesus at the resurrection of the dead (Philippians 3:8-11). May this be our example for when we die. Monica embodied the negro spiritual well, "Oh, when I come to die, Give me Jesus."

It is my prayer for you, that in life or death, your life is centered on Jesus. May he be your only hope and highest joy.

CONCLUSION

As I said in the beginning of our journey together, the goal of this book is for you to understand the Christian faith. Once you understand the Christian faith, you will see that it is more glorious and enjoyable than you ever knew. In many ways, this whole book has been one big presentation of the good news about Jesus (the gospel), the center of the Christian faith.

We know of the good news about Jesus from the Bible. We explored the Bible itself and its importance in your life. The Bible is Yahweh's amazing guidance, and we ought to let it saturate us. In order for God's word to saturate us, we must figure out how to interpret it. In spite of those who interpret the Bible wrongly, the Bible brings a life-giving message to African Americans. God is inviting us to trust that his word is life-giving. Through the Bible, God relates to us.

In order to understand the good news, you have to understand who God is and who we are in relation to him. God reveals these things to us in the Bible. What does he reveal? God is everything you need, and he is satisfying. He invites us to delight in him. However, this is difficult to believe because the pain of our lives tempts us to distrust God. In spite of how things might seem, God is at work in our lives, and he invites us to trust him. God has done and is doing all kinds of things, but one of the most glorious things God did was create humanity. This glorious God created us with a wonderful design and created us for himself. This is why your highest purpose is to glorify and enjoy God. However, this wonderful design was ruined by sin. In fact, sin is your greatest problem, which is the bad news of our lives. We fall so short of glorifying and enjoying God and have made a mess of everything through our own evil. Death, sinfulness, and pain define the world. As a consequence, God's just punishment has been declared over the world and his anger is toward it.

Now we come to the good news. God loves his enemies. History is the story of God rescuing humanity. Jesus is the climax of history, and we ought to stand in awe of his saving work on our behalf. Why did God rescue us through Jesus? Jesus is the only one who is uniquely qualified to save you as both God and human. Also, he is the perfect savior as our prophet, priest, and king. He lived the perfect life, died, rose again, and ascended into heaven for us. He lived the life we couldn't live; he died the death we should have died; he rose from the dead so that we might rise from the dead; and he ascended over all things so that we might ascend over all things. There is no one else who can save us.

How do we receive and enjoy this good news? We must respond to it. We must respond to it by having faith in Jesus. It is the Holy Spirit who gives us new life to even be able to respond to the good news. When we have faith in Jesus, we can enjoy all of God's blessings promised in his covenants. God blesses you through Jesus in this life, so we must spend our lives enjoying these blessings. God also blesses you through Jesus in the next life, so we must face death boldly knowing he will bless us there and after.

I initially wrote this book with college graduation day in mind. You have likely spent three to five years in your college campus ministry learning these truths, but now the harder task is before you on graduation day. You must not only know these truths but also *live* these truths for a lifetime. What's the first step? Find a healthy church in your city. This will be your Christian community. It is ordinarily impossible to live out these truths outside of a Christian community. Find a church that is centered on the Bible, personally cares for its members, regularly prays for you, and regularly baptizes and does the Lord's supper. Often, we can get overwhelmed with joining a church. Feel free to relax. You don't have to stay in the same church for the rest of your life, but you do need to be a part of one. Ask your campus ministry leaders for recommendations on a good church. Then, join one; lock arms with other Christians; and watch God grow you.

NOTES

WHY SHOULD I READ THIS BOOK?

1. Barna Group and Impact 360 Institute, *Gen Z: The Culture, Beliefs and Motivations Shaping the Next Generation* (Barna Group, 2018), 26.
2. Matthew Anderson, *Presbyterianism; Its Relation to the Negro* (Philadelphia: John McGill & Co., 1897), 178.
3. Biographical details taken from Walter Strickland, "Introduction to Plain Theology for Plain People," *Plain Theology for Plain People*, (Bellingham: Lexham Press, 2017), vii-xii.
4. Boothe, *Plain Theology for Plain People*, 3.

1. CAN I GET SOME HELP WITH . . . EVERYTHING?

1. Every time you see "LORD" in the Bible in all caps, it is a substitute for the personal name of God. "God" is the title, and "Yahweh" is his name. Long story, short: throughout history, at some point, Jewish scribes stopped saying God's name out-loud when they read it because they were fearful they would use it lightly. They began saying "Lord" whenever they read his name as a substitute for his actual name.
2. Details largely taken from Valerie Cooper, *Word Like Fire*, (Charlottesville: University of Virginia Press, 2011); Simmons and Thomas, *Preaching with Sacred Fire: An Anthology of African American Sermons from 1750 to the Present*, (New York: W.W. Norton & Company, Inc., 2010); and Maria Stewart, *Meditations from the Pen of Mrs. Maria W. Stewart*, (Washington: Enterprise Publishing Company, 1879).
3. Cooper, 17.
4. Maria Stewart, "Religion and the Pure Principles of Morality," in Cooper, 44-47.
5. Westminster Shorter Catechism Question 1
6. Kevin Shillington, *History of Africa*, 4 ed. (London: Red Globe Press, 2019) 111-112.
7. The meaning of words sometimes change over time, the word "testament" in the English language no longer refers to the concept of a covenant. It now refers to the concept of a will for someone's personal property upon death. Regardless, know that "Old Testament" is referring to the old covenant and "New Testament" is referring to the new covenant.

2. GOD IS TEXT MESSAGING ME?

1. Carl Ellis, *Free At Last?* (Downers Grove: IVP, 2020), 168.
2. David Walker, *David Walker's Appeal*, ed. Sean Wilentz (New York: Hill and Wang, 1995), 43.
3. Wole Soyinka, *Of Africa* (New Haven: Yale University Press, 2012), 93.
4. An apostle was one of Jesus' original, foundational disciples.
5. Cedric Robinson, *Black Movements in America* (New York and London: Routledge, 1997), 153.
6. Howard Thurman, *Jesus and the Disinherited* (Boston: Beacon Press, 1996), 3.
7. Ibid., 36.
8. John Jea, *The Life, History, and Unparalleled Sufferings of John Jea*, (Self-published, 1811), 5.
9. Jea, 37.
10. Jea, 42.

3. FIRST DATES AND HEART BREAKS

1. Benjamin Mays, *The Negro's God: As Reflected in His Literature* (Eugene: Wipf & Stock, 2010), 252.
2. Ta-Nehisi Coates, *Between the World and Me* (New York: Spiegel and Grau, 2015), 79.
3. That part of the world was then under the dominion of the Roman Empire, but the Romans did not draw their maps with the same lines and the same names. We call the whole continent "Africa," but we actually get that name from what was a small Roman province called "Africa" on the northern coast of the continent. We have adopted the name of that province as the name of the continent itself. Thagaste would have been right outside of the province of "Africa."
4. Augustine, *Confessions*, trans. R.S. Pine-Coffin, (New York: Penguin Books, 1961), 21.
5. John H. Walton, Victor H. Matthews, and Mark W. Chavalas, *The IVP Bible Background Commentary: Old Testament*, Accordance electronic ed. (Downers Grove: InterVarsity Press, 2000), 116.
6. "Hold to God's Unchanging Hand" in Gwendolin Sims Warren, *Ev'ry Time I Fell the Spirit*, (New York: Henry Holt and Company, LLC, 1997), 119.
7. Augustine, 68.

4. BUT WHY DO CERTAIN THINGS HAPPEN?

1. Irwyn Ince, *Beautiful Community*, (Downers Grove: IVP, 2020), 32.
2. A process used to determine the will of God. When someone had to make a decision in which God neither obligated nor forbade a certain thing, they would do something that would be "random," like our current-day process of drawing the shortest straw or flipping a coin.

3. James A Levernier, "Phillis Wheatley (ca. 1753–1784)," *Legacy*, 1996, Vol. 13, No. 1 (1996), accessed March 28, 2023, University of Nebraska Press pp. 65-75. https://www.jstor.org/stable/25679186

4. Phillis Wheatley, "Thoughts on the Works of Providence", in *Poems on Various Subjects, Religious & Moral*, (1773), 31.

5. Ibid., 32.

6. Ibid., 34-35.

7. Esau McCaulley, *Reading While Black* (Downers Grove: IVP Academic, 2020), 130.

5. WHEN THE LIGHTING ON GOD'S SELFIE IS JUST RIGHT

1. We were all created as God's children as image-bearers, but as we will see, sin ruined all of that.

2. John H. Walton, Victor H. Matthews, and Mark W. Chavalas, *The IVP Bible Background Commentary: Old Testament*, Accordance electronic ed. (Downers Grove: InterVarsity Press, 2000), 715.

3. Ince, 55.

4. "Gentiles" is another words for "nations." They were nations other than Israel.

5. It is called the "Mosaic" law because God gave them to Israel through Moses.

6. Biographical details taken from Sam Roberts, "Rev. C. Herbert Oliver, Civil Rights Activist, Dies at 96," *New York Times*, Dec 13, 2021, https://www.nytimes.com/2021/12/11/us/rev-c-herbert-oliver-dead.html

7. C. Herbert Oliver, *No Flesh Shall Glory: How the Bible Destroys the Foundations of Racism* (Phillipsburg: P&R Publishing, 2021), 86.

8. Boothe, 28.

6. WHY IS LIFE SO HARD?

1. Wheatley, "On Recollection," in *Poems on Various Subjects, Religious & Moral* (1773), 48.

2. Ibid.

3. Boothe, 29.

4. Soyinka, 54.

5. Ibid., 61.

6. Ibid., 67.

7. Ibid., 68.

8. Soyinka, 69.

9. "Ride On, King Jesus" in Warren, 75.

7. SEASON 3 FINALE

1. Stewart in Cooper, 47-48.

8. DOUBLE MAJOR, AIN'T NOTHING MINOR

1. Much of biographical material taken from John R. Tyson, *The Great Athanasius: An Introduction to His Life and Work*, (Eugene, OR: Cascade Books, 2017), xxi.
2. Athanasius, *On the Incarnation*, Popular Patristics Series 3 (Crestwood, New York: St. Vladimir's Seminary Press, 1996), 26.
3. Ibid., 29.
4. Athanasius, 34.
5. Athanasius, 46.
6. Ibid., 43.
7. "Go, Tell It on the Mountain," in Warren, 44.
8. "He Arose" in Warren, 50.
9. The scriptures don't have the same slavery as American chattel slavery. This is why many of your translations say "bondservant" instead of "slave." They want to reflect with their language the difference between our conception of slavery and the one that existed in the greco-roman world.

9. CAN HE GET THE JOB DONE?

1. Athanasius, 33.
2. Athanasius, 52.
3. "I Know It Was the Blood" in Warren, 56.
4. "Nobody Knows de Trouble I've Seen" in Warren, 68.
5. "Go Down, Moses" in Warren, 41.
6. Athanasius, 58.
7. "Ride On, King Jesus" in Warren, 74.
8. "I Am on the Battlefield for My Lord" in Warren, 122.
9. "Sinner, Please Don't Let Dis Harves' Pass" in Warren, 80.

10. SPECIAL DELIVERY!

1. "I Want Jesus to Walk with Me," in Warren, 59.
2. "Sweet Jesus," in Warren, 87.
3. "Glory, Glory Hallelujah!" *Ev'ry Time I Feel the Spirit,* 39.
4. Augustine, 181.

11. BLESSINGS ON BLESSINGS

1. Thurman, 39.
2. "There is a Balm in Gilead," in Warren, 93.
3. "This Little Light of Mine," in Warren, 96.
4. Stewart, 78.
5. Stewart, 65.

12. HEY, LET ME GET YOUR PASSWORD

1. "Give Me Jesus," in Warren, 37.
2. Remember, don't mistake the heavenly realms with heaven. The heavenly realms is the Bible's way of talking about the spiritual realms, where all spiritual beings, both good and evil, operate. This is why Ephesians 3:10 and 6:12 mention that "rulers," "authorities," "cosmic powers over this present darkness," and "spiritual forces of evil" are in the heavenly realms.
3. "Oh, Freedom" in Warren, 71.
4. "My Lord, What a Morning," in Warren, 67.
5. "I Want to Be Ready," in Warren, 60.
6. "Oh, Freedom," in Warren, 72.
7. "Deep River," in Warren, 30.
8. Augustine, 192.
9. Augustine, 198-199.
10. Ibid., 200.

Made in United States
North Haven, CT
17 April 2023